Foundations of English

(11)

DOUGLAS HILKER

SUE HARPER

Harcourt Canada

Toronto Orlando San Diego London Sydney

Canadian Cataloguing in Publication Data

Hilker, Douglas
       Foundations of English 11

Includes index.
ISBN 0-7747-1494-8

1. Readers (Secondary).   Harper, Sue, 1952- . II Title.

PE1121.H5385 2001   428.6   C00-932873-4

Authors

Douglas Hilker
Writing Team Leader for the Ontario Curriculum Policy Document for English and Lead Developer for the Ontario Secondary School Grade 11 Literacy Test

Sue Harper
Former Head of English, John Fraser Secondary School, Mississauga, ON, and Developer for the Ontario Secondary School Grade 11 Literacy Test

Reviewers

The authors and publisher gratefully acknowledge these reviewers for their contribution to the development of this project:

Tish Buckley, Notre Dame Secondary School, Halton Catholic District School Board, Burlington, ON
Dave Chambers, Monsignor Paul Dwyer Catholic High School, Durham Catholic District School Board, Oshawa, ON
Linda Henshaw, John Fraser Secondary School, Peel District School Board, Mississauga, ON
Gillan Richards, Secondary Coordinator, Algoma District School Board, Sault Ste. Marie, ON
Judi Symes, Northview Heights Secondary School, Toronto District School Board, North York, ON
Joe Szekeres, Monsignor Paul Dwyer Catholic High School, Durham Catholic District School Board, Oshawa, ON

Project Manager: Ian Nussbaum
Developmental Editor: Su Mei Ku
Editor: Jennifer Mallory
Production Coordinator: Jonathan Pressick
Copy Editor: John Eerkes
Proofreaders: Jane A. Clark, Margaret Allen, Dianne Broad
Permissions Coordinator, Photo Researcher: Mary Rose MacLachlan
Permissions Editor: Karen Becker
Cover Design, Interior Design, and Art Direction: Sonya V. Thursby, Opus House Incorporated
Page Composition: Carolyn Hutchings Sebestyen
Cover Illustration: Kevin Ghiglione/i2i art inc.
Printing and Binding: Friesen Printers

 Printed in Canada on acid-free paper

1 2 3 4 5   05 04 03 02 01

> Contents

> Unit 3: Media

> Unit 4: The Reference Shelf

> Alternative Groupings
of the Selections

> Genres

> Authors

According to Country of Origin or Cultural Background

> Themes

> To the Students

The purpose of this book is to help you further develop your literacy skills to increase your chances of success in your personal lives, in school, and in the world of work. You will have an opportunity to read short stories, poems, dramas, novel excerpts, comic strips, articles, speeches, and informational texts. The voices you will hear when you read represent a wide variety of experiences from Canada and from around the world.

The selections and activities invite you to:

Think
- about new ideas
- critically and creatively
- about your own and others' values

Apply
- previous knowledge
- learned skills

Understand
- a variety of types of texts
- explicit and implicit meanings in what you read
- new ways of thinking about ideas and issues

Write
- using the writing process
- in a variety of forms for a variety of purposes and audiences
- in your own and others' voices

Research
- independently and with a group
- using electronic, print, and human resources

Speak and Listen
- in pairs, in small groups, and as a class
- in formal and informal situations

Create and Evaluate
- media works
- presentations

Reflect
- on your own work
- on the work of your classmates

This book is divided into four units.

Unit 1, "Books Are Quiet Friends," reviews some skills you acquired in Grade 10 and introduces you to important skills you will be working on throughout this year.

Unit 2, Literature, contains five parts, each having a theme: "Learning with Purpose," "Who Am I?" "A Different Drummer," "Love Like the Ocean," and "Ineffable Beauty." In each of these parts, you will read a variety of types of writing, from short stories to informational texts. Each of the themes explores ideas and issues relevant to contemporary young Canadians.

Unit 3, Media, focuses on furthering your understanding of the impact of the media on you and on the world around you.

Unit 4, The Reference Shelf, gives you information, rules, and tips for using language in oral, written, and visual forms. You will also find information about life skills that are important to your success at work, school, and home.

The Glossary provides definitions of key words and phrases that are used in the activities and that you will encounter throughout your study of English. Glossary terms appear in boldface in the activities.

In Units 1 through 3, the activities are divided into the following sections:

Before Reading: You will think, talk, or write about something that will help you read and understand the selection that follows.

Responding: You will talk or write about the way in which the selection has affected you and how the writer has made you feel the way you do.

Understanding: You will practise reading skills such as understanding implicit and explicit meanings, recognizing elements of both fiction and non-fiction, and interpreting ideas and information in texts.

Thinking about Language: You will work with specific aspects of language: grammar, vocabulary, voice, intent, and structure.

Extending: You will be asked to extend your knowledge and understanding of your reading through writing, oral presentations, and media creations.

A Note about the Icons: You will notice two different icons in a number of activities. This icon indicates language and grammar activities. This one indicates media-related activities. Since most of the activities in Unit 3 are media-related, the media icon is not used in that unit.

Where to Go from Here

It is important for you to be aware of your progress throughout this English course. Although your teacher will continually assess your skills and knowledge, it is important that you also monitor your progress. Here are some things you can do to evaluate your successes and your weaknesses:

- Keep track of your marks on tests, assignments, and group projects.
- Make a list of the comments that you have received from your teacher and your peers.
- Keep a portfolio of your own work that includes written reflections on how you think you are doing.
- Keep a log of the reading you have done throughout the course.
- Keep a response journal in which you can write both the responses asked for in the selections and those you generate yourself.
- Keep a list of new words and their definitions.
- Keep a list of the spelling errors that you have made on assignments and the correct spelling for those words.
- Keep a list of grammatical errors that you have made on assignments.
- Keep track of your homework, making sure that you have specific directions for each assignment.

Enjoy this book, and good luck in your learning this year.

Sue Harper

Doug Hilker

UNIT 1

Family Circus

BIL KEANE

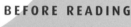

BEFORE READING

In your notebook, make a chart describing the differences between television, radio, and books. In a third column, explain under which conditions you are most likely to use each of these media.

After Reading

RESPONDING

1. Explain why you agree or disagree with the role of thinking in each of the media described in this comic strip.

UNDERSTANDING

2. Explain whether you would describe this comic strip as mainly humour or as propaganda.
3. In one paragraph, explain the differences in the balloons over the boy's head and the girl's head. In a second paragraph, explain the purpose of the differences.
4. Identify the **audience** you think the artist has in mind for "Family Circus." Give reasons for your choice.

THINKING ABOUT LANGUAGE

5. The boy in this comic uses the word "hafta." With a partner, brainstorm a list of other words that people would misspell if they wrote them down as they are usually pronounced. Write the correct spelling of the word next to the incorrect one. Post your list as part of a bulletin board display about the relationship between correct pronunciation and correct spelling.

EXTENDING

6. Explain whether you think there is any gender **bias** in this comic strip. Be prepared to discuss your conclusions with the class.
7. Add another frame to this comic strip, in which the boy describes what a computer is like. Display your frame on a class bulletin board.
8. Prepare a short presentation to the class about your favourite newspaper cartoon or comic strip series.

A Eulogy and a Poem

BEFORE READING

As a class, **define "eulogy."** Brainstorm a list of the types of things that might be included in a eulogy.

Justin Trudeau: A Son's Eulogy

"...what a dad."   JUSTIN TRUDEAU

Friends, Romans, countrymen.

I was about six years old when I went on my first official trip. I was going with my father and my Grandpa Sinclair to the North Pole. It was a very glamorous destination.

But the best thing about it was I was going to be spending lots of time with my dad. Because in Ottawa he just worked so hard.

One day, we were in Alert, Canada's northernmost point, [a] scientific, military installation that seemed to consist entirely of low, shed-like buildings and warehouses. Let's be honest: I was six. There were no brothers around to play with. And I was getting a little bored because Dad still somehow had a lot of work to do.

I remember a frozen, windswept Arctic afternoon. And I was bundled up into a Jeep and hustled out on a special, top-secret mission.

I figured I was finally going to be let into the reason for the existence of this high-security Arctic base. I was exactly right.

We drove slowly through and past the buildings, all of them very grey and windy. And we rounded a corner, and came upon a red one.

We stopped. I got out of the Jeep and started to crunch across toward the front door, but I was told no — to the window.

So I clambered over the snowbank, boosted up to the window, rubbed my sleeve across the frosty glass to see inside, and as my eyes adjusted to the gloom, I saw a figure, hunched over one of many worktables that seemed very cluttered.

He was wearing a red suit with a furry white trim. And that's when I understood just how powerful and wonderful my father was.

[Applause]

Pierre Elliott Trudeau. The very words convey so many things to so many people: statesman, intellectual, professor, adversary, outdoorsman, lawyer, journalist, author, prime minister.

But more than anything, to me he was Dad. And what a dad.

He loved us with a passion and a devotion that encompassed his life. He taught us to believe in ourselves. To stand up for ourselves. To know ourselves, and to accept responsibility for ourselves.

We knew we were the luckiest kids in the world, and that we had done nothing to actually deserve it.

It was instead something that we would have to spend the rest of our lives to work very hard to live up to.

He gave us a lot of tools. We were taught to take nothing for granted. He doted on us but didn't indulge. Many people say he didn't suffer fools gladly. But I'll have you know he had infinite patience with us.

He encouraged us to push ourselves, to the limits. To challenge anyone and anything. But there were certain basic principles that could never be compromised.

As I guess it is for most kids in Grade 3, it was always a real treat to visit my dad at work. As on previous visits, this particular occasion included a lunch at the parliamentary restaurant, which always seemed terribly important and full of serious people that I didn't recognize.

But at eight, I was becoming politically aware. And I recognized one whom I knew to be one of my father's chief rivals.

Thinking of pleasing my father, I told a joke about him. A generic, silly little grade school thing. My father looked at me sternly, with that look I would learn to know so well.

And said: "Justin, [in translation] we never attack the individual. We can be in total disagreement with someone without denigrating them as a consequence." And, saying that, he stood up, took me by the hand, and brought me over to introduce me to this man.

He was a nice man, who was eating there with his daughter, a nice-looking blonde girl, a little younger than I was. He spoke to me in a friendly manner for a bit, and it was at that point that I understood that having opinions that are different from another does not preclude being deserving of respect as an individual.

Because simple tolerance, mere tolerance, is not enough. We need genuine and deep respect for each and every human being, notwithstanding their thoughts, their values, their beliefs, their origins.

That's what my father demanded of his sons, and that's what he demanded of his country. He demanded this out of a sense of love. Love of his sons. Love of his country. And that's why we love him so.

The letters, the flowers, the dignity shown by the crowds in bidding their farewells — all of this as a thank you for having loved us so much [end translation].

My father's fundamental belief in the sanctity of the individual never came from a textbook. It stemmed from his deep love for and faith in all Canadians, and over the past few days, with every card, every rose, every tear, every wave, and every pirouette, you returned his love.

It means the world to Sacha and me. Thank you.

We have gathered from coast to coast to coast. From one ocean to another, united in our grief to say goodbye. But this is not the end. He left politics in '84, but he came back for Meech, he came back for Charlottetown, he came back to remind us of who we are and what we're all capable of.

But he won't be coming back anymore. It's all up to us—all of us—now.

The woods are lovely, dark and deep. He has kept his promises and earned his sleep.

Je t'aime, papa.

Stopping by Woods on a Snowy Evening

ROBERT FROST

Whose woods these are I think I know.
His house is in the village though;
He will not see me stopping here
To watch his woods fill up with snow.

My little horse must think it queer   5
To stop without a farmhouse near
Between the woods and frozen lake
The darkest evening of the year.

He gives his harness bells a shake
To ask if there is some mistake.   10
The only other sound's the sweep
Of easy wind and downy flake.

The woods are lovely, dark and deep,
But I have promises to keep,
And miles to go before I sleep,   15
And miles to go before I sleep.

After Reading

RESPONDING

1. Using a **graphic organizer**, list the words and phrases, thoughts, and emotions that Justin Trudeau's eulogy triggered in you. Compare your response with a partner's response.
2. The last **stanza** of Robert Frost's **poem** is often quoted in **speeches**, as it is in Justin Trudeau's eulogy. Give reasons why these lines resonate with many people. Explain whether you feel the quotation from this poem is used effectively in the eulogy.

UNDERSTANDING

3. In your notebook, describe the main and supporting ideas in this eulogy.
4. Justin Trudeau includes two personal stories from his childhood. In a short opinion paragraph, explain how these stories add to or detract from the effectiveness of his eulogy. Be prepared to present your opinion to the class.
5. Write an interpretation of Robert Frost's poem that explains who the **narrator** is, what he is doing, and how he is feeling.
6. Identify the meter and **rhyme scheme** of this poem. (See The Reference Shelf, pages 246–249.) Explain how both relate to the ideas expressed and how they contribute to the **mood** of the poem.

THINKING ABOUT LANGUAGE

7. Reread the eulogy. With a partner, look closely at the transitions that are used to create unity and coherence. Make a list of the transitions under the headings "thought transitions" and "word transitions." (See The Reference Shelf, pages 267–269.)

8. On page 8, Justin Trudeau implies a difference between tolerance and respect. As a class, using the text and your own personal experience, define each of these words, showing how they are similar and how they are different.

EXTENDING

9. a) In a small group, using electronic and/or print resources, examine the coverage of Pierre Elliott Trudeau's death by two different newspapers on the same day. (You can use any dates between September 29, 2000 and October 3, 2000.) Be sure to look at:
   - the number of **articles** in each paper
   - the number of letters to the editor
   - the **topics** of the articles
   - the **bias** of the newspaper
   - the number of photos included
   - the types of photos included

   b) Write a **report** on your findings, using clear subtitles for each section. Take your writing through the writing process in preparation for submission.

Busted

HARLAN HOWARD

BEFORE READING

With a partner, discuss whether enough is done for people who are poor or "down on their luck" in your community. Decide what assistance programs society should keep, change, or add in order to help its neediest citizens. Be prepared to present your ideas to the class.

My bills are all due and the baby needs shoes, and
    I'm busted
Cotton is down to a quarter a pound, but
    I'm busted
I got a cow that went dry and a hen that won't lay   5
And a big stack of bills that gets bigger each day
The county's gonna haul my belongings away, 'cause
    I'm busted

I went to my brother and asked for a loan, 'cause
    I'm busted   10
I hate to beg like a dog without his bone, but
    I'm busted
My brother said, 'There ain't a thing I can do
My wife and kids are all down with the flu
And I was just thinking of calling on you, and   15
    I'm busted.'

Well I am no thief but a man can go wrong, when
   he's busted
The food that we canned all last summer is gone,
   and I'm busted   20
The fields are all bare and the cotton won't grow
Me and my family got to pack up and go
But I'll make a living, just where I don't know
'Cause I'm busted
I'm broke…no bread…I mean like nothin'   25
   …forget it…

After Reading

RESPONDING

1. Choose one word that best describes the speaker in these song lyrics. In a paragraph, give specific examples from the poem to support the word you chose.

UNDERSTANDING

2. Make a list of the problems facing the speaker in these song lyrics.
3. In your notebook, write the advice you would give to the speaker if you knew he was about to steal food to feed his family.
4. With a partner, discuss the repetition of the words "I'm busted" in these lyrics. Determine whether the repetition increases or decreases the sympathy the reader feels for the speaker. Be prepared to report on your discussion to the class.

THINKING ABOUT LANGUAGE

5. With a partner, discuss the last two lines of the lyrics with the four sets of ellipses. Determine what this tells the reader about the speaker. Be prepared to report on your discussion to the class.

EXTENDING

6. **Debate** the following resolution: "Be it resolved that the courts should take extenuating circumstances into consideration when sentencing offenders." (See The Reference Shelf, pages 278–279.) You may need to do additional research to prepare arguments for the debate.

Pampered Teens Don't Have It Bad

"We, the young people of today, are a marginalized group."

SAROJINI MCKENNA

BEFORE READING

1. Read the title of this **essay**. Do you agree or disagree with its message? As a class, discuss your opinions, using examples wherever possible.

2. With the class, **define** "marginalized" as used in the above quotation from the essay.

Give me a gang fight. A biker war. Just don't tell me little Susie is carrying a gun to school.

Such is the cry from parents frightened and bewildered at the trend of rising school violence.

And while weapons offences in schools are reportedly up, the truth is, society prefers crimes committed by drugged-out, gang-warring black men than by suburban schoolgirls. It is easier to understand and accept that impoverished minorities commit crimes: they are marginalized from society and its norms.

But what explains the anger and aggression of middle-class youth? Well, what society accepts about minorities or drug addicts may be equally applicable to bankers' sons and lawyers' daughters. The children of the middle class are not mainstream at all.

We, the young people of today, are a marginalized group. But before you think this is another whiny complaint about eagle-eyed store clerks and their prejudicial treatment of teenagers, listen up. Young people are marginalized because adults treat us with kid gloves.

There is a pervasive, if elusive notion in our society that you cannot expect much from a teenager. They will inevitably spend hours on the phone or in Internet chat rooms. They are engrossed in their own worlds and efforts to involve them in practical concerns will be unsuccessful.

Teenagehood is a dark, tumultuous tunnel, but eventually teens will emerge on the other side and re-enter society. For now, however, parents should tiptoe around teens.

Seeking to be the "turned-the-bad-kid-around" educator, doormat teachers offer

after-school help with pitiful, if endearing, constancy.

And it is a self-fulfilling prophecy. Treating young people differently than one would treat anyone else inevitably pushes us to the margins of society: a place where neither normal responsibilities nor expectations apply.

Of course, not all young people are living this life of luxury, namely the nearly 1.5 million impoverished children growing up in Canada, as reported by Statistics Canada last year.

Ask any squeegee kid or foster child over 16 (the age at which Children's Aid renounces responsibility for foster children), and they'll tell you no one is making life easier for them. Even more reason to wonder why privileged teens don't always seem much happier.

Some of the most jaded, embittered teenagers I know are the ones whose lives ostensibly should be running smoothly. Their parents take care of everything: give them money, drive them everywhere, do the grocery shopping and the cooking.

These kids wouldn't know a gas bill from their elbows. Does this sound like real life? No. In real life, everyone, no matter how young, does what they can to contribute to the running of their own lives. These teens, however, inhabit an unearthly world devoid of real independence or responsibility.

Like many a celebrity before them, when the practicalities of life are miraculously taken care of, teens such as these can easily lose focus and go off the rails.

I do not believe teenagers the world over are similarly disconnected from the realities of their own lives.

By the time my Indian grandmother was my age, 17, she was married and had two children. Rural kids labour on their families' farms after school and during the summer. New-immigrant teenagers translate everything, from report cards to tax returns, for their parents. Scores of 12-year-old African children are caring for younger siblings as the AIDS epidemic kills their parents.

Some of these examples are tragic, and I would never advocate foisting on young people responsibilities too onerous for them to handle. That is simply abusive.

But you know what else is abusive? Driving your 15-year-old kid to school every day.

After Reading

RESPONDING

1. "Young people are marginalized because adults treat us with kid gloves." Find this statement in the **essay**. Write a **journal** entry responding to this statement.

UNDERSTANDING

2. Find the writer's evidence in this essay for saying that it is the parents' fault that pampered teens do not take responsibility for anything.
3. This essay is about increasing school violence. With a partner, reread your journal and your answer to activity 2. Write a description of the author's **thesis**. Is the thesis **implicit** or **explicit**? Explain how you arrived at your understanding of the thesis.
4. Describe the **voice** in this essay. Explain how this voice could backfire on the writer, depending on the **audience** reading the essay.

THINKING ABOUT LANGUAGE

5. Reread the essay, and find examples of the writer using questions.

EXTENDING

6. Using print and/or electronic resources, find incidents of violence among Canadian young people. Choose one story, and write a **report** on the case using the following headings: introduction, the incident(s), the outcome, conclusions.
7. a) Imagine that the principal asks you what can be done about violence among teenagers in your school and community. In a small group, propose an action plan. Some things you might want to include are poster campaigns, guest speakers, Crime Stoppers, and the involvement of local merchants and community groups.
   b) Present your action plan, carefully laid out so that the information in it is logical, easy to read, and clearly labelled with headings or subtitles.
   c) Have another group read your plan to look for the above three qualities.

Small Change Can Add Up to a Big Loss

"With a little planning, you can avoid costly transactions."

ELLEN ROSEMAN

BEFORE READING

As a class, brainstorm the pros and cons of a student in Grade 11 having access to a credit card or a bank debit card.

You're short of money, so you stop at an automated teller machine, or ATM, to make a withdrawal. That quick cash can often cost you $1, $2, even $3 a pop, depending on whose ATM you use and what kind of account you have. Do it every weekend and you may pay $150 a year in fees.

That's no small change.

Even virtual institutions that advertise "no-fee accounts" still charge for each withdrawal you make at another institution's ATM.

And if you use one of the new generic or "white label" machines, you'll pay an additional $1 to $2, on top of the $1.25 fee for Interac, the national electronic payments network shared by the country's financial institutions.

If you want to save money, check into whose slot you're sliding your card. With a little planning, you can avoid costly transactions.

As a frequent ATM user, you should have a bank account that provides a number of services for a flat monthly fee, or keep the minimum balance your bank requires in order to waive certain fees. Without one or the other, you may pay 30 cents to $1 for each ATM transaction, even if you use your own bank's machine.

Deal with an institution whose ATMs are convenient to your home, office or shopping areas. Count up the Interac charges on your monthly statements. Consider switching if the cost is too high.

Industry Canada, which publishes an annual report on bank service charges, has developed five typical consumer profiles.

One customer has two monthly ATM withdrawals at institutions other than his or her own bank. So does the connected consumer, who never goes into a branch.

But the convenience consumer, whose time is at a premium and who disregards where transactions are made, makes eight withdrawals a month from another institution's ATM.

If you fit that profile, find a bank with ATMs on your normal route. Recognize you won't go out of your way if the weather is chilly or you're in a hurry.

White-label machines are multiplying fast. Thousands are in stores, shopping malls, and restaurants, operated by private firms.

You can find out whether you're dealing with a generic ATM. A message on the screen asks if you're aware of the extra charge and allows you to abort the transaction.

Use your bank debit card to pay for purchases whenever possible. When you swipe a card through a point-of-sale terminal and key in a personal identification number, or PIN, money is automatically transferred from your account to the store's account.

You should have a service package that includes debit-card transactions.

When using a bank card at an ATM at a store, shield your PIN as you enter it. Someone who looks over your shoulder to get your PIN and later steals your card can take everything from your account.

With a stolen debit card, you may be on the hook for the full amount lost. You're more likely to be held liable if you haven't taken care of your PIN. It's your electronic signature.

Many people don't realize they have unlimited liability. They think stolen debit cards are treated the same way as credit cards, where you're on the hook for $50 at most if you report the theft right away.

After Reading

RESPONDING

1. In your notebook, identify one piece of advice presented in this **article**, and explain why you agree or disagree with it.

UNDERSTANDING

2. Create a chart for people your age that explains the similarities and differences between credit cards and bank debit cards. You may do research and add information that is not included in this article.

3. Write a one-sentence alternative headline for this article.

THINKING ABOUT LANGUAGE

4. Create a **glossary** of terms used in this article for someone unfamiliar with banking in general and electronic banking in particular.

5. In your notebook, copy sentences from this article that illustrate the following: a simple sentence, a complex sentence, a compound sentence, and a compound-complex sentence. In each case, explain why the sentence you chose is an example of a certain kind of sentence structure. (See The Reference Shelf, pages 228–230.)

EXTENDING

6. a) Write a short **essay** explaining whether credit cards help people to stay within their budget or cause them to spend more than their budget. Include several reasons or examples to support your position.

   b) With a partner, revise and edit your essay, focusing on organization, use of support, and correct spelling, punctuation, and grammar.

7. **Debate** the following resolution: "Be it resolved that young people today know the value of a dollar." (See The Reference Shelf, pages 278–279.) You may need to do additional research to prepare arguments for the debate.

Catalogue

ROSALIE MOORE

BEFORE READING

As a class, list the benefits of having a pet. In another list, record reasons for not having pets.

Cats sleep fat and walk thin.
Cats when they sleep, slump;
When they wake, pull in —
And where plump's been
There's skin.   5
Cats walk thin.

Cats wait in a lump,
Jump in a streak.
Cats, when they jump, are sleek
As a grape slipping its skin —   10
They have technique.
Oh, cats don't creak.
They sneak.

Cats sleep fat.
They spread comfort beneath them   15
Like a good mat,
As if they picked the place
And then sat.
You walk around one
As if he were the City Hall   20
After that.

If male,
A cat is apt to sing on a major scale;
This concert is for everybody, this
Is wholesale.   25
For a baton, he wields a tail.
(He is also found
When happy, to resound
With an enclosed and private sound.)

A cat condenses.   30
He pulls in his tail to go under bridges,
And himself to go under fences.
Cats fit
In any size box or kit;
And if a large pumpkin grew under one,   35
He could arch over it.

When everybody else is just ready to go out,
The cat is just ready to come in.
He's not where he's been.
Cats sleep fat and walk thin.   40

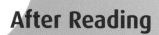

After Reading

RESPONDING

1. In a sentence, explain why the title of this **poem** is or is not appropriate to the poem. In a second sentence, suggest another title and explain why it would be appropriate.

UNDERSTANDING

2. In a paragraph, identify the main qualities of a cat that are described in this poem.
3. Explain your favourite line or lines in this poem to a partner.

4. Describe the meter and **rhyme scheme** in this poem. Explain the relationship between the information in the poem and the meter and rhyme scheme. (See The Reference Shelf, pages 246–249.)

THINKING ABOUT LANGUAGE

5. Explain the difference between the meaning of the apostrophe "s" the two times it is used in **stanza** 1.

EXTENDING

6. **Debate** the following resolution: "Be it resolved that cats make better pets than dogs." (See The Reference Shelf, pages 278–279.) You may need to do additional research to prepare arguments for the debate.

7. a) Write a poem about your favourite pet or animal. With a partner, revise and edit your poem.

   b) As a class, create an **anthology** entitled "In Praise of Our Favourite Pets and Animals."

8. With a partner, using print and/or electronic sources, research various types of cats. Create your own "Cat-alogue" that lists and describes the various types. Include pictures to help your readers visualize the kinds of cats you have included.

The Best Kind of Fear

J. WILLIAM KNOWLES

BEFORE READING

With a partner, discuss things that people pay to do that create both fear and excitement. Discuss why something that is frightening can also be exciting. Be prepared to present your ideas to the class.

Narrow winding
rock-bitten track:
the SPRONG of the suspension fork
topping out, the back wheel
slides sideways on wet root,   5
the inner ear compensates
like some pure instinct;
single-minded,
you are two fat tires,
dirt,   10
mud,
the blur of trees.

The climb:
teeth together,
snarling the air   15
into your lungs,
rubber sinks into dirt,
claws at rock;
exertion, an acid,
floods your muscles;   20
then the top:
a saving splash of water
from the bottle.

The descent:
lean back, you are   25
weightless with adrenaline,
eyes wide
with the best kind of fear,
bump,
bounce,   30
slide;
you can't turn back now,
can't re-think,
don't hesitate
or you will lose your line,   35
break an arm,
break a collar bone,
or break your neck;
just lean back
and don't brake too hard—   40
now you're alive.

After Reading

RESPONDING

1. Identify the sporting activity described in this **poem**. Write a paragraph explaining why you are or are not interested in participating in it.

UNDERSTANDING

2. For someone who has never participated in or seen this sport, explain what the following terms mean: "track" (line 2), "the climb" (line 13), "the top" (line 21), and "the descent" (line 24).
3. Explain the reference to the "inner ear" in **stanza** 1.

THINKING ABOUT LANGUAGE

4. Explain how the poet has used grammar and punctuation to try to create for the reader the experience described in this poem.

EXTENDING

5. As a parent, write a letter encouraging your son or daughter to start participating in the activity described in this poem. Have a partner read your letter and make suggestions about revising your arguments and language to make the letter more persuasive.
6. Write a series of paragraphs describing "The Best Kind of Fear" you ever experienced.
7. With a partner, prepare a business plan or **proposal** for an "adventure business" that offers people thrills and excitement in a safe way. Present your business plan or proposal to the class to see if anyone would invest in your proposed business.

No-Pear-A-Bow

"It was a woman!"

CATHY MIYATA

In the prefecture of Fukuoka-Ken, out in the lonely countryside, there is a slope, a hill really, that divides the road. You could walk to the left and go around the hill, or you could walk to the right and go around. It would save a lot of time to leave the road and climb up over the hill, but no one ever does. It is whispered that No-Pear-A-Bow is there.

One night a young man was coming home from working in the rice fields. It was late and he walked along. All he could think about was his sweet wife, waiting patiently for him to return, holding a bowl of steaming white rice for him to eat. He walked even faster.

When he got to the fork in the road, he stood and sighed. He had so far to go. To walk around the hill meant another hour or more. He cautiously looked up the slope. All seemed quiet and undisturbed.

The bamboo shoots rustled slightly in the breeze, and crickets shrilled their strange evening alarm.

"What could it hurt?" he wondered. He had never met anyone who had actually seen No-Pear-A-Bow. The poor farmer who used to own the land went mad long ago. Why should he believe the ravings of a crazy person? The occasional disappearance of someone from the village couldn't have anything to do with a hill . . .

He stepped off the road and into the weeds that smothered the steep slope. Then he stopped. "Remember No-Pear-A-Bow," a voice whispered in his head. He shivered.

"This is silly," the man said aloud, daring the voice. "I am a grown man, with a wife and child. I should not be afraid of old stories and strange rumours."

Boldly he took another step.

"Remember No-Pear-A-Bow," murmured the voice as it crept up his neck, swirled around him and was swallowed up by the shadows among the trees.

He took a step back. He looked left then right. No one was about. He thought of his bowl of delicious, steaming white rice.

"I'll run," he announced bravely to himself, and started up the hill. As quickly as he could, he wound his way between the bamboo groves and bushes. It was more work than he had expected. About halfway up, he discovered a worn path and gratefully followed that.

By the time he got to the top of the hill, he was breathless and stopped to rest. The night was still. A sliver of a moon barely lit his way, but the path was easy to see. He stood and listened. Not a sound.

"How peaceful," he thought; but then he realized even the crickets were hushed.

He was just about to move on, when a sad, whimpering sound froze him in his steps.

"A wounded animal" was his first thought, but no, it began to sound more and more human. He leaned toward the sound, straining to hear it better. His eyes grew wide and anger washed over him, for now it sounded like a child.

"Surely a baby could not have been left here alone!" Pushing aside the bushes, he moved urgently toward the noise. Deeper and deeper, through the thick yabu, he thrust, until the sound was right beside him. Lifting the branch of a great pine, he paused and stared into the darkness. It was a woman! He could see her back. She was kneeling on the ground, her head bent forward so he could not see her face. Her hair was carefully plaited and wound up over

her head. Her kimono, richly embroidered, spread out around her on the bare ground.

"*O-jo-san*," he whispered, trying to show his respect, for surely she was a woman of wealth.

"*O-jo-san*," he said louder, "please, what has happened?"

Her whimpering grew into a steady sob.

He dared not touch her, but obviously something was terribly wrong. He stepped around her to see if she was injured, but saw nothing that would indicate she was. She had her face buried in the sleeves of her gown and she would not look at him.

"*O-jo-san*," he said gently, "let me help you. I will take you down the hill. It is not safe for you to be here."

At this, her sobbing became a long, low wail and she pulled the sleeves tightly over her face.

He looked around uneasily. "Please, please," he begged, "we must leave this place. I will help you to get home."

She shook her head from side to side and screeched like a wounded crow.

"Stop that!" exclaimed the young man, for the sound was making his skin crawl. "Come now!" he insisted, "We must get out of here." Boldly he reached out and took her arms. He pulled her sleeves down, peering into her face — and gasped.

For what he saw was not a face. Where her eyes should have been there were only smooth, empty holes. Where her nose should have been, there was only a slight mound of flesh, and where her mouth should have been there was only a pinkish bubbled blister.

He stared in horror as her face melted and moulded and shaped itself into an egg! A long, jagged crack appeared down the smooth slippery surface and an eerie moan howled from inside.

The man screamed, he stumbled backwards and fell heavily to the ground. The moaning grew louder. Terrified to look at her again, he turned and tore through the brush, scratching his face and hands. Wildly, he ran among the trees, tripping over roots and falling over rotting logs. Again and again he got up and ran, the wretched sound following closely.

Ahead, he could see a light. Like a moth, he ran toward it. It was a lantern. The lantern was attached to a cart. Miraculously, there was an *udon* seller! Someone was there to help! Almost blinded by his fear, he could just make out the pedlar bending over the wares in his cart.

Screaming madly, he ran to the figure and fell at his feet.

"*Kore, kore?*" demanded the *udon* seller, his voice oddly calm. "Tell me what has happened."

The young man lay there, panting and sobbing, struggling to find the words.

"Are you hurt?" the *udon* seller demanded.

"No . . . no . . . a woman . . . a thing . . . horrible . . . horrible . . .!" he babbled between sobs.

"What sort of a woman?" the pedlar asked, but the young man could not answer.

"Look at me and speak!" the *udon* seller shouted. The pedlar grabbed the young man roughly by his shoulders and hauled him to his feet. "Look at me!" he demanded.

By the light of the lantern the pedlar forced the young man to look up. Their eyes met. The *udon* seller gasped and pulled away. He covered his face with his hands, and stumbled backwards, falling onto the road. He looked up at the young man now standing over him.

"Ahhhhhhhhhhhhhhhhhhhhhhhhhh!" And the light went out.

After Reading

RESPONDING

1. a) Keeping in mind the qualities of a good ghost story, assess whether "No-Pear-A-Bow" is a good ghost story. In your notebook, justify your assessment.

   b) Make point-form notes on what would make this a better ghost story. Discuss these ideas with the class.

UNDERSTANDING

2. With a partner, record in your notebooks what happened to the young man during his time in the forest and after he left it. Support your inferences with evidence from the story.

3. Find the clues from pages 25–27 that help you predict something terrible is going to happen to the young man.

THINKING ABOUT LANGUAGE

4. There are some Japanese words in this story. Record the words in your notebook and, from the **context** around the words, predict their meanings. Check these meanings with your teacher. As a class, discuss whether or not writers should include foreign-language words in their stories.

5. On page 25, the writer has used ellipses at the end of the paragraph. In your notebook, explain why ellipses were used. (See The Reference Shelf, page 237.)

EXTENDING

6. a) Some people believe stories that contain ghosts or magic are not appropriate for study in school. In a small group, gather evidence for or against this viewpoint. Use print, human, and electronic resources to help you support your arguments. List all your sources so that you can include them in your arguments.

   b) In your group, tape an oral **report** for your principal in which you present your ideas.

7. a) Visit the library and read another ghost story. Write a book **review** for another Grade 11 class under the following subtitles: the writer, a **summary** of the **plot** (keep this very brief), your opinion of the plot and **characters**, the way the writer has built **suspense**, and the writer's writing **style** (vocabulary, is it difficult or easy to read?).

   b) Exchange your review with a partner, who will read it and comment on the content of the review, the organization of the information, and the appropriateness of the **tone** for the **audience**.

   c) Revise your writing to prepare it for submission.

EXCERPT FROM *Night*

"With every groan of the wheels on the rail, we felt that an abyss was about to open beneath our bodies."

ELIE WIESEL

BEFORE READING

As a class, brainstorm what you know about the Holocaust.

Night is a first-person account of Second World War Nazi concentration camp horrors. This excerpt records the train trip of Jews rounded up in Sighet, Transylvania (now part of Romania) to Auschwitz, Poland.

Saturday, the day of rest, was chosen for our expulsion.

The night before, we had the traditional Friday evening meal. We said the customary grace for the bread and wine and swallowed our food without a word. We were, we felt, gathered for the last time round the family table. I spent the night turning over thoughts and memories in my mind, unable to find sleep.

At dawn, we were in the street, ready to leave. This time there were no Hungarian police. An agreement had been made with the Jewish Council that they should organize it all themselves.

Our convoy went toward the main synagogue. The town seemed deserted. Yet our friends of yesterday were probably waiting behind their shutters for the moment when they could pillage our houses.

The synagogue was like a huge station: luggage and tears. The altar was broken, the hangings torn down, the walls bare. There were so many of us that we could scarcely breathe. We spent a horrible twenty-four hours there. There were men downstairs; women on the first floor. It was Saturday; it was as though we had come to attend the service. Since no one could go out, people were relieving themselves in a corner.

The following morning, we marched to the station, where a convoy of cattle wagons was waiting. The Hungarian police made us get in — eighty people in each car. We were left a few loaves of bread and some buckets of water. The bars at the window were checked, to see that they were not loose. Then the cars were sealed. In each car one person was placed in charge. If anyone escaped, he would be shot.

Two Gestapo officers strolled about on the platform, smiling: all things considered, everything had gone off very well.

A prolonged whistle split the air. The wheels began to grind. We were on our way.

Lying down was out of the question, and we were only able to sit by deciding to take turns. There was very little air. The lucky ones who happened to be near a window could see the blossoming country-side roll by.

After two days of traveling, we began to be tortured by thirst. Then the heat became unbearable.

Free from all social constraint, young people gave way openly to instinct, taking advantage of the darkness to flirt in our midst, without caring about anyone else, as though they were alone in the world. The rest pretended not to notice anything.

We still had a few provisions left. But we never ate enough to satisfy our hunger.

To save was our rule; to save up for tomorrow. Tomorrow might be worse.

The train stopped at Kaschau, a little town on the Czechoslovak frontier. We realized then that we were not going to stay in Hungary. Our eyes were opened, but too late.

The door of the car slid open. A German officer, accompanied by a Hungarian lieutenant-interpreter, came up and introduced himself.

"From this moment, you come under the authority of the German army. Those of you who still have gold, silver, or watches in your possession must give them up now. Anyone who is later found to have kept anything will be shot on the spot. Secondly, anyone who feels ill may go to the hospital car. That's all."

The Hungarian lieutenant went among us with a basket and collected the last possessions from those who no longer wished to taste the bitterness of terror.

"There are eighty of you in this wagon," added the German officer. "If anyone is missing, you'll all be shot, like dogs. . . ."

They disappeared. The doors were closed. We were caught in a trap, right up to our necks. The doors were nailed up; the way back was finally cut off. The world was a cattle wagon hermetically sealed.

We had a woman with us named Madame Schächter. She was about fifty; her ten-year-old son was with her, crouched in a corner. Her husband and two eldest sons had been deported with the first transport by mistake. The separation had completely broken her.

I knew her well. A quiet woman with tense, burning eyes, she had often been to our house. Her husband, who was a pious man, spent his days and nights in study, and it was she who worked to support the family.

Madame Schächter had gone out of her mind. On the first day of the journey she had already begun to moan and to keep asking why she had been separated from her family. As time went on, her cries grew hysterical.

On the third night, while we slept, some of us sitting one against the other and some standing, a piercing cry split the silence:

"Fire! I can see a fire! I can see a fire!"

There was a moment's panic. Who was it who had cried out? It was Madame Schächter. Standing in the middle of the wagon, in the pale light from the windows, she looked like a withered tree in a cornfield. She pointed her arm toward the window, screaming:

"Look! Look at it! Fire! A terrible fire! Mercy! *Oh, that fire!*"

Some of the men pressed up against the bars. There was nothing there; only the darkness.

The shock of this terrible awakening stayed with us for a long time. We still trembled from it. With every groan of the wheels on the rail, we felt that an abyss was about to open beneath our bodies. Powerless to still our own anguish, we tried to console ourselves:

"She's mad, poor soul. . . ."

Someone had put a damp cloth on her brow, to calm her, but still her screams went on:

"Fire! Fire!"

Her little boy was crying, hanging onto her skirt, trying to take hold of her hands. "It's all right, Mummy! There's nothing there. . . . Sit down. . . ." This shook me even more than his mother's screams had done.

Some women tried to calm her. "You'll find your husband and your sons again . . . in a few days. . . ."

She continued to scream, breathless, her voice broken by sobs. "Jews, listen to me! I can see a fire! There are huge flames! It is a furnace!"

It was as though she were possessed by an evil spirit which spoke from the depths of her being.

We tried to explain it away, more to calm ourselves and to recover our own breath than to comfort her. "She must be very thirsty, poor thing! That's why she keeps talking about a fire devouring her."

But it was in vain. Our terror was about to burst the sides of the train. Our nerves were at breaking point. Our flesh was creeping. It was as though madness were taking possession of us all. We could stand it no longer. Some of the young men forced her to sit down, tied her up, and put a gag in her mouth.

Silence again. The little boy sat down by his mother, crying. I had begun to breathe normally again. We could hear the wheels churning out that monotonous rhythm of a train traveling through the night. We could begin to doze, to rest, to dream. . . .

An hour or two went by like this. Then another scream took our breath away. The woman had broken loose from her bonds and was crying out more loudly than ever:

"Look at the fire! Flames, flames every-where. . . ."

Once more the young men tied her up and gagged her. They even struck her. People encouraged them:

"Make her be quiet! She's mad! Shut her up! She's not the only one. She can keep her mouth shut. . . ."

They struck her several times on the head — blows that might have killed her. Her little boy clung to her; he did not cry out; he did not say a word. He was not even weeping now.

An endless night. Toward dawn, Madame Schächter calmed down. Crouched in her corner, her bewildered gaze scouring the emptiness, she could no longer see us.

She stayed like that all through the day, dumb, absent, isolated among us. As soon as night fell, she began to scream: "There's a fire over there!" She would point at a spot in space, always the same one. They were tired of hitting her. The heat, the thirst, the pestilential stench, the suffocating lack of air — these were as nothing compared with these screams which tore us to shreds. A few days more and we should all have started to scream too.

But we had reached a station. Those who were next to the windows told us its name:

"Auschwitz."

No one had ever heard that name.

The train did not start up again. The afternoon passed slowly. Then the wagon doors slid open. Two men were allowed to get down to fetch water.

When they came back, they told us that, in exchange for a gold watch, they had discovered that this was the last stop. We would be getting out here. There was a labor camp. Conditions were good. Families would not be split up. Only the young people would go to work in the factories. The old men and invalids would be kept occupied in the fields.

The barometer of confidence soared. Here was a sudden release from the terrors of the previous nights. We gave thanks to God.

Madame Schächter stayed in her corner, wilted, dumb, indifferent to the general confidence. Her little boy stroked her hand.

As dusk fell, darkness gathered inside the wagon. We started to eat our last provisions. At ten in the evening, everyone was looking for a convenient position in which to sleep for a while, and soon we were all asleep. Suddenly:

"The fire! The furnace! Look, over there! . . ."

Waking with a start, we rushed to the window. Yet again we had believed her, even if only for a moment. But there was nothing outside save the darkness of night. With shame in our souls, we went back to our places, gnawed by fear, in spite of ourselves. As she continued to scream, they began to hit her again, and it was with the greatest difficulty that they silenced her.

The man in charge of our wagon called a German officer who was walking about on the platform, and asked him if Madame Schächter could be taken to the hospital car.

"You must be patient," the German replied. "She'll be taken there soon."

Toward eleven o'clock, the train began to move. We pressed against the windows. The convoy was moving slowly. A quarter of an hour later, it slowed down again. Through the windows we could see barbed wire; we realized that this must be the camp.

We had forgotten the existence of Madame Schächter. Suddenly, we heard terrible screams:

"Jews, look! Look through the window! Flames! Look!"

And as the train stopped, we saw this time that flames were gushing out of a tall chimney into the black sky.

Madame Schächter was silent herself. Once more she had become dumb, indifferent, absent, and had gone back to her corner.

We looked at the flames in the darkness. There was an abominable odor floating in the air. Suddenly, our doors opened. Some odd-looking characters, dressed in striped shirts and black trousers leapt into the wagon. They held electric torches and truncheons. They began to strike out to right and left, shouting:

"Everybody get out! Everyone out of the wagon! Quickly!"

We jumped out. I threw a last glance toward Madame Schächter. Her little boy was holding her hand.

In front of us flames. In the air that smell of burning flesh. It must have been about midnight. We had arrived — at Birkenau, reception center for Auschwitz.

After Reading

RESPONDING

1. Write a series of paragraphs describing how the best and worst aspects of human behaviour are revealed in the events chronicled in this excerpt.

UNDERSTANDING

2. Explain why the Jewish Council would offer to organize the gathering of Jews in the synagogue at the beginning of this excerpt.
3. Explain why the author of this first-person account spends so much time describing the nocturnal ravings of Madame Schächter.

THINKING ABOUT LANGUAGE

4. Describe the **mood** of this excerpt. Refer to specific words, phrases, and sentences to explain how the mood is created and sustained.

EXTENDING

5. Read the rest of this book, *Night*, and report on specific aspects of it to the class.

6. a) Sometimes young people ask why the Jews did not resist more, why they allowed themselves to be rounded up across Europe and sent to concentration camps. Using print and/or electronic sources, research the events in Europe at the time of the Holocaust.

   b) Based on your research, write an **essay** that addresses this question. Take your essay through the writing process before submission. Be sure to create a bibliography of all the sources that you used. (See The Reference Shelf, pages 255–257.)

7. Using print and/or electronic sources, research the life of Elie Wiesel and prepare a **report** to present to the class.

What's in This Toothpaste?

"...chalk, water, paint, seaweed, antifreeze, paraffin oil, detergent, peppermint, formaldehyde and fluoride."

DAVID BODANIS

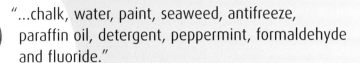

BEFORE READING

Read the information on organizing an **essay** in The Reference Shelf (pages 262–263). Look at the margin notes in this essay for examples of the structure of a well-organized essay.

Into the bathroom goes our male resident, and after the most pressing need is satisfied it's time to brush the teeth. The tube of toothpaste is squeezed, its pinched metal seams are splayed, pressure waves are generated inside, and the paste begins to flow. But what's in this toothpaste, so carefully being extruded?

Introduction

Statement of topic

Water mostly, 30 to 45 per cent in most brands: ordinary, everyday, simple tap water. It's there because people like to have a big gob of toothpaste to spread on the brush, and water is the cheapest stuff there is when it comes to making big gobs. Dripping a bit from the tap onto your brush would cost virtually nothing; whipped in with the rest of the toothpaste the manufacturers can sell it at a neat and accountant-pleasing price. Toothpaste manufacture is a very lucrative occupation.

1st ingredient (water)

Second to water in quantity is chalk: exactly the same material that schoolteachers use to write on blackboards. It is collected from the crushed remains of long-dead ocean creatures. In the Cretaceous seas (from the age of dinosaurs), chalk particles served as part of the wickedly sharp outer skeleton that these creatures had to wrap around themselves to keep from getting chomped by all the slightly larger other ocean creatures they met. Their massed graves are our present chalk deposits.

2nd ingredient (chalk)

The individual chalk particles — the size of the smallest mud particles in your garden — have kept their toughness over the eons, and now on the toothbrush they'll need it. The enamel outer coating of the tooth they'll have to face is the hardest substance in the body — tougher than skull, or

description

bone, or nail. Only the chalk particles in toothpaste can successfully grind into the teeth during brushing, ripping off the surface layers like an abrading wheel grinding down a boulder in a quarry.

what it does

The craters, slashes, and channels that the chalk tears into the teeth will also remove a certain amount of built-up yellow in the carnage, and it is for that polishing function that it's there. A certain amount of unduly enlarged extra-abrasive chalk fragments tear such cavernous pits into the teeth that future decay bacteria will be able to bunker down there and thrive; the quality control people find it almost impossible to screen out these errant super-chalk pieces, and government regulations allow them to stay in.

3rd ingredient (titanium dioxide)

In case even the gouging doesn't get all the yellow off, another substance is worked into the toothpaste cream. This is titanium dioxide. It comes in tiny spheres, and it's the stuff bobbing around in white wall paint to make it come out white. Splashed around onto your teeth during the brushing, it

what it does

coats much of the yellow that remains. Being water soluble it leaks off in the next few hours and is swallowed, but at least for the quick glance up in the mirror after finishing it will make the user think his or her teeth are truly white. Some manufacturers add optical whitening dyes — the stuff more commonly found in washing machine bleach — to make extra sure that glance in the mirror shows reassuring white.

need for other ingredients

These ingredients alone would not make a very attractive concoction. They would stick in the tube like a sloppy white plastic lump, hard to squeeze out as well as revolting to the touch. Few consumers would savour rubbing in a mixture of water, ground-up blackboard chalk and the whitener from latex paint first thing in the morning. To get around that finicky distaste the manufacturers have mixed in a host of other goodies.

3 more ingredients

To keep the glop from drying out, a mixture including glycerine glycol — related to the most common car antifreeze ingredient — is whipped in with the chalk and water, and to give that concoction a bit of substance (all we really have so far is wet coloured chalk) a large helping is added of gummy molecules from the seaweed *Chondrus crispus*. This seaweed ooze spreads in among the chalk, paint and antifreeze, then stretches itself in all directions to hold the whole mass together. A bit of paraffin oil (the fuel that flickers in camping lamps) is pumped in with it to help the moss ooze keep the whole substance smooth.

2 more to come

With the glycol, ooze and paraffin we're almost there. Only two major chemicals are left to make the refreshing, cleansing substance we know as toothpaste. The ingredients so far are fine for cleaning, but they wouldn't make much of the satisfying foam we have come to expect in the morning brushing.

next ingredient (detergent)

To remedy that, every toothpaste on the market has a big dollop of detergent added too. You've seen the suds detergent will make in a washing machine. The same substance added here will duplicate that inside the mouth. It's not particularly necessary, but it sells.

The only problem is that by itself this ingredient tastes, well, too like detergent. It's horribly bitter and harsh. The chalk put in toothpaste is pretty foul-tasting too for that matter. It's to get around that gustatory discomfort that the manufacturers put in the ingredient they tout perhaps the most of all. This is the <u>flavouring</u>, and it has to be strong. Double rectified peppermint oil is used — a flavourer so powerful that chemists know better than to sniff it in the raw state in the laboratory. Menthol crystals and saccharin or other sugar simulators are added to complete the camouflage operation.

next ingredient (flavouring)

<u>Is that it? Chalk, water, paint, seaweed, antifreeze, paraffin oil, detergent and peppermint?</u> Not quite. A mix like that would be irresistible to the hundreds of thousands of individual bacteria lying on the surface of even an immaculately cleaned bathroom sink. They would get in, float in the water bubbles, ingest the ooze and paraffin, maybe even spray out enzymes to break down the chalk. The result would be an uninviting mess. The way manufacturers avoid that final obstacle is by putting something in to kill the bacteria. Something good and strong is needed, something that will zap any accidentally intrudant bacteria into oblivion. And that something is <u>formaldehyde</u> — the disinfectant used in anatomy labs.

final ingredient (formaldehyde as a disinfectant)

<u>So</u> it's chalk, water, paint, seaweed, antifreeze, paraffin oil, detergent, peppermint, formaldehyde and fluoride (which can go some way towards preserving children's teeth) — that's the usual mixture raised to the mouth on the toothbrush for a fresh morning's clean. If it sounds too unfortunate, take heart. Studies show that brushing with <u>just plain water</u> will often do as <u>good a job.</u>

Conclusion

After Reading

RESPONDING

1. Write a response expressing your feelings about the information in this essay. How do the ingredients make you feel about toothpaste?

UNDERSTANDING

2. Write a **summary** of this essay in 100 words or less. Compare your summary with that of a partner.

3. a) Reread the essay and decide whether David Bodanis is for or against modern toothpaste. Be sure to look at the language he uses as part of the evidence to support your opinion.

   b) As a class, discuss the opinions of your classmates and arrive at a **consensus** about the writer's attitude.

4. The opening paragraph should grab the reader's attention and indicate what the reader will find in the essay. Explain how this essay's opening paragraph does both.

5. With a partner, make a list of the transition words or phrases the writer uses from one paragraph to the next. Look at both the ends and beginnings of paragraphs. Indicate in which paragraphs you have found each transition. (See The Reference Shelf, pages 267–269.)

THINKING ABOUT LANGUAGE

6. In your notebook, write five words that were unfamiliar to you before reading this essay. Find them in a dictionary, and record the **definition** of each word.

EXTENDING

7. a) What if all advertisers had to be perfectly honest when they advertised a product? In a small group, write and perform a television **commercial** for toothpaste in which you disclose the ingredients. When thinking about your commercial, consider different approaches, including using humour, using a famous person, scaring your audience (in order to get them to try your brand), and animating the toothpaste tube.

   b) When you have written and rehearsed your commercial, perform it for another group. Listen to their comments about the content and whether or not they would buy your product.

   c) Revise and rehearse your commercial in preparation for presentation.

8. Use this essay structure as a model and write an **essay** entitled "What's in This _____?" Your subject could be a food product, a fabric, a toy, or anything else for which you can find out the ingredients. Take your essay through the writing process.

Hockey Stick Is a Canadian Artefact

"About 85 per cent of today's hockey sticks are made in small towns in Ontario and Quebec."

FABRICE TAYLOR

BEFORE READING

As a class, brainstorm a list of products that people around the world associate with Canada and would tend to buy if there was a "Made in Canada" label on them.

What

The humble yet mighty hockey stick.

What About It

Despite all the hand-wringing about Canada's waning dominance in the game, we can still boast prominence in one area of hockey: the manufacturing of sticks. About 85 per cent of today's hockey sticks are made in small towns in Ontario and Quebec. Most of the rest are made in Europe and the U.S.

Ideal Qualities

The trick to making a good stick is to give it just the right flexibility and as much strength as possible, without adding too much weight. Flexibility, which gives a stick "whipping" action, can add horsepower to a slapshot. Strength comes in handy when you're getting busy with someone in front of the net, either on the giving or receiving end of a solid two-hander, say.

The shafts of most wood sticks are made of aspen, a light hardwood. The blades are made of white ash and birch. All blades are reinforced with fibreglass, as are many wood shafts.

But technology has been cruel to the wood stick. Aluminum shafts caught on in the [1980s] (when Wayne Gretzky started using one), and in the [1990s], it was composite sticks, made of space-age materials like graphite and even titanium.

Not all innovation is aimed at materials. Last year, Hespeler Hockey introduced the offset stick, which, like an offset golf club, has a kink in the shaft, a few inches up from the blade. It's meant to provide accuracy, but it takes getting used to.

Major Canadian Manufacturers

The Hockey Company (brands: Jofa, CCM, Canadien, Koho, Titan); Bauer Nike Hockey Inc. (Nike and Bauer brands; Nike bought Bauer a few years ago); Sherwood

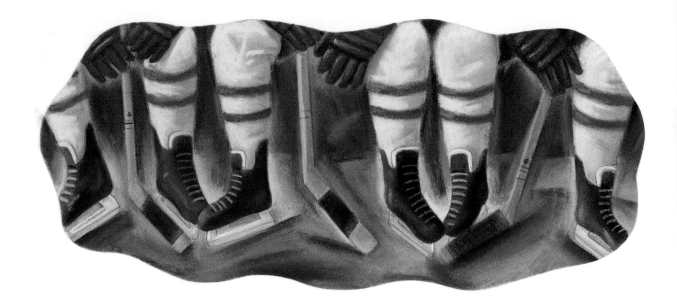

(Sher-Wood); Louisville; and Easton (which makes aluminum sticks in Mexico, of all places).

The Curve

Exactly who invented the curved hockey stick is a point of contention, but it gained wide popularity in the [1960s], the heyday of one of its more skilled users, Bobby Hull.

Curves, which add control, are limited today in the NHL to a half-inch. (In 1967, the limit was set at 1 1/2 inches.

Length Matters

The length of hockey sticks is a useful gauge to measure the increasing size of hockey players. The longest sticks today are a maximum of 63 inches. [In the 1930s], they were 53 inches long.

Patriotic Perversion

For some strange reason, roughly two-thirds of sticks sold here are left-handed, while two-thirds sold south of the border are right-handed. Americans are also much more likely to prefer non-wooden sticks.

What's in a Name

Some sticks have NHL players' names stamped on them. This means the stick's blade has the same curve and shape as the player's.

After Reading

RESPONDING

1. Make a list of the ways this article says hockey sticks have changed over the years. If you know of any additional changes hockey sticks have undergone, add them to the bottom of your list.

UNDERSTANDING

2. Select two comments in this article that deal in opinion rather than objective information about hockey sticks. Write a paragraph explaining whether these opinions are appropriate in an article such as this one. Give reasons for your position.
3. With a partner, assess the usefulness to the reader of the subtitles in this article. Decide whether they should be left as they are, reworded, or removed. Be prepared to present your decisions and the reasons for them to the class.

THINKING ABOUT LANGUAGE

4. Select two words in this selection that you think are not well chosen. Using different words, revise the sentences in which they appear and give at least one reason for the change that you made.

EXTENDING

5. a) Write a letter to the National Hockey League indicating why it is or is not important to have rules governing the shape of and the materials in the hockey sticks used by professional hockey players.
   b) With a partner, revise and edit your letter in preparation for submission.
6. Using print and/or electronic sources, research another product made in Canada. Create a similar information article about the product. Use diagrams or illustrations if necessary to help your readers better understand the product.

Setting Up a Printer

BEFORE READING

With a partner, describe the hardest set of instructions you ever tried to follow. Consider what made those instructions so hard to follow. Be prepared to describe your experience to the class.

1. Unpacking the Printer

Remove the printer from its packaging. Check that you have all these items:

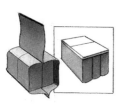

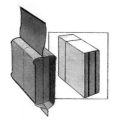

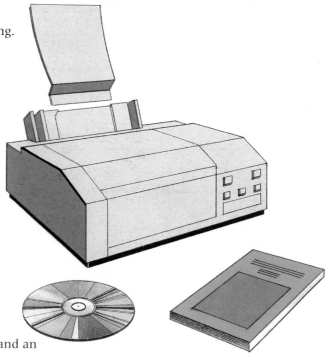

Put the printer near your computer and an available outlet. Avoid areas with high temperature or humidity, in direct sunlight or dusty conditions, and near electromagnetic interference.

☞ Note: If you need help as you set up your printer, see "Troubleshooting" in the *Printer ABC Guide*.

2. Attaching the Paper Support

Attach the paper support into the slots at the back of the printer.

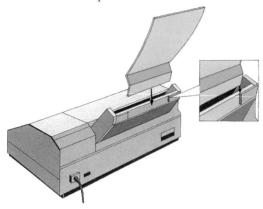

3. Installing the Ink Cartridge

1. Plug the printer's power cord into a grounded outlet.
2. Open the front cover.

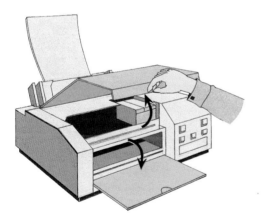

3. Press the power button to turn on the printer. The power light will flash. The ink cartridge holder will move into loading position.

 ! Don't use an outlet that is on the same circuit as a large appliance. This may disrupt the power to the printer, erasing its memory and/or damaging its power supply.

4. Disengage the arm of the ink cartridge holder.

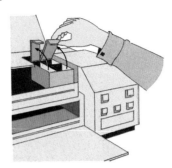

5. Remove the ink cartridge from its package.
6. Slide the ink cartridge (label facing out) into place, and engage the arm.

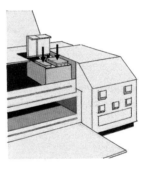

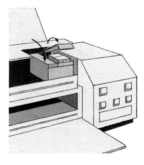

 ! If ink gets on your hands, wash them with soap and water. If ink gets in your eyes, flush them immediately with water.

7. Close front cover.

4. Loading the Paper

Load a stack of white paper, with the printable side facing up. Don't load the paper higher than the right-edge guide or the printer won't be able to grip it.

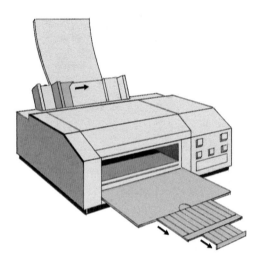

* These printer installation instructions are based on a combination of instructions from printers made by various manufacturers.

5. Connecting the Printer

1. Turn off the printer and the computer.
2. Connect the USB cable that came with your printer: one end to the printer jack, the other end to your computer. Make sure the connection is secure, then turn on your printer and computer, and run a "test" sheet.

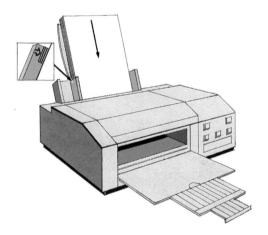

After Reading

RESPONDING

1. In a paragraph, explain why you think these instructions would be easy or difficult to follow.

UNDERSTANDING

2. With a partner, answer the following questions. Be prepared to present your answers to the class.
   a) According to these instructions, where can you get help if you have trouble following these instructions?
   b) Why are the points in the first two parts of the instructions not numbered as they are in the last three parts?
3. Identify at least three methods used in these instructions to make them clear and easy to follow. Compare your ideas with those of others in the class.
4. Identify one point in these instructions that you think could be made clearer. Explain how you would make that part of the instructions clearer.

THINKING ABOUT LANGUAGE

5. Count the number of times the term "ink cartridge" is used in these instructions. Explain why the writer of the instructions does not vary the term by using words such as "ink container" or "ink refill."

EXTENDING

6. Conduct an Internet search for the term "Plain Language." Explain how the rules of plain language apply to writing instructions such as these for setting up a printer. Be prepared to **report** on your findings to the class.
7. The next time you or your family gets something that comes with instructions, write a report on how easy or difficult it was to follow the instructions.

UNIT 2

> Literature

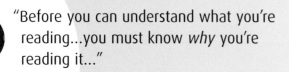

Reading with Purpose

"Before you can understand what you're reading...you must know *why* you're reading it..."

RON FRY

BEFORE READING

Read the activities that follow this **article** (page 55). On the basis of those activities, list five points you need to watch for as you read the article.

Even if you consider yourself "not much of a reader," you read *something* each and every day: a magazine article, instructions for hooking up the DVD player, telephone messages tacked on the refrigerator, notes from your latest heartthrob.

Regardless of *what* you are reading, you have a purpose that dictates *how* you are going to read it — and you read different items in different ways. You wouldn't read the DVD player instructions as you would a novel, any more than you'd read the magazine article in the same way as a grocery list. Without a purpose, you'd find yourself reading aimlessly and very inefficiently.

Unfortunately, many of the students I've talked to have not yet realized the importance of having a purpose for reading. Their lack of reading purpose can be summed up by the proverb, "If you aim at nothing, you will hit the bull's-eye every time."

Before you can understand what you're reading — and *remember* it — you must know *why* you're reading it in the first place.

DEFINING YOUR PURPOSE FOR READING

What is your purpose for reading? If the best answer you can come up with is, "Because my teacher said so," we need to come up with some better reasons. Reading a chapter just so you can say, "I finished my assignment," is relatively futile. You may as well put the book under a pillow and hope to absorb it by osmosis.

Unless you identify some purpose to read, you will find yourself flipping the pages of your textbooks while seldom retaining anything more than the chapter titles.

According to reading experts, there are six fundamental purposes for reading:

1. To grasp a certain message.
2. To find important details.

3. To answer a specific question.
4. To evaluate what you are reading.
5. To apply what you are reading.
6. To be entertained.

Because reading with purpose is the first step toward improved comprehension, let me suggest some simple techniques you can use to identify a purpose for *your* textbook reading.

FIND THE CLUES IN EVERY BOOK

There is a group of special sections found in nearly all textbooks and technical materials (in fact, in almost all books except novels) that contains a wealth of information and can help you glean more from your reading. Becoming familiar with this data will enrich your reading experience and often make it easier. Here's what to look for:

The first page after the title page is usually the *table of contents* — a chapter-by-chapter list of the book's contents. Some are surprisingly detailed, listing every major point or topic covered in each chapter.

The first prose section (after the title page, table of contents, and, perhaps, *acknowledgments page*, in which the author thanks other authors, his [or her] editor, researcher, friends, relatives, teachers, and so forth, most of which you can ignore), is the *preface*, usually a description of what information you will find in the book. Authors may also use the preface to point out unique aspects of their books.

The *introduction* may be in place of or in addition to the preface and may be written by the author or some "name" the author has recruited to lend additional prestige to his or her work. Most introductions are an

even more detailed overview of the book — chapter-by-chapter summaries are often included to give the reader a feel for the material to be covered.

Footnotes may be found throughout the text (a slightly elevated number following a sentence, quotation, or paragraph, for example, "jim-dandy"[24]) and either explained at the bottom of the page on which they appear or in a special section at the back of the text. Footnotes may be used to cite sources of direct quotes or ideas and/or to further explain a point, add information, and so forth, outside of the text. You may make it a habit to ferret out sources cited for further reading.

If a text tends to use an alarmingly high number of terms with which you may not be familiar, the considerate author will include a *glossary* — essentially an abridged dictionary that defines all such terms.

The *bibliography*, usually at the end of the book, may include the source material the author used to research the textbook, a list of "recommended reading," or both. It is usually organized alphabetically by subject, making it easy for you to go to your library and find more information on a specific topic.

Appendices containing supplementary data or examples relating to subject matter covered in the text may also appear in the back of the book.

The last thing in a book is usually the *index*, an alphabetical listing that references, by page number, every mention of a particular name, subject, and topic in the text.

Making it a habit to utilize all of these tools in your textbook can only make your studying easier.

LOOK FOR THE CLUES IN EACH CHAPTER

Every textbook offers some clues that will help you define a purpose for reading. Begin with a very quick overview of the assignment, looking for questions that you'd like answered. Consider the following elements of your reading assignment *before* you begin your reading.

Much as the headlines of a newspaper clue you into what the story is about, these elements will give insight into what the section or chapter is trying to communicate:

Chapter heads and subheads

Chapter titles and bold-faced subheads announce the detail about the main topic. And, in some textbooks, paragraph headings or boldfaced "lead-ins" announce that the author is about to provide finer details.

So start each reading assignment by going through the chapter, beginning to end, *reading only the boldfaced heads and subheads*.

For example, suppose you encountered the heading, "The Fall of Communism," in your history textbook. You might use it to formulate the following questions:

1. *What* caused the fall of Communism?
2. *Who* caused it?
3. *When* did it fall?
4. *Why* did it fall?
5. *Where* did the fall occur?

As you read the chapter, you'll find yourself seeking answers to these questions. You now have a purpose!

Often you may find headings that contain words or terms you don't recognize. Seeking to define these terms or explain a concept should then become your purpose.

This process of headline reading takes only a few minutes, but it lays the groundwork for a more intelligent and efficient reading of the chapter. You'll have some idea where the author is headed, which will help you identify the most important details and clarify where you should be concentrating your studying.

End-of-chapter summaries

If you read a mystery from start to finish, the way the author hopes you will, you're likely to get thrown off the scent by "red herrings" and other common detective novel devices. However, if you read the last page first, knowing the outcome will help you detect how the author constructed the novel and built an open-and-shut case for his or her master sleuth. You'd perceive a wealth of details about the eventually unmasked murderer that might have gone *un*noticed had he been just another of the leading suspects.

Similarly, knowing what the author is driving at in a textbook will help you look for the important building blocks for his [or her] conclusions while you're reading.

It may not be fun to read a mystery novel this way, but when it comes to textbook reading, it will help you define your purpose for reading. And further, it will transform you into a much more *active* reader, making it less likely you'll doze off while being beaten senseless by the usual ponderous prose.

Pictures, graphs, and charts

Most textbooks, particularly those in the sciences, will have charts, graphs, numerical tables, maps, and other illustrations. All too many students see these as fillers —

padding to glance at quickly, and, just as quickly, forget.

If you're giving these charts and graphs short shrift, you're really shortchanging *yourself*. Be sure to observe how they supplement the text, understand what points they emphasize, and make note of these.

Highlighted terms, vocabulary, and other facts

In some textbooks, you'll discover that key terms and information are highlighted within the text. (I don't mean highlighted by a previous student — treat such yellow-markered passages with caution!) To find the definitions of these terms, or to find the application of facts, may then be your purpose for reading.

Questions

Some textbook publishers use a format in which key points are emphasized by questions, either within the body of text or at the end of the chapter. If you read these questions *before* reading the chapter, you'll have a better idea of what material you need to pay closer attention to.

Prereading your assignment

If you begin your reading assignment by seeking out these heads, subheads, and other purpose-finding elements of the chapter, you'll have completed your prereading step. What is prereading? It is simply beginning your assigned reading by reviewing these clues and defining your purpose (or purposes) for reading.

I advise that you *always* preread every assignment! Why? Have you ever spent the better part of an evening plowing through an assignment only to finish with little or no understanding of what you just read? If the answer is yes, then you probably failed to preread it.

While the heads, subheads, first sentences, and other author-provided hints we've talked about will help you get a quick read on what a chapter's about, some of the *words* in that chapter will help you concentrate on the important points and ignore the unimportant. Knowing when to speed up, slow down, ignore, or really concentrate will help you read both faster *and* more effectively.

When you see words and phrases such as "likewise," "in addition," "moreover," "furthermore," and the like, you should know nothing new is being introduced. If you already know what's going on, speed up or skip what's coming entirely.

On the other hand, when you see "on the other hand," "nevertheless," "however," "rather," "but," and their ilk, slow down — you're getting information that adds a new perspective or contradicts what you've just read.

Lastly, watch out for payoff words and phrases such as, "to summarize," "in conclusion," "therefore," "consequently," "thus" — especially if you only have time to "hit the high points" of a chapter or you're reviewing for a test. Here's where the real meat is, where everything that went before is happily tied up in a nice bow and ribbon, a present that enables you to avoid having to unwrap the entire chapter.

PURPOSE DEFINES READING METHOD

Typically, your purpose for reading dictates how you read. There are basically three types of reading we all do:

1. **Quick reference reading** focuses on seeking specific information that addresses a particular question or concern we might have.
2. **Critical reading** involves discerning ideas and concepts that require a thorough analysis.
3. **Aesthetic, or pleasure reading**, is what we do for sheer entertainment or to appreciate an author's style and ability.

As you define your purpose for reading, you will determine which method of reading is necessary to accomplish this purpose. In the following table are some examples of types of reading, why you might read them, and the method you should use:

TYPE	PURPOSE	METHOD
Newspaper advertisement	To locate best price for car	Quick reference
Magazine	To stay aware of current events	Quick reference
Self-help book	To learn to get along better with your family	Critical
Biology text	To prepare for an exam	Critical
New issue of *Rolling Stone*	To take your mind off biology!	Pleasure

If you're a good reader or desire to be one: You will always fit your reading *method* to your reading *purpose*; you have trained or are training yourself in a variety of reading skills; you have no problem switching your method to accommodate your purpose; and you are unsatisfied reading only one type of material.

A poor reader, on the other hand, reads everything the same way — doggedly plowing through the biology assignment, the newspaper, and the Stephen King novel . . . word by painful word. Reading with purpose is both foreign and foreboding to such a person, which makes it difficult for him or her to adapt a method of reading.

BECOME AN ACTIVE READER

Reading with purpose is as vital to your comprehension and retention as oxygen is to life. It is the cornerstone of *active* reading, reading that involves thinking — that process of engaging your mind and emotions in what the author is trying to communicate. Too many readers seek to absorb information passively as their eyes move across the page. The active reader *involves* him- or herself in receiving a message — a fact, an idea, an opinion — that is readily retained because he or she had a *purpose*.

Following is a passage adapted from *101 Ways to Make Every Second Count* by Robert W. Bly (Career Press, 1999). *Preread* the passage in order to determine a *purpose* for reading. Be sure to jot down questions that may have been raised through your preread, as well as your purpose.

Learn to handle pressure and juggle projects

Are you too busy? If you've been in the corporate world for a spell, you know how difficult it can be to cope with an overload of work. Here are some suggestions for doing so.

Learn to say no. It's scary to turn down work or say no to a manager above you. But when you're truly too busy, it's sometimes the best thing to do. After all, if you take on more than you can handle and miss a deadline or do shoddy work in order to make the deadline, that will do far more harm to your relationship and reputation than saying no.

I rarely say no to current clients, unless the deadline is so tight that I cannot possibly make it. If that's the case, I ask if there's any reason why the deadline can't be a few days longer, and I usually get it. (Many deadlines are artificial and have no logic behind them.) If they cannot be flexible, I politely explain that the deadline is too short, thank them for the offer of the job, apologize for not being able to take it on, and suggest they give it to one of their other resources (freelancers, in-house staff, ad agency, production studio).

However, I frequently say no to new prospects who call me during a busy period. When they start to describe their project or ask about my service, I stop them and say, "I'd be delighted to talk with you about this project. But I don't want to waste your time, so I must tell you now that I am booked through the end of September [or whenever]. If the project is not a rush or if you can delay it until then, I'd be happy to work with you. If not, I'll have to pass."

Amazingly, the usual reaction is not anger or hostility (although a few callers get mad); instead, most are impressed, even amazed. ("You mean you are booked through September? Boy, you must be good!" one caller said today.) In fact, turning down work because you are booked frequently creates the immediate impression that you are in demand and thus tops in your field, creating an even stronger desire to work with you. Many people you turn down will call you back at the time you specify and ask, almost reverently, always respectfully, "You said call back in September. I have a project. Can you work with me now?" Try it. It works!

Set the parameters. An alternative to turning down work cold is to set the schedule and deadline according to your convenience, not theirs. "Well, I am booked fairly solidly," you tell the prospect. "I can squeeze you in; however, it will take seven weeks [or whatever] instead of the usual three to complete your project, because of my schedule. If you can wait this long, I'll be happy to help you. If not, I will have to pass on the assignment."

Again, many prospects will turn to someone who can accommodate their original deadline. However, many others will say "yes" to your request and hire you on your terms.

Get up an hour earlier. I find that mornings are my most productive time. I work best from 7 a.m., when I usually start, to 1 or 2 p.m.; after that, I slow down. If I am extremely busy, I try to start at 6 a.m. instead of 7 a.m. and find that I get an amazing amount of work done during that first extra hour. Also, it makes me less panicky for the rest of the day because I have accomplished so much so early.

Work an hour later or work one or two hours in the evenings after dinner. If you usually knock off at 5 p.m., go to 6 p.m. Or, if you generally watch television from 8 p.m. to 10 p.m., work an extra hour and a half from 10 p.m. to 11:30 p.m. I prefer the extra morning hour for client projects; evening time is reserved for my own self-sponsored projects, such as books, articles, or self-publishing.

Put in half a day Saturday morning or Saturday afternoon. If you have to work weekends, Saturday morning — say, from 8 a.m. to noon — is the best time. You get that early morning energy and get the work out of the way so you can relax and enjoy the rest of the weekend. If you are not a morning person, try Saturday afternoon. If you put the work off until Sunday, you'll probably just spend all Saturday worrying about it or feeling guilty about it, so don't. Get it done first thing and then forget about it.

Hire a temp. If you are under a crunch, consider getting temporary help for such tasks as proofreading, editing, research, typing, data entry, trips to the post office, and library research. Spend the money to get rid of unnecessary administrative burdens and free yourself to concentrate on the important tasks in front of you.

Break complex tasks into smaller, bite-size segments. Rush jobs are intimidating. If you have two weeks to work on a major brochure, but put it off until the last three or four days, the task looms large and panic can set in.

The solution is to break the project into subprojects, assign a certain amount of the task to each day remaining, and then write this down on a sheet of paper and post it on the wall or bulletin board in front of your desk.

Ask for more time. When you are just starting out, you naturally want to please co-workers and thus you agree to any deadline they suggest. In fact, you encourage tight deadlines because you believe that doing the work fast is a sign of doing your job right.

As you get older and more experienced, you learn two important truths. First, that many deadlines are artificial and can be comfortably extended with no negative effect on the client's needs whatsoever. And second, that it's more important to take the time to do the job right than to try and impress a naïve client or supervisor by doing it fast. What matters, for example, is not that the software was coded fast but that it works, meets user requirements, is reliable, and doesn't have bugs. So if you need extra time, ask for it. This is real service to the client. Doing rush jobs is not.

Get a fax machine. Before the advent of the fax machine, if I had a project due Wednesday, I pretty much had to be done with it on Tuesday at 3 p.m. so it could be printed and ready for Federal Express pickup by 5 p.m. Now with a fax machine, the job due Wednesday can be finished Wednesday at 4 p.m. and on the client's desk at 4:15 p.m. — giving me an extra day on every project.

Most corporate workers I know have fax machines. Some entrepreneurs don't. If your small business doesn't have one, get one. Don't waste time and money faxing documents at the local stationery store. Don't waste your time or other peoples' by making your fax compete with your modem and phone for use of one line; get separate lines for each. (Having the same number for phone and fax also is a sign to some people that you are not running a "real" business.)

Stay seated. Georges Simenon, author of the popular *Inspector Maigret* series of mystery novels, wrote more than 500 books. How did he do it? Simenon said that he limited his writing vocabulary to

2,000 words so he would not have to use a dictionary (there are more than 800,000 words in the English language, with 60,000 new words added since 1966). This allowed him to work continuously, without having to stop, open, and search a dictionary for a word. The key to his success then, at least in part, was working without interruption — he kept going, and didn't let anything stop him while he was hot.

You've heard the term "seat of the pants" used to describe a method of working. Although it originally referred to a person who made decisions by instinct without a lot of planning or formal study, for office workers the definition is different: You apply the bottom of your pants (your rear end) to the seat (your chair), and stay there until the work gets done.

This means getting into your chair — and staying there. No using the VCR monitor in your office to watch TV. No quick trips to the cafeteria for a snack. No gossiping around the water cooler. This sounds trivial, but is in fact an important point. To get a lot of work done, workers must stay at their workstations. For office workers, the workstation is your desk and chair. Distractions are death to peak personal productivity. It's bad enough that many distractions — drop-in visitors, emergencies, telemarketing calls — already present themselves during a normal workday. Do not seek them out deliberately.

After Reading

RESPONDING

1. In your **journal**, write about one thing you learned from reading this article and about how you can use that new knowledge in the future.

UNDERSTANDING

2. With a partner, create a chart like the one below in which you list the type of reading method, the purpose, and examples of reading you would do at home, work, and school.

Method of Reading (e.g., quick reference reading)

	EXAMPLES FROM HOME	EXAMPLES FROM SCHOOL	EXAMPLES FROM WORK
Purpose — looking for specific information that answers a specific question or concern	Reading a manual for the VCR in order to tape a program while I am out		

3. The designer of this article has provided the reader with visual aids that give the reader quick access to information in the article. Identify some of the visual aids and explain how each helps speed up reading.

THINKING ABOUT LANGUAGE

4. Italics are used several times in this article. Identify examples of italics used for naming something and italics used for emphasis. Include the page number beside your examples.

EXTENDING

5. a) In a small group, examine a textbook used for a subject other than English. Make a list of the "clues" the designer has used to make the text easier to read. Write a short description of each design clue.

   b) After rereading the article, give examples of what the designer of your text has not included that could have helped in your reading. Be prepared to give an oral **report** on your group's ideas and to take notes on the findings of other groups.

6. Think of a topic that interests you and that you would like to know more about.

   a) Visit the library, and, using a variety of electronic and print resources (the Internet, CD-ROMs, books, magazines, newspapers, encyclopedias), look at several sources that might contain information about your topic.

   b) Record the names of those sources, leaving enough space for taking notes on each one.

   c) Look at each of those sources for clues that will tell you whether or not it contains information that you can use to further your knowledge about your subject.

   d) For each source, write down whether it would be useful to you. If it would be useful, take notes on the information you can use. If not, explain how you know the source is not useful to you.

   e) Be prepared to discuss your topic and your research with a partner.

7. a) With a partner, create a poster to be displayed in your school promoting one "Tip for Reading" that Ron Fry includes in this selection. Include advertising techniques to create the most effective poster for your **audience**. Before finalizing your ideas, discuss your concepts and design with another partnership.

   b) As a class, create an evaluation form to assess each poster.

Why Write?

"Writing was a friend..."

CARYN MIRRIAM-GOLDBERG

BEFORE READING

Make a list of the types of writing you do. Consider all kinds of writing, from notes to your friends to e-mails, from diaries to homework assignments.

When I think of what writing has given me, especially when I was tumbling through my teen years, I realize there's not a basket big enough to hold the gifts. Just sitting down in a corner and filling up my notebooks inspired me, made me feel alive, carried me through the difficult times, and showed me I had something to give to the world. Writing was a friend who would meet me on the page whenever I needed to sit and talk. Your writing can help you get inspired, too. Following are twelve good reasons to write.

TWELVE REASONS TO WRITE

1. **Writing helps you discover who you are.** When you put pen to paper and pour out your thoughts, you begin to discover what you know about yourself and the world. You can explore what you love or hate, what hurts you, what you need, what you can give, and what you want out of life. This helps you better understand yourself and your place in the world.

2. **Writing can help you believe in yourself and raise your self-esteem.** The very act of making something out of nothing produces a feeling of pride and a sense of accomplishment. Knowing that you're able to fill up a journal with your

thoughts, write a story, or put together a research paper helps you believe in your own abilities, talents, and perseverance. Your increased self-confidence can inspire you to take more risks in your writing and in other creative activities.

> "I think I did pretty well, considering I started out with nothing but a bunch of blank paper." STEVE MARTIN

3. When you write, you hear your own unique voice. Poet William Stafford once said that a writer is not someone who has something to say as much as someone who has *found a way to say it.* Writing allows you to communicate in your own words and voice, without the filters and blocks you might use when talking to people you want to please, avoid, connect with, impress, or run from. Writing also gives you an opportunity to listen to your own distinctive voice, recognize it, and know it better.

> "Writing is a way of cutting away at the surface of things, of exploring, of understanding." ROBERT DUNCAN

4. Writing shows you what you can give the world. As you write, you can explore your particular talents, interests, and passions. What are you good at? What do you feel compelled to throw energy into? What do you want to improve? Writing allows you to delve deeper into yourself and put into words what it is you want to be and do. It helps you find your calling.

5. As you write, you seek answers to questions and find new questions to ask. Because writing forces you to sit and think, it can be a way of finding answers to questions in your life. Writing is introspective by nature; it gives you the opportunity to carefully review choices and decisions about everything from what to study, to who to hang out with, to how to tell someone what's on your mind. In the process of writing about your issues and examining your questions, you may find answers that are right for you.

> "I like to write when I feel spiteful; it's like having a good sneeze." D.H. LAWRENCE

6. Writing enhances your creativity. Creating anything means asking questions, dwelling in doubt and confusion, and finally reaching a breakthrough. When you write, you immerse yourself in the creative process. The more practice you get, the more easily you can transfer these skills to other areas of your life (school, activities, a job) that require creative solutions.

7. You can share yourself with others through writing. Many people believe that the written word allows for more freedom of expression than the spoken word. Writing lets you reveal aspects of yourself that don't always come across in face-to-face communication, phone conversations, or class discussions. Your writing self, in contrast to your talking self, has more time to reflect on what you believe, what you want to say, and why you think or feel a certain way.

8. **Writing gives you a place to release anger, fear, sadness, and other painful feelings.** Feelings are intense. They can hurt you to the core. (According to writer Oscar Wilde, their main charm is that they don't last!) When you're feeling angry, scared, upset, or depressed, it helps to get these emotions on paper rather than bottle them up. Writing is a safe way to release your feelings, explore them, and begin to cope.

What I Want to Write About:
1. How I felt when my teacher called on me, even though my hand wasn't raised!
2. Feeling shy

9. **You can help heal yourself through writing.** It's no secret that many writers derive at least some healing benefits from writing. Whether it's their career, passion, hobby, or all three, writing offers writers a way to examine their wounds and, if they want, share them with the world. You, too, can take what has hurt you and turn it into something that helps you. The very act of creating can be a way to heal.

10. **Writing can bring you joy and a way to express it.** It's fun to put into words what's important and meaningful to you, then read what you've written. But the *process* of writing can be fun, too. It's exciting to put words onto paper and fill up pages with your ideas and opinions, not knowing exactly what you're going to say or what will come next. When you allow yourself to relax and see what happens on the page, you experience the thrill of creative expression.

11. **Writing can make you feel more alive.** The words, the images, the delight or grief that surfaces, the discoveries, the answers or questions that come to you as you write — all of this helps you feel more alive. Writing, like any art, is a way to connect with yourself, other people, and the world. In doing so, you may feel more involved, engaged, and interested in life. You may even be compelled to embrace it wholeheartedly.

12. **You can discover your dreams through writing.** Through the quiet and solitary act of writing, you can discover your greatest dreams (not what you or other people *think* they should be, but what *really* calls to you). You can think about these dreams, what it would take for them to become real, and what you can do to start making things happen. Then you can write your way there.

"Lift up your eyes upon this day breaking for you. Give birth to a dream." MAYA ANGELOU

After Reading

RESPONDING

1. Write a brief note to the writer of this **article**, telling her your feelings about writing.

UNDERSTANDING

2. Look at the article's twelve reasons to write. Cluster these reasons under three or four new subtitles.

3. The designer of this text has used a variety of design techniques to make the reading easier and more visually interesting. With a partner, select three techniques and explain the impact they have on the reader.

4. a) Choose one of the twelve reasons to write. Using the writer's **point of view** and examples from your own life, write a **personal essay** on how writing has helped or could help you. Your essay should have an introduction, a body, and a conclusion. Remember that personal stories and quotations from others can help create interest in what you are writing.

   b) Word-process your essay and use a spelling- and grammar-check program to review your writing and correct your errors.

THINKING ABOUT LANGUAGE

5. Choose five words from the article for which you do not know the exact meaning. Write them in your notebook, and try to create a **definition** for each word based on its context. Check your definition against the dictionary's definition.

EXTENDING

6. Think of a job you might like to do when you finish school. Using human, print, and electronic resources, find out what types of writing are required in that job. Create a poster that presents all the types of writing required and includes a description and an example of each type of writing. Be prepared to display your poster in your classroom.

The Sentence: EXCERPT FROM
Angel Square

"It seems strange, a moose with a camera."   BRIAN DOYLE

BEFORE READING

In your notebook, record a memorable incident that occurred during your early years in grade school.

School wasn't getting along with me very well lately. And I wasn't getting along very well with it.

It pretty well started back when I was in grade five and Miss Strong just laughed at me when I said I wanted to be a writer when I grew up.

She didn't really laugh, I guess, she just made a kind of sound with her mouth like you would if you were blowing a little feather or a hunk of fluff off your upper lip just under your nose.

Or maybe it was way back in grade four when we had the I.Q. test. They gave all the grade fours an I.Q. test and I was the only one who had to go back the next day and do it over again. I saw Miss Frack and Miss Eck discussing mine. They were standing facing each other talking about my test. I knew because they looked over at me a couple of times. They both had huge chests and they were standing kind

of apart so their chests wouldn't bounce off each other.

They looked like two huge robins discussing a worm.

There was a lot of sighing and then they came and told me that I'd have to do the test again the next day. By the looks on their faces I figured they were saying that they knew I was stupid, sure, but could I possibly be that stupid? Could I be something subhuman? You'd have to be in a coma or something to score that low.

But Dad said that maybe I scored so high that the test couldn't record it — maybe I blew out all the tubes in the thing and they figured only a genius could score that high and they figured something went wrong with their test because even Albert Einstein couldn't score that high.

And they say he invented the atomic bomb.

That made me feel a bit better.

But I didn't really blame Miss Strong for laughing when I said I wanted to be a writer.

After all, I was the second worst writer in the class.

Melody Bleach was the worst writer in the class. Her main problem was she never had a pencil and she couldn't write with a pen and a nib because she pressed too hard.

Dad said the reason was, she wasn't organized.

And she always put her tongue out when she tried to write after she borrowed a pencil or the teacher gave her one.

She'd stick her tongue between her teeth when she was trying to think of what to write. Some of the kids would laugh at her and make fun of her.

I laughed at her too but I also felt sort of sorry for her.

Specially when she wet herself. That was in grade three, I think. Melody wet herself. She was too scared of Miss Frack

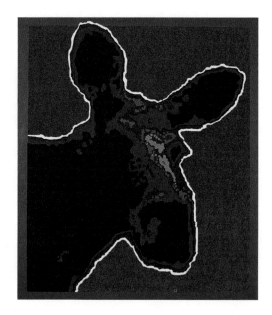

or Miss Eck, or whoever it was, to ask if she could leave the room.

So she just sat there and the water ran down off the seat into a pool on the floor under her desk. And the water ran down her cheeks from her eyes. There was water running out of her from both ends.

I think Dad was right. Her main problem was that she wasn't organized. Dad always says, get organized and you can't go wrong.

Suddenly I heard Blue Cheeks saying my name. Everybody was looking over at me. And Blue Cheeks was getting bluer. He was asking me about a grammar sentence. He was writing on the blackboard but he was looking at me.

Blue Cheeks could turn his head *right* around without moving his body. His head would start turning slowly and it would keep turning and turning until it was facing the other way. Then it would start back until it was back almost to the same spot. He could turn his head left and right so far that he could cover the whole 360 degrees without moving his shoulders. His head must have been on a swivel or something.

He would write grammar sentences on the board so that we could copy them out and then tell him what was wrong with them.

All the sentences he ever wrote on the board were wrong.

Every day we wrote down hundreds of sentences that were wrong.

Some of them were quite funny but if he heard anybody laughing or snorting, old Blue Cheeks's head would start coming around, slowly, slowly. And we'd all sit there, hypnotized by how far his head could come around.

I used to think it would unscrew and tumble right off onto the floor.

But then, of course, if that happened he could catch it just before it hit because his hands hung down there near the floor anyway.

Somebody must have coughed or something and he looked around and couldn't catch anybody so he noticed I was in a trance and picked me as his victim. I must have been staring into the blackboard like I was hypnotized. Dad said later that I must have looked like a cow watching a train go by.

"You! What is wrong with this sentence?"

He was pointing at the sentence he had just written on the board.

"Read the sentence, please," he said.

I read it. "Ralph edged closer as the moose sniffed suspiciously and snapped the picture," the sentence said.

"Well?" said Blue Cheeks.

I looked at the sentence again.

"Tell us, Mr. Daydreams, what is wrong with this sentence."

"It's something to do with the camera," I said.

"It's something to do with the camera, is it?" His head was right around facing me full-on now and his shoulders were still facing the blackboard. It seemed impossible.

"And the moose," I said, "and something to do with the moose."

"The camera and the moose," said Blue Cheeks, sarcasm dripping off his lips like syrup.

"And Ralph," I said, just to make sure, "there's something wrong with Ralph too."

"And what do you suppose it is that is wrong with Ralph?" said Blue Cheeks.

"He hasn't got the camera," I said.

"And who has the camera?"

"The moose seems to have the camera."

"And why has the moose got the camera instead of Ralph?"

"I don't know, sir. It seems strange, a moose with a camera."

"Why has the moose got the camera?"

"Maybe he took it from Ralph?"

"Why hasn't Ralph got his own camera?" Blue Cheeks's face was dark blue now.

"Maybe it *isn't* Ralph's camera!" I said, thinking I was on to something. "Maybe Ralph hasn't got a camera and the moose has a camera and Ralph's sneaking up on the moose to steal his camera!"

"Read the sentence again!"

"Ralph edged closer as the moose sniffed suspiciously and snapped the picture." I almost knew it off by heart now.

"What is wrong with that sentence?"

Behind me sat Geranium Mayburger, the dumbest girl in the school. Geranium loved to whisper answers to people. Specially people in trouble.

"Hooves," she whispered behind me. "A moose can't take a picture because his hooves are too big for the button."

"Five seconds," said Blue Cheeks, "or you stay and write lines!" He sounded like he was choking. I was desperate.

"A moose could never hold a camera properly or snap a picture because of its large and clumsy hooves," I said, trying to make the best sentence I could.

I knew I was doomed, so I sat down.

Blue Cheeks gurgled, "One hundred lines — 'I must learn my grammar'!"

A few minutes later the bell rang for recess and I was suddenly alone.

After Reading

RESPONDING

1. Explain whether the first sentence provides an effective beginning for this excerpt.

UNDERSTANDING

2. Explain how the **image** in the excerpt's fifth paragraph (page 61) captures both the physical and emotional aspects of the moment being described.

3. The **narrator** is writing about a time when he first knew he wanted to be a writer. Describe one quality of his writing in this excerpt that indicates he has become a good writer.

THINKING ABOUT LANGUAGE

4. "Ralph edged closer as the moose sniffed suspiciously and snapped the picture." In your own words, explain what is grammatically wrong with this sentence and how it can be fixed.

EXTENDING

5. In your notebook, write a few paragraphs explaining whether the narrator of this excerpt would have made a good teacher. Find reasons in the excerpt to support your position. Include an introductory and concluding sentence. Have a classmate read your writing and give you suggestions for revision.

6. The narrator's father blames the problems Melody Bleach has at school on lack of organization. Explain to a partner one problem you once had that you solved through better organization. Be prepared to present your experience as an organizational tip to other members of the class.

7. a) The sound made by Miss Strong that is described in the third paragraph (page 61) is an example of non-verbal communication. With a partner, brainstorm a list of ways in which people communicate without using words.
   b) Write a short **script** in which non-verbal communication plays as important a role as words do.
   c) Rehearse and present your script to the class.

8. a) Write a **story** about your own early school years. You might want to base it on the incident you wrote about in the "Before Reading" activity.
   b) As a class, collect all the stories and create an **anthology** entitled "Memories of Our Early School Years."

Maths

DEEPAK KALHA

BEFORE READING

With a partner, explain how a good knowledge of English can help you in math class. Be prepared to present your ideas to the class.

What do you minus,
and from where?
I ask my teacher,
but he don't care.

Ten cubic metres   5
in square roots,
Or how many toes
go in nine boots?

Change ten decimals
to a fraction   10
Aaaaaaaaaaaahhhhhhhhhh!
is my reaction.

After Reading

RESPONDING

1. Write a brief paragraph explaining a similar situation that you might have had with math or any other school subjects.

UNDERSTANDING

2. Explain why you think the **narrator** of this **poem** is better at English than at math.
3. With a partner, make up the math test that might have led to the feelings in the last **stanza**. Be prepared to present your test to the class.

THINKING ABOUT LANGUAGE

4. Identify and correct the grammar error in this poem. Explain why you think the poet included this error in the poem.

EXTENDING

5. Write a letter to your math teacher explaining (a) your greatest success this year in math class and (b) an area that you think you will need extra help with to understand. With a partner, revise and edit your letter for submission.

The Skills Employers Want

"...employers want good basic academic skills and much more."

BEFORE READING

As a class, make a list of the skills you think employers want.

Many employers say that the most important skills for any employee are reading, writing, and computation. With increasing regularity, employers are telling the media, "Give me people who can read, write, and do simple math and I'll train them for the jobs I have available." But probing further, one finds that employers want good basic academic skills *and much more. . . .*

So what are [some of] these basic workplace skills that employers want? They certainly include basic skills associated with formal schooling. But academic skills such as reading, writing and arithmetic comprise just the tip of the iceberg.

Employers want employees who can learn the particular skills of an available job—who have "learned how to learn."

Employers want employees who will hear the key points that make up a customer's concerns (listening) and who can convey an adequate response (oral communications).

Employers want employees who can think on their feet (problem-solving) and who can come up with innovative solutions when needed (creative thinking). . . .

This is a prescription for a well-rounded worker who has acquired a number of discrete skills and who has the capability to acquire more sophisticated skills when necessary.

THE FOUNDATION: KNOWING HOW TO LEARN

Knowing how to learn is the most basic of all skills because it is the key that unlocks future success. Equipped with this skill, an individual can achieve competency in all other basic workplace skills, from reading through leadership. Without this skill, learning is neither as rapid nor as efficient and comprehensive. . . .

Learning is now a fact of life in the workplace. Even routine jobs are evolving as the demands of the workplace expand.

Competitive pressures compel employers to shift employees between jobs and responsibilities, putting a premium on the ability to absorb, process, and apply new information quickly and effectively. The complexity, amount, and availability of information compound the issue. . . .

COMPETENCE: READING, WRITING AND COMPUTATION

Basic academic skills — reading, writing and computation — have long been revered as the keys to success in society and the workplace. In theory these skills have been essential, but in practice workers have often succeeded because of "a strong back and willing hands."

The workplace of the past was one in which those with limited academic achievements could succeed. Jobs often required going through the motions of a regularized process or repetitive interaction with machines. In that workplace, illiteracy and innumeracy could be hidden or ignored.

But today's workplace is one that increasingly involves interaction with sophisticated, computerized machinery that requires good reading skills for efficient use. The introduction of approaches such as statistical process control (SPC) demand higher mathematical skills. And writing is frequently the first step in communicating with customers, interacting with machines, documenting competitive transactions, or successfully moving new ideas into the workplace. . . .

Reading tasks on the job…require the reader to be analytical, to summarize information, and to monitor one's own comprehension of the reading task. This is an interpretive approach that requires the reader to have active involvement with the reading task. . . .

Workplace writing relies on analysis, conceptualization, synthesis and distillation of information, as well as clear, succinct articulation of points and proposals. . . .

Workplace math skills are taught contextually to reflect their actual use on the job; instructional materials simulate specific job tasks. Building on the prior math knowledge of the learner and emphasizing problem identification, reasoning, estimation, and problem-solving, this approach has been shown to produce the quickest, most effective results in employee performance.

Most employers today cannot compete successfully without a workforce that has sound basic academic skills. Workers spend an average of 1 $\frac{1}{2}$ –2h per workday engaged in reading forms, charts, graphs, manuals, computer terminals, and so on. Writing remains the primary form of communication for transmitting policies, procedures, and concepts. Computation is used daily to conduct inventories, report on production levels, measure machine parts or specifications, and so on.

Deficiencies in such basic workplace skills create barriers that impair an employer's ability to meet strategic goals and to be competitive. . . .

COMMUNICATION: LISTENING AND ORAL COMMUNICATION

Reading and writing are essential communication tools, but it is through listening and speaking that we interact most frequently. The average person spends 8.4 percent of communications time writing, 13.3 percent reading, 23 percent speaking, and 55 percent listening.

Workers spend most of their day in some form of communication. They communicate with each other about procedures and problems and they relay information to and receive it from customers. Success on the job is linked to good communications skills. In fact, recent studies have indicated that only job knowledge ranks above communication skills as a factor for workplace success. . . .

Employees who lack proficiency in oral communication and listening skills are handicapped as to their learning and communicating abilities, and their personal and professional development. Business leaders estimate that deficiencies in these skills cost employers millions each year in lost productivity and errors.

ADAPTABILITY: CREATIVE THINKING AND PROBLEM-SOLVING

Problem-solving skills include: the ability to recognize and define problems; to invent and implement solutions; and to track and evaluate results. Cognitive skills, group interaction skills, and problem-processing skills are all crucial to successful problem-solving. . . .

New approaches to problem-solving, organizational design, or product development all spring from the individual capacity for creative thinking. In the workplace, creative thinking is generally manifested as creative problem-solving or creative innovation. Often a group activity, creative problem-solving is characterized by effective teamwork, the examination of problems in new ways, and the invention of new solutions to existing problems. Either an individual or a group activity, creative innovation refers to the development of new activities that expand markets and improve such elements as productivity. . . .

GROUP EFFECTIVENESS: INTERPERSONAL SKILLS, NEGOTIATION, AND TEAMWORK

In the past two decades, there has been a tremendous increase in the use of teams in the workplace. The team approach has been linked conclusively to higher productivity and product quality, as well as to increased quality of worklife. . . .

Whenever people work together, successful interaction depends upon effective interpersonal skills, focused negotiation, and a sense of group purpose. The quality of these three factors defines and controls working relationships.

[Good] interpersonal skills [allow] the employee to recognize and improve the ability to judge and balance appropriate behavior, cope with undesirable behavior in others, absorb stress, deal with ambiguity,

listen, inspire confidence in others, structure social interaction, share responsibility, and interact easily with others.

Such skills are essential to successful **negotiation**. Conflicts, both major and minor, are a fact of worklife. They can sap productivity and short-circuit strategic plans.

The key to diffusing potential conflict situations is to enhance employee negotiating skills at all levels. . . .

Interpersonal and negotiation skills are the cornerstones of successful **teamwork**. Teams are organized in the workplace so that appropriate talents and skills can be directed through group effort to accomplish vital tasks and goals. This pooling of resources, however, frequently requires team members to have an array of skills that individual or routine jobs do not demand.

Quality teamwork results when team members know how to recognize and cope with various and unique personalities and when each has a sense of the cultures and approaches that other team members represent. Team members also need an understanding of group dynamics, which evolve and change as the team approaches its goal. Lastly, team members must be aware of the technical skills that fellow members have and how those skills can be applied.

Teamwork can only occur when team members provide and receive feedback in a focused manner. Individuals gather and process information in personalized ways; good teamwork calls for the recognition and use of certain valuable differences between members of the team. . . .

After Reading

1. Based on your reading of this **article**, make a list of employment skills that you think you already have. Beside the skill, write a brief note on how you acquired that skill.

UNDERSTANDING

2. Make point-form notes on the five skills discussed in this article. (Someone who has not read the article should be able to read your notes and understand the writer's main ideas.)

3. a) Think about your own work experience or your experiences in school or with other organizations. In a **personal essay**, explain which of the five skills described in this selection you think is the most important to success.

   b) Exchange your work with a partner who has a different skill listed as most important. Have him or her comment on your content (especially the arguments you have used in the body of your essay), organization, and your level of language. Prepare your essay for submission.

4. In a small group, think of possible solutions to each of the following problems. Before deciding on your final solution, brainstorm the issues surrounding the problem, the unknowns in the situation, and a variety of solutions.

   • Kevin is always late for work. He generally has someone cover for him so his boss doesn't notice. He doesn't know the boss has been keeping track for two weeks. Kevin really needs the job. The reason he has been late is that he has to babysit his little brother every day after school until his father gets home. The boss wants to simply fire Kevin, even though when he is there, Kevin is a good worker.

   • Sarita has been working at a company for three weeks. She is a good worker, always checking with her supervisor when she feels uncertain about a procedure. Her boss wants to change Sarita's job to fill a position that has been left vacant. It involves running a machine. The boss gives Sarita the manual for the machine and asks her to familiarize herself with the operating of the machine. Sarita does not read well enough to understand the manual. What should she do? The new job will give her more experience and slightly higher pay.

THINKING ABOUT LANGUAGE

5. In a small group, have each person choose one paragraph from the article. For each of these paragraphs, make a chart that examines the level of language and the **tone** of this article.

In your chart, describe the vocabulary, the sentence lengths, the sentence types, and the degrees of formality of the tone. Compare your group's findings with those of another group.

EXTENDING

6. a) In a small group, describe situations in the workplace that demonstrate the need for the basic skills listed in this article. Perform a series of **dramatizations**, some with positive outcomes and some with negative outcomes.

   b) After you have completed your performances, be prepared to answer questions about your **characters'** attributes, areas for improvement, their motivations, and their actions in the situations. As well, be ready to talk about what each of the characters could do to improve himself or herself in the workplace.

7. **Interview** a person who has a job you would like to do or a job you admire. Design ten questions that will help you understand the amount and the type of mathematics, reading, writing, listening, and speaking he or she has to do daily. Write your interview in **report** form that you might present orally to the class or submit for evaluation.

Strategies: Decision-Making Patterns

BEFORE READING

As a class, review the steps of a good decision-making strategy.

There are many decision-making patterns. We'll list some in a moment that you might recognize in your own behavior. Most of us have a tendency to use one or more of these patterns from time to time. Do you? Some of the patterns most often used are described below. See if you can think of other examples for each. Take them from your own experience, from examples in this book, or from any other source you'd like.

WISH PATTERN

Definition: Choosing an alternative that could lead to the most desirable result, regardless of risk.

Example: You choose someone to marry hoping to change her bad habits.

ESCAPE PATTERN

Definition: Choosing an alternative in order to avoid the worst possible result.

Example: You do not go to a party because you are afraid everyone will laugh at the way you dance.

SAFE PATTERN

Definition: Choosing the alternative that is most likely to bring success.

Example: You take an art class knowing you are a good artist, rather than taking another subject in which you do not know how well you will do.

IMPULSIVE PATTERN

Definition: Giving a decision little thought or examination; taking the first alternative; not looking before you leap.

Example: You move out of your dormitory room into an apartment without first determining the advantages and disadvantages.

FATALISTIC PATTERN

Definition: Letting the environment decide; leaving it up to fate.

Example: You do not take the time to learn to swim before you go on a dangerous boat trip.

COMPLIANT PATTERN

Definition: Letting someone else decide, or giving in to group pressure.

Example: You go to a party because your friend wants to.

DELAYING PATTERN

Definition: Postponing action and thought; procrastinating.

Example: You leave your graduation requirements until the last semester.

AGONIZING PATTERN

Definition: Getting so overwhelmed by alternatives that you don't know what to do.

Example: You need to decide where you will go to college and you have so many college catalogues that you can't make up your mind.

PLANNING PATTERN

Definition: Using a procedure so that the end result is satisfying; a rational approach.

Example: You decide to take a job with a company at which there is much potential for advancement.

INTUITIVE PATTERN

Definition: Making a choice on the basis of vague feelings, or because "it feels right."

Example: You choose a college because you like the campus. You don't talk to the instructors in your program, or find out about financial aid.

Which pattern do you think you use the most?

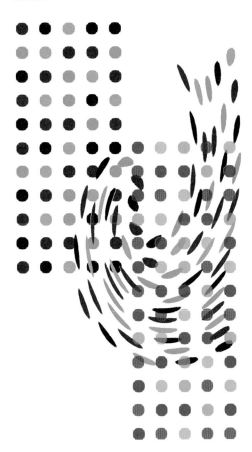

After Reading

RESPONDING

1. In your notebook, identify one decision-making pattern described in this selection that you have used. Explain whether, in general, it results in decisions that please you.

UNDERSTANDING

2. Choose five decision-making patterns in this selection, and write another example for each pattern. Be prepared to read your examples to the class.
3. With a partner, decide which one of the decision-making patterns in this selection is the least effective. Be prepared to give reasons for your choice to the class.

THINKING ABOUT LANGUAGE

4. With a partner, decide which decision-making pattern is most effectively titled and which is least effectively titled. Give a reason for each choice, and suggest a better name for the one with the least effective title. Be prepared to **summarize** your conclusions for the class.

EXTENDING

5. Identify another weak decision-making pattern that you have used or observed others using, and describe it in the same format used in this selection.
6. Using the decision-making patterns described, assess the decisions made by a **character** or characters in a **narrative** you have studied this year.

7. Identify celebrities or characters in popular films and television programs who exhibit a decision-making pattern described in this selection. Use specific examples to support your choices. Be prepared to discuss your ideas with the class.

Toughest Interview Questions Should Be Your Own

"The point of a job interview is to help each party learn more about the other."

MICHAEL STERN

BEFORE READING

As a class, brainstorm a list of ways a person should prepare for a job **interview**.

When you're applying for a job or getting ready to face an interview, most people worry about what questions they are likely to be asked.

But if you're serious about landing the job, you should make sure that the toughest questions you face come from yourself.

To put your best foot forward in any job interview, you need to prepare yourself by facing up to tough questions in at least three fundamental areas.

> What is the message I want to get across to the interviewer or prospective employer? What three or four pieces of information about myself do I want to make sure I bring out?

Few candidates do much preparation for a job interview, but those who don't are making a mistake. You should never try to "wing" an interview—or any other important presentation. To make the best impression, you have to know exactly what you want to say.

Make a list of the points you want to get across. Think of your interests, your abilities and your accomplishments. What have you done that can help this company move forward?

If you're applying for a job in the aviation industry, your message may be that you've worked in that industry, or that you've had experience in other fields that are rapidly deregulating, or in other industries that have faced wholesale consolidation.

Whatever your message, think about the best way to communicate it. You should have a few facts or stories you want to bring out, and you should never finish an interview until you've done so. Maybe you just want to drop the names of a few industry leaders who know your work. Maybe you have an anecdote that shows how you took charge of a troubled situation—preferably one much like those that your prospective employer currently may be facing—and turned it around.

But remember this: if you never get around to making your points, the interviewer can't read your mind.

Your best chance will probably come when the interviewer asks you how you think you can contribute to the company. Be prepared.

You'd be surprised how many candidates act as if they never saw these questions coming. If you're prepared properly, you will turn these questions into opportunities to showcase your best material.

If the interviewer's questions don't seem to be heading in a direction that would let you cite your accomplishments, it's okay to subtly take the initiative. Answer any question the interviewer asks, fully and honestly, but don't hesitate to segue into areas that give you a chance to tell your story or underline your experience.

> Ask yourself, "What are my 'must-haves' in this job? What do I need to learn about this company, my prospective manager or my colleagues, so that I can determine if this is the place—and the opportunity—for me?"

Everyone has a bottom line when considering acceptance of a new job. Maybe you absolutely need good "chemistry" with your boss. Perhaps you've had enough of the buggy-whip industry and feel the need to join a company with a future. Maybe you absolutely need to earn $75,000 a year, or you want a flexible organization that will let you work from home one or two days a week.

Knowing your "bottom line" demands is useful for evaluating any organization or job offer. You can do preliminary research to find out what sort of future the company has, or ask around to learn what sort of person your boss might be.

But be realistic. Keep your "must-haves" down to three items. Tops. Any more, and you're not likely to be working soon.

> Ask yourself, "What questions do I hope the interviewers won't ask?" And then prepare your responses to them—just in case.

Remember going into exams and praying that they wouldn't ask anything about photosynthesis, or the origins of World War I? Most people approach interviews the same way—aware that they have a few weak spots that they hope nobody will probe.

Everyone's weak points are different. Maybe there's a two-year gap in your résumé that you hope no one will notice. Perhaps you're not eager to explain why you've had six jobs in five years, or you always flub questions like: "What are your weaknesses?" Or maybe you just never know how to handle the question, "How much money are you looking for?"

Face up to your fears. Prepare for your interview by coming up with plausible, positive answers to questions like these. Good bosses and experienced interviewers have a way of sensing weak points in any presentation, so presume you'll need answers to all your worst-nightmare questions.

Your average bookstore, or any one of hundreds of career-related Web sites

(Yahoo! is a good place to start) will have resources that can help you anticipate the questions you might be asked, and to frame positive responses.

Finally, here's a question you should not ask yourself prior to an interview: "Do I really want this job?" Good question. But don't ask it too soon.

Many people do, and they often talk themselves out of exploring a potentially promising opportunity.

My advice: don't make up your mind prematurely. The point of a job interview is to help each party learn more about the other. Maybe you'll discover something that will impress you so much that commuting a little longer, or changing jobs for the same salary becomes much less of a concern. And the career you save may be your own.

TIP

The reference shelves and business department of your local public or university library are still good places to search for hard data on companies and industries. Many fields are served by specialized directories, with names, addresses and titles of possible job contacts. Large libraries subscribe to trade magazines that offer up-to-date news on particular industries, and may also have companies' annual reports.

After Reading

RESPONDING

1. In a paragraph, explain one idea or job interview strategy presented in this **article** that was new to you.

UNDERSTANDING

2. Explain which of the three main categories of advice in this article apply to your **résumé** and **covering letter** as well as in the job interview. (See The Reference Shelf, pages 289–290.)
3. In a paragraph, explain which piece of advice in this article will be the most challenging for you to follow.

THINKING ABOUT LANGUAGE

4. Write a brief **definition** or explanation of the following phrases used in this article: "put your best foot forward," " 'wing' an interview," "segue into areas," "good 'chemistry' with your boss," "buggy-whip industry," "bottom line," and "worst-nightmare questions."

EXTENDING

5. With a partner, **role-play** two contrasting job interviews: one that follows the advice in this article, and another that does not. Be prepared to present your role-plays to the class.

Summer Jobs

"Unlike working at traditional places...
having an out-of-the-ordinary job...leaves a lasting
impression."

CAMILLE BAINS

BEFORE READING

In your notebook, describe your ideal summer job.

When Jane Alkhouri thinks of her summer job two years ago, she can't help but laugh.

"The place was a *Gong Show*," Alkhouri says of the job she landed after graduating from high school. It was in a lab that promised balding people a fresh crop of hair.

"You had to apply these funny-looking solutions on their heads . . . and then you'd have to put a heat cap on their heads for 15 minutes and repeat the procedure twice."

The lab drew customers through newspaper advertisements, but didn't provide any guarantees on hair growth.

Besides listening to silly stories from desperate clients, Alkhouri also had to put up with an eccentric boss.

"If her scalp got itchy, she'd just get one of the solutions and rub it on her own head, just for no reason," Alkhouri says.

"She also wanted to start a part-time dating agency to make extra money and wanted to know if I'd help."

Alkhouri, now a third-year humanities student at the University of Calgary, said "no thanks" and quit.

It's that time of year again when students are looking for summer jobs to give them work experience and cash.

Unlike working at traditional places such as concession stands, service stations or day camps, having an out-of-the-ordinary job such as Alkhouri's leaves a lasting impression.

Although she can make fun of her job now, the experience taught her to start looking for summer work as early as possible, says Alkhouri, who hopes one day to work in advertising or journalism.

She's not alone when it comes to quirky stories about summer jobs.

When Lyle Baker was 16, he worked as a quarry for the Vancouver police department's dog squad.

68 Pine Street
Cooksville
P7A 5X3

June 12, 1999

Ms. Holly Peters
Manager
Cool Threads Clothing Store
25 Main Street
Cooksville
A1B 2C3

Re: Application for salesperson

Dear Ms. Peters: ❶

I am interested in applying for the position of salesperson at the Cool ❷
Threads Clothing Store, which was advertised in the June 10 edition of
the Cooksville News.

As a high school student, I have developed organizational and ❸
communication skills through my involvement in school sports and
by coaching junior soccer. By specializing in economics and accounting,
I also understand how business operates. I have enclosed my résumé
with further details.

I would enjoy being a part of your company and am available for an ❹
interview at your convenience. You can contact me at 555-1212 or
leave a message at 555-1234. I look forward to hearing from you.

Sincerely,

Jane Dough

Jane Dough

COVERING LETTER TIPS

Address your covering letter to the person responsible for hiring. Don't use Dear Sir/Madam or To Whom It May Concern. Call the business and get the exact name and title of the person. Ask for the correct spelling.

Paragraph 1: State your interest in the company and the type of job you want. If you learned of the job through an advertisement, refer to it in the opening paragraph.

Paragraph 2: Highlight the experience and skills you can offer the company. Use dynamic verbs like accomplished, created, improved, produced, specialized, organized, established. Refer to your résumé for further details.

Paragraph 3: Request an interview and leave a number where you can be reached. Have others check the letter for spelling or grammatical errors.

Baker's job was to hide — in an abandoned building or up a tree — before police officers let their dog-in-training loose to find him.

His only protection was a padded leather arm piece and a plastic baseball bat that he whacked the dog's rear end with to protect himself.

"I was the actual prey," Baker says of the summer job that he got through friends. It lasted part time for two years while he finished high school.

Sometimes there was a change in routine during the 8 p.m. to 4 a.m. shift when police officers responded to emergency calls, he says.

Neatness counts.
Do it on a computer or typewriter and use quality paper.

Keep it short.
One page is ideal. Briefly describe your skills and experience. Employers are looking for energetic people who can communicate well, solve problems, learn how to use technology, and who work well with others. Be sure to include any references that show you have these skills.

"If they got a call to go chase a speeding car or something, they would throw me out at the corner of the street and I had to wait there until they came back for me."

Baker, who now works as a painter, chef, and trade show mover, says it's been 23 years since that unforgettable job. He still sports a scar on his ankle from when a dog pulled him from a tree.

Heather Anne Britton landed her job through a technical college, where an instructor recommended her because of her outgoing personality.

As a park naturalist at the Okanagan Lake Provincial Park in British Columbia, Britton gave talks on wildlife, conducted nature walks, caught bats and fed a rattlesnake.

She had to keep the snake food — dead mice and rats — in her home freezer.

"I was living with somebody else and I had to clearly mark the box, 'Dead mice, do not eat.'"

Britton also had to ensure a neighbouring cat didn't eat the mice she would thaw out on the sidewalk.

An unusual summer job can provide benefits besides being the source of entertaining stories. Britton says her job helped her develop new skills, as well as giving her the chance to work in an environment she loved.

"It was an awesome experience; it got me out there believing that I could actually do something."

Want to learn more? Check out these Internet sites:

www.campusaccess.com/campus_web/career/c2job.htm
Mainly for university students, but includes advice on finding a job that anyone can use.

www.studentjobs.com
Site of the Student Employment Network, an organization that helps students in their job searches.

parkscanada.pch.gc.ca/Employment/jobs/english/students_e.htm
If you want a job in one of Canada's national parks, this is the site for you.

THE ART OF FINDING A JOB

Looking for a summer job? Here are some tips:

Getting started:
Write your résumé to target a specific job. Don't use the same résumé for all jobs.

Free résumé help:
Try your local Human Resources Centre for Youth. Call 1-800-935-5555 for the address.

Job postings:
At community centres, churches, YWCA/YMCA Boys' and Girls' Clubs, local Human Resources Centre for Youth.

Consider:
All your past experiences, including babysitting, paper routes, volunteer work, computer skills, participation in team sports.

Likely places to look:
Concession stands, video arcades, parks, day camps, service stations, farms, fast food restaurants.

Where:
Think about how you are going to get to work. Is there a bus nearby?

Network:
Let teachers, parents' friends, neighbours and other acquaintances know you're looking for work.

After Reading

RESPONDING

1. Choose one of the jobs mentioned in the **article**. Sketch or describe a cartoon that captures the humour in that job. The humour might be entirely visual or the cartoon could be accompanied by a caption.

UNDERSTANDING

2. Heather Anne Britton said there were many benefits to her job as park naturalist. With a partner, describe what benefits could be gained from working in a hair-growth lab or as a police-dog quarry.

3. Examine the **layout** of the covering letter portion of the article. Explain the techniques the designer has used to make the page inviting and readable.

THINKING ABOUT LANGUAGE

4. Look closely at each sentence in the covering letter. For each, describe the sentence length (i.e., number of words), the sentence type, and the sentence order. In a paragraph, make general observations about this writer's **style**.

EXTENDING

5. a) Write a newspaper job advertisement for the ideal summer job you described in the "Before Reading" activity. In your advertisement, include the qualifications and work experience necessary, and a small job description. Keep the advertisement short: under 50 words.

   b) Write a **résumé** and **covering letter** for this job. (See The Reference Shelf, pages 289–290.) Exchange your advertisement, résumé, and letter with a partner. Critique your partner's work for content and layout.

   c) Post your advertisements, letters, and résumés in the classroom.

Who Am I?

BRIAN HENRY

Then there was silence
No more screams of terror
No more pain
of having to bear chains
A nation forgiven for its difference: 5
A people permitted to dream again

Frolicking in the light of freedom
I feel their suffering
I know the fight is not over
Afflicted with oppression and poverty   10
my brethren from every corner of
the terrestrial planet
call for me
call for help
and I will go   15
for their pain is in my blood

Once dressed in filthy rags;
hair ragged like sheep's wool
shackles branding my wrists and ankles
I cowered before my master's whip   20
crying like a child, as every lash scorched and
tore through my flesh.
In the midst
of blood, dirt, and bugs
I discovered anguish   25
I was taught to endure

So strong I am
So glorious my existence
my blackness a shield against evil
I am here because seas of blood   30
parted, and I passed through
I will not fold when faced with controversies
I will not bend to wickedness
I will not turn a cold shoulder to injustice   35
I will stand strong
I will persevere
I am a man
A black man

After Reading

RESPONDING

1. In a personal letter to the poet, Brian Henry, tell him how you feel about his **poem**.

UNDERSTANDING

2. a) The poem breaks down into four parts: lines 1-6, 7-16, 17-26, and 27 to the end. With a
      partner, reread each part and explain its meaning.
   b) Decide whether the poet's references to different time periods and historical events are
      effective. Record your reasons.

3. Ask your teacher to explain "Everyman." Show how the **narrator** thinks of himself as an "everyman."

THINKING ABOUT LANGUAGE

4. a) Look up and record the **definitions** of the following words: oppression (line 10), terrestrial (line 12), shackles (line 19), cowered (line 20), anguish (line 25).

   b) In a paragraph, explain how understanding the vocabulary in a poem helps the reader to understand the meaning of the poem.

EXTENDING

5. a) Choose one of the following **topics** on which to write a research **report**: Nelson Mandela; the slave trade to the United States; Harriet Tubman; Africville, Nova Scotia; Louis Farrakhan. Create a research plan for your work. Keep detailed notes on the resources you have used. In your research report, use subtitles that will help your reader easily see what types of information you are including.

   b) Take your report through the writing process.

I and Africa

LILLIAN ALLEN

BEFORE READING

1 a. As a class, **define "typography."**

b. Without reading this **poem**, list the different ways the poet has used typography in her poem.

```
I
      dream
            like no one
                              heart
can    hold    the    warmth
the breath of the sun                    5


I      feeeeeel        music

my body carries the rhythms
of  A    F    R    I    C    A
            sweet
a rising crest of strength & laughter    10
my soul swells with her song
      FREEDOM, she sings
I     hear         her        calling
```

and when the music finds its source
      it   play s   15
         through me   l
                       d
my   heart   beats i
                  p
             a   20
          r

I   and   Africa   are   one

After Reading

RESPONDING

1. a) In your notebook, explain the feelings the **narrator** has for Africa. Use words from this poem as well as your own words as evidence.

   b) Explain whether or not the poet made you feel anything for Africa.

UNDERSTANDING

2. With a partner, look closely at each special use of typography. For each example, explain the effect its use has on the meaning and on the emotion in the poem. Compare your ideas with those of the rest of the class.

THINKING ABOUT LANGUAGE

3. This poem has almost no punctuation. Write it in proper sentences, with the correct punctuation, adding words where necessary. As a class, discuss which is more effective for this poem, standard Canadian English or the English the poet chose to write in. Why?

EXTENDING

4. With a partner, create a 15-second radio **commercial** for tourism in the Africa of this poem. Write an explanation of the content and the **implicit** and **explicit meanings** contained in the commercial. Rehearse, record, and present your commercial to the class.

Attitudes: How Will Yours Affect Your Future?

"Your opinions will create your attitude toward relationships and work."

BEFORE READING

With a partner, discuss the role of attitude in attaining success in school. Be prepared to present the key points of your discussion to the class.

Your life choices are affected by attitudes—your own, and the world's. Because these attitudes play such an important part in your life, we must examine them carefully. Men and women today have more freedom and choices than ever before. Sometimes it can be confusing.

Since the changing role of women will affect your future, it's important to know how you feel. Your opinions will create your attitude toward relationships and work. To help sort out your opinions, complete the following exercise.

You will need to copy the chart into your notebook, or obtain a photocopy from your teacher. Put a check mark in the column that best describes how you feel.

ATTITUDES INVENTORY

Instructions: Put a check mark in the column that best describes how you feel.

	STRONGLY AGREE	AGREE	UNDECIDED	DISAGREE	STRONGLY DISAGREE
1. Women with preschool children should not work outside the home.					
2. The mother should be awarded custody of the children when a couple is divorced.					
3. Divorced men should not have to assume support for their children.					
4. Boys are more intelligent than girls.					
5. If a working couple buys a house, the husband should make the house payments.					
6. At work, women are entitled to use sick leave for maternity.					
7. If a woman works outside the home, she should be responsible for the housework as well.					
8. I would vote for a woman for prime minister if she were the best candidate.					
9. Women are less responsible than men.					
10. It is important for a man to be "masculine" and a woman to be "feminine."					
11. Men should not cry.					
12. Money spent on athletics should be evenly divided between boys and girls.					
13. Both men and women can be good doctors.					
14. Wives should make less money at their jobs than their husbands.					
15. Boys should have more education than girls.					

	STRONGLY AGREE	AGREE	UNDECIDED	DISAGREE	STRONGLY DISAGREE
16. Women should not hold jobs on the night shift.					
17. Men should not do clerical work because they lack the necessary dexterity.					
18. Women can be capable administrators.					
19. Women should concentrate on finding jobs in the fields of nursing, teaching, clerical and secretarial work since they already possess these skills.					
20. A wife and husband should take turns staying home with a sick child.					
21. A single man is not capable of taking care of an infant.					

As you look back over your answers, take a moment to think about why you feel the way you do. Talk to your friends about your thoughts. Then think about your answers again.

By constantly examining your feelings, you continue to grow and learn.

After Reading

1. After completing this questionnaire, reread your answers. In your notebook, describe what a stranger might think about you solely on the basis of the answers you gave.

UNDERSTANDING

2. In your notebook, complete the following sentence: This questionnaire focuses on attitudes about _____. In a paragraph, explain your answer.
3. With a partner, select five items in this survey and imagine you are a politician who wants to get elected in your community. Draft the politician's responses to each of the five items for an upcoming speech. Give reasons for the responses you selected.
4. With a partner, select five items in this survey. Explain the answers an employer in a large company with both male and female staff would expect from a prospective employee.

THINKING ABOUT LANGUAGE

5. Explain why the word "should" appears frequently in a survey on attitudes.
6. Look at the Values Survey on pages 95–100. Explain the difference between an "attitude" and a "value" as the terms are used in the two surveys. Consult a dictionary if necessary.

EXTENDING

7. With a partner, create a similar Attitude Inventory focused on another topic. Be prepared to present your work to the class.

Values Survey

BEFORE READING

As a class, **define** values. Where do values come from? How do they influence us in our daily lives, in school, and in our jobs?

Copy this chart into your notebook, or obtain a photocopy from your teacher. Check the columns that most closely match your feelings.

	VERY TRUE	SOMETIMES TRUE	NOT SURE	NOT TRUE
1. I would rather have a large expensive house than own a work of art.				
2. I like to go places with my friends.				
3. I'd really like to travel to faraway places.				
4. I think music and art should be required in our schools.				
5. It is important that my family does things together.				
6. I like to make things.				
7. I would rather be president of a club than just a member.				
8. I'd like people to know that I've done something well.				
9. I like to read books that help me understand people.				
10. If I had talent, I'd like to be on TV.				
11. Having an expensive car is something I'd really like.				

	VERY TRUE	SOMETIMES TRUE	NOT SURE	NOT TRUE
12. If I could, I'd like to make a movie that would make people aware of injustice, and would improve the conditions it described.				
13. I'd rather be rich than married.				
14. I like writing stories, plays, or poetry.				
15. I like to try things I've never done before.				
16. I enjoy doing different things.				
17. It is important to be proud of what I do.				
18. If my friends want to do something that I think is wrong, I will not do it.				
19. I'd like to accomplish something in life that will be well known.				
20. A strong family unit is essential.				
21. I would disobey a boss who asked me to do something against my principles, even if it meant being fired.				
22. It is important for me to have a good understanding of history.				
23. If I could, I'd like to be prime minister.				
24. It would be fun to climb mountains.				
25. It is important for me to live in beautiful surroundings.				
26. I like to go to parties.				
27. It is important to have very good friends.				
28. I would rather make gifts than buy them.				
29. I am very close to my mother, father, or both.				
30. I like to attend lectures from which I can learn something.				
31. It is more important to stick to my beliefs than to make money.				
32. I would rather make less money at a job I know would last than take a chance with a job that might not last but pays more.				
33. I would like a lot of expensive possessions.				

	VERY TRUE	SOMETIMES TRUE	NOT SURE	NOT TRUE
34. I would rather be free to move around than be tied down by a family.				
35. I like to feel that I am in charge in a group.				
36. It is important to have an appreciation for art and music.				
37. I like to write.				
38. I'd look forward to taking a job in a city I had never visited before.				
39. Having children is important to me.				
40. I'd like to understand the way a TV works.				
41. I'd like to be able to decide what and how much work I will do during a day.				
42. I'd like to do something that helps people.				
43. I'd like to be famous.				
44. I'd rather be a judge than a lawyer.				
45. I do not think I'd like adventurous vacations.				
46. I would like to have works of art in my home.				
47. I would like a job that gives me plenty of free time to spend with my family.				
48. I could not be happy with a job in which I did not feel good about myself.				
49. I get very nervous when I'm forced to take chances.				
50. I would rather be a boss than a worker.				
51. It is important to share activities with friends.				
52. If I knew how, I would make my own clothes.				
53. I would rather not have to answer to a boss.				
54. Gaining knowledge is important to me.				
55. I'd rather work for a well-established company than a new company that hasn't established itself.				
56. Money can't buy happiness, but it helps.				
57. Being rich would be the best thing about being a movie star.				

	VERY TRUE	SOMETIMES TRUE	NOT SURE	NOT TRUE
58. Being famous would be the best thing about being a movie star.				
59. The best thing about being a movie star is that I'd be doing something creative.				
60. I like to be able to make my own decisions.				
61. Getting to travel would be the best thing about being a movie star.				
62. I'd like to nurse people back to health.				
63. I would like helping tutor people having trouble at school.				
64. I feel more comfortable in places I've seen before than in new places.				
65. I'd like to work at a job in which I help people.				
66. I enjoy spending an evening with my family.				
67. I'd rather work at a job that is not very interesting but pays a lot, than one that is interesting, but pays little.				
68. I would like to write a book that would help people.				
69. I want to be able to travel if the opportunity arises.				
70. If I had the talent, I'd like to be a famous rock star.				
71. I like reading to gain insight into human behavior.				
72. It is important to share your life with someone.				
73. If you don't take chances, you'll never get anywhere, and I like to take chances.				
74. I'd rather be a leader than a follower.				
75. The world would be a terrible place without beautiful things.				
76. It is important to try to learn something new every day.				
77. I would feel I was doing something worthwhile if I helped a friend with her problems.				
78. I especially like things I make myself.				

	VERY TRUE	SOMETIMES TRUE	NOT SURE	NOT TRUE
79. A close family is important to me.				
80. I think it is important to donate to the needy.				
81. I enjoy looking at beautiful scenery.				
82. The best thing about winning a gold medal at the Olympics would be the recognition.				
83. I like to go on hikes (or bike rides) with my friends.				
84. I have strong beliefs about what is right and wrong.				
85. It is important to have a family with whom to discuss problems.				
86. I'd like an exciting life.				
87. I prefer working by myself rather than as part of a team.				
88. I'd like to know all that I can about the workings of nature.				
89. I think it's wrong to help a friend cheat on an exam, even if I know he will fail if I don't help.				
90. Having a job I know I can keep is important to me.				
91. I'd like to have enough money to invest for the future.				
92. I don't like someone assigning me tasks to do.				
93. I do not like being alone very much.				
94. I like to take charge of organizing activities.				
95. I think saving money for the future is very important.				
96. When I've done something I'm proud of, it's important that other people know.				
97. I would rather make less money at a job in which I choose my own work, than make more money at a job in which someone tells me what to do.				
98. People should contribute a small amount of money to be used to decorate public buildings.				
99. I don't like to take risks with money.				

	VERY TRUE	SOMETIMES TRUE	NOT SURE	NOT TRUE
100. I like thinking of something that's never been done before.				
101. I would not like a job in which I travelled a lot and could not have lasting relationships.				
102. If a teacher accidentally left test answers where I could see them, I would not look.				
103. I like people to ask me for my opinion when trying to decide the best way to handle a situation.				
104. If I could, I'd like to make a movie that people would think is beautiful.				

Go back to the beginning of this exercise. Above the words "Very True," write a 9. Above the words "Sometimes True," write a 6. Above the words "Not Sure," write a 3. Above the words "Not True," write a 0. Do the same for each page of the exercise.

Copy the scoring chart that follows or obtain a photocopy from your teacher.

To add up your score, write the numerical value of the response you selected against each question number written below. For example, if on number 5 you selected "Sometimes True," put a 6 on the line next to the number 5. When all the lines have been completed, total the numerical responses under each values heading.

Family		Adventure		Knowledge		Power	
5	____	3	____	9	____	7	____
20	____	15	____	22	____	23	____
29	____	16	____	30	____	35	____
39	____	24	____	40	____	44	____
47	____	38	____	54	____	50	____
66	____	61	____	71	____	74	____
79	____	73	____	76	____	94	____
85	____	86	____	88	____	103	____
Total	____	Total	____	Total	____	Total	____

Moral Judgment and Personal Consistency

17	_____
18	_____
21	_____
31	_____
48	_____
84	_____
89	_____
102	_____
Total	_____

Money or Wealth

1	_____
11	_____
13	_____
33	_____
56	_____
57	_____
67	_____
91	_____
Total	_____

Friendship and Companionship

2	_____
26	_____
27	_____
51	_____
72	_____
83	_____
93	_____
101	_____
Total	_____

Recognition

8	_____
10	_____
19	_____
43	_____
58	_____
70	_____
82	_____
96	_____
Total	_____

Independence and Freedom

34	_____
41	_____
53	_____
60	_____
69	_____
87	_____
92	_____
97	_____
Total	_____

Security

32	_____
45	_____
49	_____
55	_____
64	_____
90	_____
95	_____
99	_____
Total	_____

Beauty or Aesthetics

4	_____
25	_____
36	_____
46	_____
75	_____
81	_____
98	_____
104	_____
Total	_____

Creativity

6	_____
14	_____
28	_____
37	_____
52	_____
59	_____
78	_____
100	_____
Total	_____

Helping Others

12	_____
42	_____
62	_____
63	_____
65	_____
68	_____
77	_____
80	_____
Total	_____

For which category is your total the highest? That's the value most important to you at present. However, values can change, and in fact, usually do. For this reason, you may wish to take the Values Survey again in a year or two.

What do the categories mean? Descriptions of each category follow.

FAMILY

Someone with a very high score in this category greatly values the closeness of a family. Parents and children feel close to each other and spend much time together. "Family" can also mean other persons or friends who are close to you, if you choose not to join a traditional family. Your inner circle of acquaintances is important. You are a people person. If you score high in this area, you will want a job that allows you plenty of time at home where you can enjoy family and friends. Your work hours should be consistent and stable. You probably would not be happy as a travelling sales representative, a forest ranger, or a monk.

ADVENTURE

In contrast to the preceding, a career that calls for a lot of travel may be just right if you value adventure. You certainly would not be satisfied with a job in which the routine is the same day after day. Your score shows that you would like to have varied job duties and that you are comfortable taking risks.

See how easy this is? But, oops! What if you have high scores in two categories? Could you have a happy family life and lots of adventure, too? It's possible. Here is where you have to make some choices and spend time comparing careers. Which do you value more? If you're an adventure-loving family man, you may have to settle for hang gliding on weekends, or making an expedition through the wilderness each summer, rather than being a foreign correspondent or an international jewel trader.

KNOWLEDGE

If you value knowledge, you will want a career that lets you keep on learning. Teaching is an obvious choice, but you might also consider doing research—scientific, historical, political, or whatever. Being a journalist who covers different stories every day and spends time reading reports and interviewing people might be a good choice.

POWER

It's hard to find an entry-level job with a lot of power, but if that's what you value, you'll want to make sure that there's plenty of room for advancement in your chosen field. You should prepare yourself to take a leadership role by pursuing advanced education or by learning more skills in your field. Or, you might want to start your own business. That way you can be president immediately—even if you're the only employee!

MORAL JUDGMENT AND PERSONAL CONSISTENCY

If you scored high in this category, you'll want to make sure that your career choice is one you feel is worthwhile; that is, one you can be proud of, no matter what other values it mirrors. For example, if you also had a high adventure score, you would probably be more satisfied as a Peace Corps worker than as a bomber pilot.

MONEY

Obviously, if money is your top value, you will look carefully at potential earnings for any job you take. Since making a lot of money usually entails spending long hours on the job, you should consider your other values in choosing a field that will hold your interest. You may have little time for family, friends, or outside hobbies. Check the salary levels for a wide range of jobs before starting to narrow your choices.

FRIENDSHIP AND COMPANIONSHIP

If friendship and companionship are important to you, your job should involve working closely with others. Being shut away in a laboratory or sitting in a cubicle with an adding machine will probably hold few charms for you. If you get along well with others and can easily talk with people you don't know well, you might consider working in sales or public relations. If having time for close friendships outside of work is important, though, you won't want a job that involves a great deal of travel or overtime.

RECOGNITION

Is recognition what you want? If so, you'll do best choosing something for which you have a talent, something that will let you work to develop the talent. Of course, some fields have more potential for recognition built into them than others. There may be very few world-renowned bus drivers, but the fact remains that in many communities there are bus drivers *everyone* knows and respects. It often depends on how you do your job, not just what job you do.

AESTHETICS

People who score high in aesthetics (love of beauty) like to be surrounded by beauty. If this describes you, you might be happy as an interior designer or an art dealer. You might like being a forest ranger at a national park or an executive in a plush office. You would almost certainly be unhappy as a garbage collector or coal miner.

CREATIVITY

Writers and artists are often thought of as creative, but creativity is an important asset in other fields as well. If you value creativity, you will want a career that gives you room to make choices and decisions, to put your ideas into effect, and to evaluate the results of your efforts. You probably wouldn't be happy in a job that is rigid or inflexible. You might find a use for your creativity as program director for a senior citizens' group, as an engineer in a large research firm, or as a landscape architect.

HELPING OTHERS

People who value helping others have traditionally become educators or clergymen. But, there are many other options. Doctors, social workers, psychologists, counsellors, writers, politicians, dieticians, speech pathologists, and physical therapists are just a few of the career possibilities for those scoring high in this area.

INDEPENDENCE

If you value independence and freedom, you should be wary of careers that are rigidly supervised or scheduled. Some sales representative positions allow you a great deal of freedom. People who work on a freelance basis, or as consultants, may be able to decide where, when, and how much work they will do.

SECURITY

Careers with well-established companies, or those in areas that are basic to human needs and not likely to become obsolete, are good choices for someone who values security. Such a person is usually happier with clearly defined work.

Re-examine your values throughout your life to make sure you aren't working hard and giving up things that are important to you for the sake of something you no longer value.

After Reading

RESPONDING

1. Once you have scored your answers to the survey, look at the three values on which you scored the most points. Write your reactions to your results. Do you think those results reflect who you are and what you value?

UNDERSTANDING

2. Compare your value scores with those of a partner. Try to explain any similarities and differences between the two of you.
3. Make point-form notes about each category of values. You may work with a partner, but you each need to create your own notes.
4. As a class, discuss the following question: Do you think there is one value that teens tend to value most? Do you think there is a value that 30- to 50-year-olds value most? What about 50- to 70-year-olds? What types of events in a person's life might influence his or her values?
5. With a partner, decide whether or not this **informational text** is well designed. Make notes on the positive and negative aspects of the design.

THINKING ABOUT LANGUAGE

6. Describe the **tone** of the section on "Adventure." In your notebooks, write down the types of language in the section and a description of the sentences that create that tone.

EXTENDING

7. Using your survey results, name several jobs that would fulfill your top three values and keep you happy, according to your survey results. Create a chart on Bristol board, or a computer, that looks like the following one to post in your classroom. Before posting your chart, read it to another classmate to make sure your published work is error free.

JOB NAME AND DESCRIPTION	HOW IT FULFILLS VALUE #1 (NAME THE VALUE)	HOW IT FULFILLS VALUE #2 (NAME THE VALUE)	HOW IT FULFILLS VALUE #3 (NAME THE VALUE)

Everyone Talked Loudly in Chinatown

"I started to play with friends who weren't loud and who weren't Chinese."

ANNE JEW

BEFORE READING

As a class, discuss ways in which a teenager's family values can sometimes be in **conflict** with the values of his or her peers. In your notebook, explain the best way to resolve one of these conflicts.

Lately I have been walking home from school in the sunshine with Todd. It's October and the leaves have turned, though the temperature hasn't changed since the end of August. My father says the reason for this is there were two Junes in the Chinese calendar this year. I wonder if that makes this year thirteen months long or if one month is left out to fit it into the regular calendar. But I don't ask. He would launch into a long, boring explanation of the history of the Chinese calendar and say it was superior to the Western calendar. If it was anyone else, I would probably ask.

Todd is very good looking. All the girls at school think so, and it makes me feel good when they turn to look at us walk down the hall together. Sometimes on our walk home we stop at the park to sit on the swing and talk. Actually Todd talks a lot and I listen. He usually describes his daily visit to the vice principal, the cars he wants, and the bands he likes. There is a Led Zeppelin logo drawn onto the back of his jean jacket in black felt which kind of bothers me.

"Have you ever really listened to their lyrics? They just make so much sense." It's his favourite band.

I try hard to stay interested in what he says and ask him questions, but mostly I end up nodding my head and saying, "Uh huh, uh huh." He doesn't seem to mind my quietness though. His eyes are clear blue, almost like glass, and it's hard to describe the feeling I get when he looks at me. My whole body feels like it's melting to the ground, and I'm always surprised to see that it hasn't.

Today Todd walks me to the beginning of my block as usual and then crosses the street to go on. My mother would start to ask questions if she saw us together.

As I enter the house I pass my grandmother's room to go upstairs. She is lying in there dying. I throw my bag into my room and head into the kitchen. I take out a bag of chips from the cupboard and pour a glass of orange juice and join my brother in the living room where he is watching a rerun of *The Brady Bunch*. It's the one where Jan refuses to wear her glasses and smashes into the family portrait with her bike. After a while I forget about the Bradys and start to daydream about Todd.

The next thing I know, my mother is waking me up to feed my grandmother, whose hands shake all the time so she can't do it herself. My brother and I take turns every night.

I stand by the window in the kitchen waiting for my mother to put the food onto the dinner tray. I draw hearts encircling Todd's initials and mine on the steamed glass.

"Hey, what are you doing?" she asks. I quickly wipe away the evidence.

"Nothing."

Her dinner is basically the same every night — soup, rice with water, steamed vegetables, salted fish and a thermos of tea. When I go into the room she is sleeping with the quilt drawn up to her chin, which is usually how I find her now. Before, my mother would move her to an armchair by the window where she could watch people walk by or she would watch the new television set my father bought for her. Her favourite shows were *The Roadrunner* and *The Beverly Hillbillies*, both of which I couldn't stand. She would point and laugh and mumble something in Chinese. She didn't understand them, but I think she liked their movements. Now she stays in bed, too weak to get up.

She looks really old. I think she's almost eighty-four, but no one knows for sure. They didn't have birth certificates in China then, and she had to lie about her age when she came over to Canada. Her skin is bunched up like fabric and it just kind of hangs from her cheekbones. But it feels thin and soft. I touched it once when she was asleep. Her hair is grey and white and oily. It's combed back making her forehead look like a shiny grapefruit. The lobes of her ears have been stretched by the weight of gold earrings I have never seen her take off. She is hardly moving. She almost looks as if she were dead already.

"Grandmother, it's time to eat rice."

She briefly opens her eyes and then closes them again.

"Grandmother, it's time to eat rice," I repeat a little louder.

She opens her eyes again, and I bring the tray closer for her to see. She starts to sit up, and I put down the tray to help her. After I prop her up onto some pillows, I tuck a paper napkin into the neck of her pajamas and begin to feed her. I really hate doing it and I always want it to be over as soon as possible. Luckily she has been eating less and less. I have been begging my mother to do it instead, but so far she hasn't given in.

"You're not the one who has to bathe her and change the sheets. Don't be so bad. You are the only one she has treated well. She is going to die soon anyway."

My mother can't wait for my grandmother to die. She is always telling my brother and me how she was treated like a slave by grandmother when she first married my father.

"Why didn't you stand up for yourself?" I ask.

"Oh, you don't know what it was like then."

We start with the soup. The spoon makes a clanging noise as it knocks against her teeth, sending a shiver through me. She still has all of them, which is amazing since my mother already has false front teeth. She doesn't chew the food very much though. It stays in her mouth a while, and then she makes a great effort to swallow. I try to show her how to chew by making exaggerated movements with my mouth, but she just ignores me. She finishes the soup, and we start on the rice in water. Some of it dribbles out of her mouth so I have to scrape it off her chin and spoon it back in like I'm feeding a baby. I feel disgusted and guilty and I don't know why. I also feel guilty for not spending more time with her and for not wanting to spend more time with her. Todd would die if he knew I had to do this.

She is a grown-up who has always taken care of me, but now I have to take care of her. It bothers me. She used to be different.

When I was little, she would take me to Chinatown every weekend. We would go to a small pastry shop at the corner of Pender and Gore. I would have a Coke and a coconut bun while she had tea with the owners. I had to call them Uncle and Auntie although they weren't related to us. They spoke to each other about the people they knew: who was dying, who was dead, whose daughter-in-law was lazy. They drew out their words into sighs and shook their heads at the misfortunes of others. Sometime they would comment on me, looking at me as if I couldn't see or hear them.

"Look at that high nose. She doesn't look Chinese."

"She is such a shy, cute girl."

I usually watched the customers, the bell tinkling above the door as they came and went. Most were short, chubby women with unmade faces and hair. They always looked tired and reminded me of my mother. They carried plastic shopping bags with different shop logos on them in Chinese characters, and their children would run around them as they tried to order. They would scream out their orders and at their children at the same time.

There were also old stooping men with brown spots on their faces and the odd gold front tooth, and old women with straight grey hair pinned back over their ears. The old people were always buried under layers of clothing no matter what season it was.

Each time we left, the owners would give me a box of barbecued pork buns to take home.

"Lin, thank Uncle and Auntie."

"Thank you Uncle and Auntie."

"What a cute girl."

My grandmother was very popular in Chinatown. While we shopped we would be stopped every few feet by her acquaintances. Everyone talked loudly and waved their arms. I couldn't understand why they had to be so loud. It seemed uncivilized. She also took me to visit her friends and I would occupy myself with extra game pieces while they played mah jong.

But as I started to grow up, I stopped going to Chinatown with her, where it was too loud, and then I stopped spending time with her altogether. I started to play with friends who weren't loud and who weren't

Chinese. This upset my mother. She was suspicious of all other cultures. My best friend for a long time was a German girl who lived up the block. Everything was neat and orderly at her house, and her mother was a quiet, pleasant woman who offered me green apples from their tree. My mother only bought red ones in Chinatown.

Grandmother eats the rest of the rice and some vegetables and then motions me to stop. I wipe her mouth and chin and help her to lie down again. She closes her eyes, and I turn out the light and climb the stairs to my own dinner.

On our walk home from school the next day, Todd asks me to see a movie with him. I lie to my parents and tell them I am going with my girlfriend Sandra. She swears not to say anything to anyone.

Todd pays for the movie and the popcorn, and we sit in the back row of the theatre. He puts one arm around me, balances the bucket of popcorn on his knee, holds his drink between his legs, and eats and drinks with his other hand. I am impressed. I usually gorge myself on popcorn, but I feel compelled to eat one kernel at a time.

Halfway through *The Great Santini* and after we've finished the popcorn, Todd offers me a Certs. Then after a while he turns to me and kisses me on the lips. He opens his mouth on mine and not knowing what to do, I open my mouth. I feel his tongue moving around in my mouth, so I move my tongue around in his. He still tastes faintly of popcorn under the flavour of the Certs. Just as I'm becoming used to the new sensation, he stops and kisses me on the lips and turns back to the movie. I can feel saliva clinging to the edge of my mouth and not wanting to wipe it away with my hand I press my face into his shoulder hoping his shirt will absorb the moisture. It works.

As we leave the theatre, Todd takes hold of my hand. I am quickly beginning to fall in love.

"Now that was a great movie. That Robert Duvall guy is one harsh dude. What'd you think? Did you like it?"

"Yeah, I thought it was quite good."

"Yeah, it was great."

My hand feels good in his, but his strides are twice as long as mine, so our mismatched rhythms make us bounce along instead of walk. By now I am truly in love and I let him take me all the way home. Only the living room light is on so we sit in the darkness of the carport in the back. Todd kisses me again and we move our tongues around. I am lost in the kissing until a car's headlights shine at us as it pulls into the driveway.

"Oh my God! It's my mother!"

I grab Todd's arm, and we run to the front of the house.

"Go! Hurry up!" He quickly kisses me and runs up the block. I stand around debating whether to go inside or escape to Sandra's house. I finally decide to go in. My mother and father are standing in the living room.

"How can you be so fearless! Going out with a white boy!" screams my mother.

My father walks up to me, his eyes wide with anger and slaps me on the face. Automatically I slap him back. He is stunned and I take the opportunity to run into my room. I expect him to come charging after me, but I am left alone for the rest of the night. It is only when the last light is turned out that I start to cry.

When I wake up hours later, my eyelashes are clumped together with dried tears. I didn't draw the curtains, so the moon shines into my room. Everything looks calm and quiet covered in moonlight. It comforts me. Todd, my father—it seemed to happen so long ago.

Only the hum of the fridge can be heard as I creep out into the hallway. I slowly climb down the stairs to my grandmother's bedroom. I imagine the sound of movement as I enter, but I stop and there is nothing. It is dark, so I feel my way over to the window and draw the curtains back a little. She is so still in the moonlight. I go to her and touch her face. It is soft, but cool. The shadows make it look almost ghostly. I take her hand, bony and fragile, and find she has no pulse. I drop it instantly and stand back to stare at her. She is dead, I think. I stare at her face expecting it to move, but somehow it looks peaceful. I take her hand again, kneel beside the bed, and rest my head against her. Soon I am asleep.

After Reading

RESPONDING

1. In your notebook, explain why the **narrator** feels comforted and relaxed in the last two paragraphs of this **story**.

UNDERSTANDING

2. In a small group, make a list of things that Todd and the narrator have in common. Reach a conclusion about what attracts them to each other. Be prepared to present your conclusion to the class for further discussion.

3. Reread this story, making note of the details used to describe the Chinese family. Explain whether you think the author has used stereotypes to describe her **characters** and their lives.

4. Explain what the specific references to television shows and the movie add to this story.

THINKING ABOUT LANGUAGE

5. The narrator says she has feelings of love for Todd. Select three words she uses to describe him or his actions that make you wonder if this is true. Explain why each word raises a doubt in your mind about her real feelings.

EXTENDING

6. With a partner, create a **dialogue** between the narrator's mother and father after the narrator escapes to her room. Be prepared to present your dialogue to the class.

7. As one of her best friends, write a letter to the narrator explaining why you do or do not think Todd is a good partner for her. Exchange your letter with a partner for revision and editing comments.

8. Assuming that the grandmother does not die at the end of this story, write a **narrative** about the narrator feeding her grandmother dinner the day after her date with Todd. Use some **direct speech** by the narrator to her grandmother in your narrative.

EXCERPT FROM
Welcome to the Ark

STEPHANIE S. TOLAN

BEFORE READING

1. The ark is a famous Biblical ship. As a class, discuss what you know about the story of Noah's ark.

2. On the basis of your discussion, and considering the title of this excerpt, brainstorm what this novel might be about.

April 15, 1999

Phenom Vanishes

PARIS (AP)—Fifteen-year-old Miranda Ellenby, known to the world through her mother's best-selling book, *Phenom in the Family,* has disappeared from an academic conference on language and culture where she was to present a paper. She is the youngest person ever to be asked to participate in the elite international gathering. Ellenby was last seen by a doorman at her hotel yesterday when she left "for a walk" shortly after dawn. "We were to meet for breakfast," said Dr. Miriam Freidenberg, her companion and adviser at Harvard, where Ellenby is pursuing a doctorate in Romance languages and literature, "but she never appeared." French police have been joined in their investigation by Interpol. The girl's distraught father, Dr. Walter Ellenby, who has built a multi-million-dollar business aimed at teaching parents how to create geniuses, arrived in Paris this morning to join the search.

April 15, 1999

MIRANDA

In the late-afternoon sun, the girl in blue jeans and sneakers and a flowered warm-up jacket, her hair pushed up into a gold beret, was very still. Leaning over the bridge rail, she watched a *bateau-mouche* churn by beneath, stirring the dark water as it passed. She kept her head turned away from the figures moving on the busy sidewalk behind her. Among the stories of border conflicts and terrorist bombings, the morning papers in three languages had been full of her disappearance, her publicity photo from the conference brochure smiling out from the pages.

She sighed and reached into her jacket pocket to pull out an orange. It was the last remnant of the food she had bought yesterday — cheese, bread, fruit, pastries, sparkling water. The rest she had consumed in the shabby pension in Montmartre where she had spent the night. The concierge had asked no questions, accepting her accent, the way nearly everyone did, as Parisian, with a shadow of something that hinted, perhaps, of a country childhood.

She had not meant to run away. She had meant only to take a walk, as she had told the grandfatherly doorman who fussed about the dangers of the city and the chill of the misty morning air. But when it was time to go back she had found she couldn't. Something drew her on, farther and farther from the hotel, finally to have breakfast alone at a sidewalk café, watching people as the city woke up and went about its business. And then on again, first along the Seine, then into side streets, watching the people. Always watching the people. The woman pushing a baby carriage, the lovers leaning against a tree in a tiny park, their arms twined around each other. The old men on a bench, arguing in a dialect she could barely understand, one gesturing with his cigar, the other with a folded newspaper.

She had a sense that she was looking for something, something all those other people seemed to have. She didn't even know for certain what it was, only that in spite of speaking their language, the thing that should have made her one of them, she didn't have it. Had never had it.

Now she began peeling the orange, dropping the first bit of peel into the river below and watching the spot of color bob sideways in the fading wake, dipping and turning as it moved toward the line of foam and debris along the muddy bank beneath the bridge. The rest of the peel she put into her pocket.

As she separated the segments, she thought about last night, the first night of her life when no one, not Mother or Daddy, not Miriam, not Dr. James, had been with her, or even known where she was. The first night of her life she had ever been truly alone.

She had sat by the window of the little room with the stained ceiling, staring out over the rooftops of Paris, silvered by moonlight. By morning she had made a decision. She would go back, of course. About that she had no choice. She would not explain her leaving — how could she when she didn't fully understand it herself? She would greet their questions with silence and let them invent their own stories. This evening she would present her paper on schedule. And when the conference ended she would fly home with Miriam.

But she would not continue the life her mother and father had planned for her.

When Miranda had finished the orange, her hands and mouth sticky with the juice, she turned toward the street and began to walk back to the hotel, keeping her head down, her eyes on her feet. As she walked, unnoticed among the hurrying people, even by the soldiers patrolling with their guns slung over their backs, she thought about what she had understood in the long, drifting quiet of the moonlit night. She had started learning languages all those years ago in a desperate search for her native tongue. She had never found it. She suspected now she never would.

October 7, 1999
ELIJAH

Beneath a bush in the corner of a playground shadowed by two towering apartment buildings a small boy in tattered blue jeans and a too-small jacket sat, writing with one dark brown finger in the dirt. T-O-N-D-I-S-H-I. He spelled it out and drew a line around it, the name of the world he had built in his mind and filled with animals and people of his own design.

Early this morning the growling sound had begun in his head and he had hurried outside, to this refuge he had swept clean of broken glass and stones. All summer when the growl began — the growl that meant the man would be yelling soon, throwing things, looking for a reason to hit or punch or kick — he had done his best to get outside, to hide here with the smell of dirt and green leaves and tell himself stories of Tondishi, a world of open skies and mountains and meadows like the ones he remembered from before they came to the city.

Sometimes he made it out, sometimes he didn't. Soon, he knew, the leaves would fall and this safe place would be gone. Even if he could get out of the apartment in time, he would have to find somewhere else to hide. Now he wrote S-A-M-S-O-N slowly in the dirt, the Bible name he had borrowed for the wild-living, cave-dwelling Tondishi hero he liked best, a tall, strong, dark man who had no need to hide, whose story he had been telling himself this morning.

The growl had grown, as it so often did now, into a roar, so loud in his head that he couldn't think. He had lost his hold on the story. The roar meant that the man inside was yelling now, smashing things against the walls. He hoped his mother had left, but he couldn't be sure. He'd tried to warn her in the old way, thinking the warning at her as hard as he could, but she hadn't understood. She hardly ever understood anymore. He struggled to find the sense of her through the roaring in his head. It was there, a fragile thread of warmth that, before the man came into their lives, had glowed bright and strong. His mother was still inside, frightened, making herself as quiet and as small as she could.

Suddenly there was a flash, so vivid it seemed to blind him, even though it was inside his head, had nothing more to do with his eyes than the roar had to do with his ears. He blinked. Darkness. And silence, so sudden, so complete that it nearly knocked him over. Frantically, he searched for the thread of warmth, knowing the truth even as he searched. It was gone. Gone. There was nothing but cold, darkness, silence.

Then the roar exploded like a bottle against a wall. He wrapped both arms around his head, as if to shut it out. Beneath the roar the darkness was as empty as it had been the night Mama Effie died.

Mama, too, was gone. He was alone. Tears filled his eyes and spilled over.

For a long, long time Elijah did not move. Then he raised his head, rubbed out the letters in the dirt, wiped his nose on his jacket sleeve, and filled his mind with a white fog that blotted out thoughts and memories and, when they came, the sound of the sirens.

January 26, 2000
TARYN

Snow swirled against the windows of the Laurel Mountain Center for Research and Rehabilitation, so that the distant mountains, the lake, even the nearest trees were blotted out in the white turbulence. The wind howled around the corners of the building.

In the arts and activities room a little boy, huddled under a table, began to beat his head against the table leg and moan with the wind. Other voices joined him, some children stamping feet, others pounding on the tables, until the cacophony overrode the sound from outside. The art therapist and her assistant hurried from child to child, murmuring, patting, calming.

Next to the window a small hand was pressed against the cold glass. A child with hair that fell in a fine black sheet down her narrow back sat still and silent, peering out into the storm. She frowned in concentration and raised the other hand to press it, too, against the glass. The snow whispered against the window, a tiny sound she could just pick out beneath the background din. The snow had stories to tell, stories of silent mountains, sleeping trees, the frozen surface of the lake and the life suspended far beneath. Stories of cold and darkness and danger.

She leaned to touch her forehead to the window, shivering in the draft. And felt something else, something far beyond the storm, beyond the mountains. It was not a voice, not a sound or even a vision. The child closed her eyes to focus. It was no use. As she tried to bring it in it skidded sideways, out of reach. A change was coming, she thought, an important change. But she couldn't make it clearer than that. She opened her eyes again, listening to the whispers of the snow. The winter stories were stories of waiting. She could wait. It was the most important thing she had learned here.

Laurel Mountain Center for Research and Rehabilitation

PATIENT NUMBER	LAST NAME FIRST NAME M.I.		DATE ADMITTED
5042	Ellenby, Melinda K.		6/5/00

LEGAL STATUS AT ADMISSION	AGE	SEX	RACE
Involuntary	16y, 3m	F	W

HOME ADDRESS	EDUCATIONAL STATUS AT ADMISSION	CITY & STATE OF BIRTH
50 Green Meadow Dr. Waltham MA 02154	B.A. + grad. work	Waltham, MA

FATHER'S NAME	ADDRESS PHONE	OCCUPATION
Walter J. Ellenby	50 Green Meadow Dr. Waltham, MA 02154 617-555-4307	Prof. – Harvard Pres. – Phenom, Ltd.

MOTHER'S MAIDEN NAME	ADDRESS PHONE	OCCUPATION
Elizabeth Stern	(see above)	Writer Dir. – Phenom, Ltd.

PARENT'S MARITAL STATUS	PERSON TO NOTIFY IN EMERGENCY	RELATIONSHIP
M	Walter or Elizabeth Ellenby 617-555-4307	Parents

ESTABLISHED DIAGNOSIS	DIAGNOSTIC IMPRESSION AT ADMISSION
Referring phys. suggests possible borderline personality	No diagnosis possible.

ADDITIONAL NOTES REGARDING ADMISSION INTERVIEW

Subject totally uncooperative. Spoke only to insist on her "Miranda rights."

PREVIOUS HOSPITALIZATION	INSTITUTION	DATES: FROM TO
None		

ADMITTING PHYSICIAN	SIGNATURE	DATE
Harlan Turnbull	*Harlan Turnbull*	6/5/00

JOURNAL — MIRANDA ELLENBY
June 6, 2000—10:30 P.M.

It was the interview I did with KIDS TODAY magazine—
where I said I was an alien—that pushed them over the
edge. From the moment they read it, they started looking
at me funny. Really funny. Not like the way they looked
at me when I shaved my head. This was out of the sides
of their eyes, and there was desperation in it. Up till
then, they'd figured I was just doing an adolescent
number on them. After the interview they put it all
together, everything I'd done since Paris, and came to
the conclusion that I was having a mental meltdown.
Maybe they're right. For the smartest kid the world, it
was a pretty stupid mistake.
   It never occurred to me that anyone would think I was
really crazy. Or that looking crazy in public would
demolish (PTURFLUKT!) the Ellenby empire. If Mother and
Daddy made me what I was before, now it would look to
all the world as if they'd made me nuts, too. Who would
sign up for another workshop? Who would buy another
book?
   Mother must have worked fast to get them that
appearance on Delia Shevin's CNN talk show for the very
day the magazine would hit the stands. Craziness was
never mentioned, of course. Teen rebellion was their
story. "Adolescence is a difficult period for any child,
doubly so for a prodigy, and Miranda needs some time
away from the public spotlight." Right. So very quietly,
with lots of security, they dumped me here.
   Once they decided I was crazy nothing I said would
change their minds. Crazy people can't plan their lives,
of course—everybody knows that. Besides, kids—no matter
how smart they are—have no power in the world. None.
   Did I believe the alien story when I told the woman
who was doing the interview? Do I now? It isn't such a

bad explanation, given how different I am from them—from everybody. I could have been traded for Baby Ellenby by the aliens I really belonged to right there in the hospital before anybody knew the real one well enough to notice the difference. Left on earth by aliens, waiting for them to come back and take me home.

When I was little I used to stand and stare up at the stars and wonder which one of them held the solar system that was my real home. I toyed with the idea that Mother and Daddy were in on the switch—a way to get a baby and fortune and fame at the same time. Of course, if they'd been in on it, they wouldn't have sent me here. Besides, I think they really believe they made me what I am. After all, they got me a psychologist and all those tutors and let me go to college when I was nine. Hardly standard parenting practice. Nobody seems to notice that no matter how many parents take the Ellenby workshops, their kids just don't manage to turn out like me. Phenom, Ltd. is right. The phenomenon is limited to me.

So here I am at the Laurel Mountain Center for Research and Rehabilitation (a private nuthouse), with nobody to talk to except shrinks and loonies. Writing my journal on the computer the shrinks agreed to install in my private room (got to give Mother and Daddy that— they're sparing no expense), writing in Muktuluk so I don't have to worry about any tricks they might have built into the system to spy on me.

It's like when I was little and wrote my diary in Muktuluk so Mother and Daddy's snooping wouldn't do them any good. I'd figured out that there were two uses for language—to connect people who speak it and to keep out people who don't. I used to talk in Muktuluk, too. Nobody understood it was a whole language, grammar, syntax, and all. They thought I was just playing.

Of course, I had to quit speaking it and erase all my computer discs when I was ten and Mother's book came out. The army of psychologists and linguistics people that descended on me after the book would have had a field day if they'd found it. They were freaked enough that I knew so many real languages. It would have been even worse if they'd known I made one up on my own when I was three.

I never stopped thinking in Muktuluk, though, and growing it. So there aren't many ideas I can't express this way—and some I can't manage properly in any other language. No need to hide Muktuluk now—what can happen to me that's worse than being committed?

Judging from the people I've met so far—especially Turnbull, the head shrink—I can safely assume nobody here is going to be able to come up with a translation, even if they have some way of finding this. The big problem here, like everywhere else, won't be whether anybody's sharp enough to figure me out, but whether I can suffer the fools gladly. Or suffer them at all.

Hey, up there on Home Planet, time to beam me up. Joke's over. Experiment's done. I want to come home now. Do you hear me?

After Reading

RESPONDING

1. In a **journal**, write about a time when you felt like an alien. What had happened? How did you feel about yourself? How did you act toward others?

UNDERSTANDING

2. The writer introduces each **character** with his or her own **short story**. In a small group, describe the physical appearance of each young person as he or she is introduced. In your notebook, take point-form notes on your impressions of each person on the basis of this physical description. Your notes should look like the sample below:

Name: Miranda Ellenby
Physical description: - blue jeans, sneakers, flowered warm-up jacket
*   - leaning on a bridge, keeping her head turned away from people*
*   near her*
Impression:

3. Using no more than two sentences for each character, **summarize** his or her story so far.
4. a) The writer has chosen a newspaper **article**, a short **biography**, a page from a log book, and an excerpt from a diary to start her novel. Explain why she might have wanted to include so many approaches to telling her story.
   b) Make point-form notes about the effect these changing **styles** had on you as a reader. Be ready to talk about the effect as a class.

THINKING ABOUT LANGUAGE

5. The language in each type of writing listed in activity 4 is unique. With a partner, look closely at each of the styles. Make a chart in your notebook like the one on the following page, and fill it in. Be sure each of you has a copy of the chart in your own notebook. Compare your chart with that of another pair of your classmates.

WRITING TYPE	DESCRIPTION OF VOCABULARY USED	TONE/HOW IT WAS CREATED
Newspaper article		
Biography		
Log		
Diary		

EXTENDING

6. You have been asked to turn this excerpt into a **script** for a movie. With a partner, brainstorm the following issues before you start:
   - whether you should present the screenplay in the same order as the novel
   - what point is the best point at which to start? (What should you introduce first? What will grab the **audience**'s attention and interest immediately?)
   - a list of the scenes you would include (you can add something that is not in the story)
   - how you would work in **dialogue** (there is very little in the excerpt that you have read)

   Write the script using "Medicine Woman" (pages 133–138) as your model. When you have completed your first draft, trade your script with two of your classmates. Read the script, looking for interest in the opening scene, use of dialogue, **character** development, language, and flow. Exchange comments, then revise your script, and prepare it for submission or publication.

7. In your notebook, make a list of the possible directions in which this story could go. Create a **graphic organizer** for one of your ideas, and follow that storyline to the end. (See The Reference Shelf, pages 259–261.)

A Different Drummer

HENRY DAVID THOREAU

BEFORE READING

As a class, discuss the **conflict** many people feel between trying to stay true to their individual personalities or family values and trying to fit in with the styles and values of their peers or neighbours. Which is more important?

If a man does not keep pace
with his companions,
perhaps it is because he hears
a different drummer.

Let him step to the music   5
he hears,
however measured
or far away.

After Reading

RESPONDING

1. In a sentence, identify the main idea of this **poem**.
2. In your notebook, explain one way in which you march to the sound of a different drummer.

UNDERSTANDING

3. Each sentence or **stanza** of this poem has a different purpose. Identify
   a) what is explained in the first sentence or stanza; and
   b) what advice is given in the second sentence or stanza.

THINKING ABOUT LANGUAGE

4. With a partner, discuss how this poem would need to be rewritten to be more inclusive.

EXTENDING

5. Identify a celebrity who you think "hears a different drummer." Give reasons for your choice.
6. **Debate** the following resolution: "Be it resolved that it is better to fit in than to stand apart from the crowd." (See The Reference Shelf, pages 278–279.) You may need to do additional research to prepare arguments for the debate.
7. Research the life and times of Henry David Thoreau. Prepare a **report** to the class, describing his life at Walden Pond and his basic philosophy of life. Include stories from Thoreau's life that illustrate his values and ideas.

The Men That Don't Fit In

ROBERT W. SERVICE

BEFORE READING

In your notebook, **define** "fitting in." Do we have to fit in to be successful in life?

There's a race of men that don't fit in,
    A race that can't stay still;
So they break the hearts of kith and kin,
    And they roam the world at will.
They range the field and they rove the flood,   5
    And they climb the mountain's crest;
Theirs is the curse of the gypsy blood,
    They don't know how to rest.

If they just went straight they might go far;
    They are strong and brave and true;   10
But they're always tired of the things that are,
    And they want the strange and new.
They say: "Could I find my proper groove,
    What a deep mark I would make!"
So they chop and change, and each fresh move   15
    Is only a fresh mistake.

And each forgets, as he strips and runs
  With a brilliant, fitful pace,
It's the steady, quiet, plodding ones
  Who win in the lifelong race.   20
And each forgets that his youth has fled,
  Forgets that his prime is past,
Till he stands one day, with a hope that's dead,
  In the glare of the truth at last.

He has failed, he has failed; he has missed his chance;   25
  He has just done things by half.
Life's been a jolly good joke on him,
  And now is the time to laugh.
Ha, ha! He is one of the Legion Lost;
  He was never meant to win;   30
He's a rolling stone, and it's bred in the bone;
  He's a man who won't fit in.

After Reading

RESPONDING

1. In a journal, write how you feel about the **narrator**'s view of men who do not fit in. Do you think these men exist? If so, where?

UNDERSTANDING

2. a) Write a statement of the **theme** of this **poem**. Choose words and phrases from the poem that support your statement of this theme.
   b) Explain whether or not you agree with the writer's **point of view**.
3. Describe the **mood** of this poem. Show how the writer has used word choice and rhythm to create this mood.

THINKING ABOUT LANGUAGE

4. Look up the following words: kith (line 3), kin (line 3), rove (line 5), fitful (line 18). In your notebook, identify the part of speech for each word, write a **definition** of the words, and use each word in a sentence that conveys its meaning.

5. Research the history of the word "gypsy." Show how the negative-**image** portrayal of the gypsy in this poem is a stereotype.

EXTENDING

6. In a small group, research the life of Robert Service. Divide the presentation into parts (e.g., the **topics** he covered in his writing, the **style** of his poetry, his family, his schooling, other interesting facts about him). Using your information, design for the class an effective interactive presentation on this famous poet.

7. a) With a partner, think of a product that could use the image of this kind of man in its advertisements. Create a brief sales talk to convince the president of the company that this man's image is perfect for selling the product. (See The Reference Shelf, pages 279–281.)

b) Design a television commercial or magazine advertisement using one or more of these "men that don't fit in" to sell your product. Perform your commercial or display your advertisement to the class.

c) As a class, comment on the commercials and advertisements, focusing on how well each has used the image of "the men that don't fit in."

Anne Frank

JOANNE STANBRIDGE

BEFORE READING

As a class, brainstorm a list of the facts you and classmates know about the life of Anne Frank.

When autumn cracks November sky
Or watching silver seagulls soar,
And much, and much I long to fly,
I think of you.

 And grief, and why? While others grew,   5
 You, cripple-winged, never flew.
 You had to cower, had to hide;
 When August glowed, you, locked inside,
 From grimy windows loved the sky
 And longed for sun, and longed to fly.   10

When feather snow shines Christmas white
Or watching rain on blackbird wet,
And much, and much I yearn for flight,
I think of you.

 And grief, and why? A secret door   15
 Shut you far away from war
 And kept them out, the ones who dared
 To hate the faith your people shared,
 And locked you in from boundless sky
 And caged you up, and grief, and why?   20

When April meadows shimmer wide
Or watching sparrows flicker past,
And much, and much I long to glide,
I think of you.

    And grief, and why? On shattered wings   25
    You clung to wild imaginings
    And, trapped inside, you searched for you,
    You scrambled and you struggled through.
    And then your pen, mid-sentence, dropped
    And even dream-world freedom stopped.   30

When August sun blazed hot, a torn
And broken, bloodied raven cried.
Much, and much he longed to soar,
The silent day that Anne Frank died.

(translation)
"This is a photo as I would wish
myself to look all the time. Then
I would maybe have a chance to
come to Hollywood."
Anne Frank, 10 Oct. 1942

After Reading

RESPONDING

1. Identify the times when the **narrator** of this **poem** thinks of Anne Frank. What do all of these times have in common?

UNDERSTANDING

2. What do you think the narrator of this poem admires about Anne Frank?
3. Explain the pattern of the **stanzas** of this poem in terms of the ideas expressed.

THINKING ABOUT LANGUAGE

4. Select one adjective and one verb in this poem that you think are particularly well chosen. In each case, explain what makes the word effective.

EXTENDING

5. Read an encyclopedia entry about Anne Frank. In a paragraph, give one reason why so many people admire her and discuss the reason.

6. If you have never read *The Diary of Anne Frank*, read it and write a **review** of it for the school newspaper. Work with a partner to revise and edit your review before submitting a final copy for publication.

Yes, It Was My Grandmother

LUCI TAPAHONSO

BEFORE READING

As a class, make a list of 15 career categories (e.g., health care professional, teacher, mechanic). Individually, label each career as "male," "female," or "both." As a class, discuss any careers you labelled as solely "male" or "female."

Yes, it was my grandmother
who trained wild horses for pleasure and pay.
People knew of her, saying:
   She knows how to handle them.
   Horses obey that woman.   5

She worked,
skirts flying, hair tied securely in the wind and dust.
She rode those animals hard and was thrown,
time and time again.
She worked until they were meek   10
and wanting to please.
   She came home at dusk,
   tired and dusty,
   smelling of sweat and horses.

She couldn't cook,   15
my father said smiling,
your grandmother hated to cook.

Oh Grandmother,
who freed me from cooking.
Grandmother, you must have made sure   20
I met a man who would not share the kitchen.

I am small like you and
do not protect my careless hair
from wind or rain—it tangles often,
Grandma, and it is wild and untrained.   25

After Reading

RESPONDING

1. In a **journal**, describe what you admire about the grandmother in this poem.

UNDERSTANDING

2. The poet breaks several stereotypes about women in this poem. With a partner, list each stereotype and explain how the poet breaks it.
3. Explain why the poet's choice of **narrator** is a good way of revealing the **character** of both the grandmother and the granddaughter.

THINKING ABOUT LANGUAGE

4. Copy the entire second **stanza**. For each sentence, identify the sentence type and the phrases and clauses used in the sentence. As a class, discuss the effectiveness of using a variety of sentences in any type of writing.

EXTENDING

5. a) Using "Yes, It Was My Grandmother" as a model, write a **poem** about an interesting person in your family. Talk to other family members about this person's life and, if possible, speak to the person.
   b) Exchange your poem with a partner who will look at the content and the way you have followed the original poem as a model. Use your partner's comments to revise your work. Prepare your poem for publication in your classroom.

Medicine Woman

"I guess it *was* good sauce. I'm sweating like a pig."

RICHARD DEMING

CHARACTERS

Jed Harmon, a key witness in a criminal's trial
Marcia Harmon, Jed's wife
Sgt. Harry Cartwright, Jed's bodyguard
John Minor, another man assigned to follow Jed
George Tobin, John's partner

Marcia Harmon is in the kitchen of a small house by a lake. She is stirring some spaghetti sauce. Her husband Jed and Sergeant Harry Cartwright enter dressed in fishing clothes.

Jed: That sauce smells good. But why are you making it? You must not have much faith in my fishing skills.

Marcia (*teasing*): You didn't have much luck this morning.

Harry: Late afternoon is when the fish bite around here.

Marcia: If you catch some fish, I'll put this sauce in the freezer. But in case you have your usual luck, you won't go hungry.

Jed (*grinning*): What about those two nice bass we had for dinner last night?

Marcia: What about the nice baloney we had the night before?

Jed: Be prepared to freeze that stuff. (*He kisses her.*) We'll be back about 6:00, honey.

Harry: I'll look around outside before you go out, Jed.

Jed: Mark Flager couldn't know where I am, Harry. Why don't you relax and enjoy yourself?

Harry: I'll relax after you testify in court tomorrow. Meanwhile, my job is to make sure you stay alive to talk. Wait here. (*He opens the back door and goes outside.*)

Marcia: I'll be glad when this is over. Each morning, I wonder if I'll be a widow by night.

Jed: How could Flager's men ever find me way out here? We're safe. I'll even be sorry when it's over. I'm enjoying the fishing.

Marcia: But it's not fair. Why should you have to hide out from gangsters?

Mark Flager should be the one who is haunted and hunted.

Jed: He's not exactly running around free. He's in jail. After I identify him tomorrow, he'll be on his way to prison.

Marcia: His gunmen are still free, though. I wish you hadn't seen him throw that bomb.

Jed: I'm glad I saw it. No one should get away with throwing a bomb in a crowded restaurant. He killed four people and injured nine others. If he goes free, his gang will be able to control the whole restaurant business.

(*Harry comes back in.*)

Harry: There's no sign of anyone around.

Marcia: I hope you have good luck. But if you don't, we can always eat spaghetti.

(*The men laugh and go outside. Marcia watches them walk to the lake and get into a small boat. Then she hears a car drive up. She goes into the living room and looks out the front window. She sees two men get out of a car and head for the front door. She puts the burglar chain on the door and opens the door a crack.*)

Marcia: Yes? Who are you?

John: I'm Sergeant John Minor of the district attorney's office, ma'am. (*He shows her a badge.*) My partner here is Officer George Tobin. Are you Mrs. Harmon?

Marcia: Yes. Just a moment, please. (*She takes off the chain and opens the door.*) Has something happened, Sergeant?

John: The D.A. doesn't like to take chances. He wants us to follow your husband and his guard into town tomorrow. Do you have enough room to put us up for the night?

Marcia (*letting them walk in*): There are two bedrooms. My husband and I share one. One of you can share the other with Sergeant Cartwright. The other one can sleep on the couch here.

John: That will be fine. I know Cartwright. I'll share his room. George, you can have the couch.

(*George nods. He is sweating and trembling.*)

Marcia: Let me take your coats. You must be hot.

John: I'm fine.

George: Me, too. (*He wipes his face with a handkerchief.*)

John: I think George is coming down with a cold. He's been having chills and fever.

Marcia: Would you like some aspirin?

George: No, thanks. I'll be all right.

John: We saw a boat pulling out as we drove up. Are your husband and Cartwright out fishing?

Marcia: Yes. They'll be back at 6:00. Excuse me a moment. I'm cooking spaghetti sauce, and it's time to stir it.

(*She leaves the room, and the men sit down. She returns and sits down. All three seem uneasy.*)

Marcia: Would you like some beer?

John: We don't drink on duty.

(*There is a short silence.*)

John: How did you and your husband find this place, Mrs. Harmon?

Marcia: It's the summer house of my department head, Dr. Peterson. I work at a hospital.

John: It's a fine hideout. We had trouble finding it, even with directions. It's far from everything, isn't it?

Marcia: Yes. We have to drive 20 miles for groceries. That's a little too far away for me.

John: Your troubles will be over tomorrow. (*He sniffs.*) That spaghetti sauce smells good.

Marcia: I made it in case my husband and the sergeant don't catch any fish. If they do, I'll put it in the freezer. But if you two don't like fish, you can have spaghetti instead.

John: I'd prefer spaghetti.

Marcia: How about you, Mr. Tobin?

George (*looking sick*): Spaghetti is my favorite food.

Marcia: I'd better stir it again, or it will burn. (*She goes into the kitchen. The phone rings, and John answers it.*)

John: Hello? (*Pause.*) You want to speak to Dr. Harmon?

(*Marcia appears.*)

John (*to Marcia*): I didn't know your husband is a doctor.

Marcia: He isn't. I'm the doctor. (*She takes the phone.*) Hello? (*Pause.*) Hi, Dr. Peterson. (*Pause.*) That was one of the police officers who are guarding us. (*Pause.*) Yes, everything is fine. Thank you for letting us stay here. (*Pause.*) Jed gives his testimony tomorrow. I want to be in court with him. So I won't be back at work until the day after. (*Pause.*) Okay. Thanks for calling. Good-bye. (*She hangs up.*)

John: So you're a lady doctor? And you can cook, too.

Marcia (*noticing spots of sauce on her apron*): I'm afraid I'm not a very neat cook, though. I'd better wash these spots out before they stay for good.

(*Marcia leaves, going toward the bathroom. George hurries into the kitchen. He takes off his coat, and we see a gun in a shoulder holster. He turns on a burner on the stove. He puts some white stuff into a spoon and heats it over the burner. He fills a hypodermic needle with liquid from the spoon. Then Marcia enters.*)

George (*startled*): I'm having a shot of insulin. I'm a diabetic.

Marcia: Oh. May I help you with the shot?

George: I'm used to doing it myself, thanks.

(*While George gives himself the shot, Marcia reaches under the sink. She takes a can of rat poison and hides it behind a curtain on the windowsill. Then she adds some spice to the spaghetti sauce. George packs up his things and returns to the living room. Marcia quietly goes to the living room door and listens to the men.*)

John: You fool! She's a doctor. She knows you weren't taking a shot of insulin.

(*Marcia enters the room. Both men stare at her.*)

John: I guess you figured us out.

Marcia (*nodding*): Insulin doesn't have to be heated in a spoon. Heroin does. Mr. Tobin's sweating and shaking were signs of addiction. I doubt that a member of the D.A.'s office would be a heroin addict. So I assume that you're Mark Flager's men.

John: You don't seem very scared about it.

Marcia: I am. But in my work, I've learned to control my emotions. May I ask what your plans are now?

George: We don't have any plans until 6:00, Doc.

Marcia: I assume you plan to kill my husband. You can't leave witnesses, so you'll probably kill Sergeant Cartwright and me, too.

John: We hoped we could keep things friendly until the last minute. If you sit down and stay quiet, we can still keep it friendly. Otherwise, we'll have to tie you up. (*Marcia sits on the couch. The clock ticks loudly. It is 4:15. No one says anything for about 15 minutes.*)

John: Isn't it time to stir that sauce again?

Marcia: Why should I? None of us will live to eat it.

George: My buddy and I will, Doc. How soon will it be ready?

Marcia: It's ready now. It gets better the longer it cooks, though.

John: There's no point in letting good sauce go to waste. We'll have it about 5:00. Go stir it, George. And look out the window while you're there. If the fish aren't biting, those guys may return early.

(*George goes into the kitchen. He returns in a minute.*)

George: The boat is still way out there. That sauce smells good. I could eat any time.

John: Do you know how to cook spaghetti?

George: I think you just boil it in water.

John: Maybe we'd better let her cook it.

(*He turns to Marcia.*) How long does the spaghetti take, Doc?

Marcia: First, the water has to boil. Then it takes about eight minutes for the spaghetti to cook. You'll find a large pot in the cabinet by the stove.

John: You must not have heard me, Doc. *You* are going to cook it. Or would you rather be tied up?

Marcia: I guess cooking for you is the lesser of two evils. (*She goes into the kitchen. The two men follow her. She gets out a large pot. John looks out the window.*)

John: Is that their boat? It looks as if they're heading in.

Marcia (*looking out*): I can't tell from so far away. Anyway, it's moving too slowly to be heading in.

John: Even if they *are* heading for shore, it will take them 45 minutes. I guess we can relax.

(*John and George sit at the kitchen table. Marcia fills the pot with water and puts it on the stove. When the water boils, she adds the spaghetti. John gets up to look out the window again.*)

John: They're still a quarter of a mile out.

(*Marcia sets two plates on the table.*)

George: Aren't you going to eat with us, Doc?

(*Marcia doesn't answer. She continues to set the table.*)

George: Some beer would go well with the spaghetti.

(*Marcia gets two beers from the refrigerator. She also sets out bread, butter, and grated cheese. She drains the spaghetti. Then she serves it, with the sauce, onto the two plates.*)

Marcia (*sarcastically*): Is there anything else you'd like?

John: I guess we're set. Go ahead, George, while I take another look.

(*George starts eating, while John looks out the window. Then he sits back down at the table.*)

John: They're moving slowly. They'll be half an hour yet. (*He joins George in eating.*)

George: This is good sauce.

John: Yes, Doc, but you make it awfully spicy.

Marcia: My husband likes it spicy. He says if it doesn't make you sweat, it's not good sauce.

(*The two men eat in silence. It doesn't take them long to clear their plates.*)

John: I guess it *was* good sauce. I'm sweating like a pig. (*He gets up and goes to the window.*) We timed that just right. They're close to shore now.

George (*taking out his gun*): We'd better let her have it. She might try to warn them by screaming.

Marcia: It wouldn't be very wise for you to do that. It would be like committing suicide. I'm the only doctor within 20 miles.

John: What are you talking about?

Marcia: Do you feel a slight burning in your stomach? Is your sweat turning cold? Look at each other. Can you see each other turning a bit green? These are the first signs of phosphorous poisoning.

(*The two men stare at each other. Then they stare at Marcia.*)

John: What are you getting at, Doc? Spit it out fast.

(*Marcia reaches behind the kitchen window curtain. She pulls out the tin can she hid there earlier. She shows them the label, which says "Rat Poison."*)

Marcia: I realized you were Mark Flager's hired killers when I saw George giving himself a shot. So I put this in the spaghetti sauce. I can save your lives, if you let me. In another 15 minutes, no one will be able to save you.

George: Give us the cure fast, or I'll kill you!

Marcia: No, you won't, because you're dead if you do. I'll give you the cure as soon as you put your guns on the table.

(*They stare at her, but don't move. She continues.*)

Marcia: The basic chemical in rat poison is phosphorous. Every second, more of it enters your blood. By now, your stomachs must be burning, and you must be feeling dizzy. You don't have time to argue.

(*The two men stare at each other. Then they clutch their stomachs and put their guns on the table. Marcia picks up the guns, takes them to the door, and throws them outside. She gets out a bottle from under the sink. She pours out some liquid into two glasses and hands them to the two men.*)

Marcia: The first step is to stop the phosphorous from entering your blood. This will do it. It's turpentine. Drink it down.

(*The men drink the turpentine.*)

Marcia: Now you need something to clear out your stomachs. (*She fills two more glasses with warm water. Then she stirs in some dried mustard.*)

John: Hurry up, Doc! My stomach is on fire!

Marcia: There's no hurry now. You have to wait for the phosphorous to react with the turpentine. Take these glasses into the bathroom. Don't drink this liquid until I tell you to.

(*They grab the glasses and stumble toward the bathroom.*)

(*About 10 minutes later, Jed Harmon and Harry Cartwright walk in the back door — without any fish. Marcia is waiting for them.*)

Marcia: We have a couple of visitors. They're patients of mine. (*She leads them into the bathroom. John and George are kneeling by the bathtub, looking weak. They have been throwing up.*)

Harry: It's Johnny Minor and George Needle! They're Mark Flager's top killers. What in the world is wrong with them?

Marcia: They ate some of my spaghetti sauce. It had a lot of red pepper in it.

Jed: Did that make them sick?

Marcia: Not exactly. Their imaginations did the job. They believed that I had put rat poison into the sauce. I described how rat poison would make them feel, and they imagined they felt the signs. They thought I was a doctor of medicine. I didn't explain that I'm really a doctor of psychology.

THE END

After Reading

RESPONDING

1. In a paragraph, explain what point in this **drama** is the most **suspenseful**. Give reasons for your choice.

UNDERSTANDING

2. In a short **essay**, explain whether this drama would be more effectively performed on radio, television, or the stage. Give reasons for your choice.

3. A drama as short as this one needs to be very well structured. With a partner, divide the drama into four parts: background or set-up for the **plot**, rising action or complication, turning point or crisis, and resolution or denouement. Be prepared to explain to the class the lines at which each section begins and the reasons for your choices.

4. Write Sergeant Harry Cartwright's police report about the events presented in this drama. Be prepared to read your report aloud.

5. In a small group, rehearse and present all or part of this drama for the class.

THINKING ABOUT LANGUAGE

6. Explain the difference between the words in this drama that are in bold, those in italics, and those that are in neither bold nor italics.

EXTENDING

7. Read the Attitudes Inventory on pages 92–93. Then read the conversation between John Minor and Dr. Marcia Harmon just after he answers the telephone. Explain how John's comments **foreshadow** the fact that he is not a trained police officer, even though he has said that he is.

8. Do some research to find out whether Dr. Marcia Harmon would have been charged with murder if she had put rat poison in the spaghetti sauce and one or both of Flager's men had died. Prepare a **report** on your findings to present to the class.

Watching the Sun

AMON SABA SAAKANA

BEFORE READING

Some people wake up bright and cheery; others wake up slowly and in a less-than-cheery mood.
In a small group, discuss the advantages and disadvantages of both ways of waking up. Be prepared
to present the main points of your discussion to the class.

i wake to a yellow fire
a blazing light hanging
on my face
like a dream of floating balloons
dancing on my nose   5
& thru the wooden slats of jalousies
i see the leaves
of the mango tree playing
from fresh caresses of the wind
& in the sky   10
a dizzying blueness
that makes me want to sleep

i wake to a yellow fire
a blazing light hanging
on my face   15
whistles of keskidees
gently bringing me to life
& sounds of footsteps
like the charm of water-falls
to this smell of fried bakes   20
& salt-fish

& this yellow fire of dream
turns into the smiling face
of my mother

After Reading

RESPONDING

1. Identify one possible place where the **narrator** of this **poem** might live. Identify two details in the poem that support your choice.

UNDERSTANDING

2. In a single word, describe the **mood** of this poem. In a paragraph, justify the word you chose.
3. Identify an example of a **simile** and a **metaphor** in this poem. Explain what two things are being compared in each case.

THINKING ABOUT LANGUAGE

4. Look up any new or unfamiliar words used in this poem, and create a **glossary** to accompany each.
5. This poem is written in two run-on sentences without standard punctuation. In a paragraph, explain why the poet might have chosen to write in this manner. In a second paragraph, explain whether the poem's punctuation and grammar make it more or less meaningful for you.

EXTENDING

6. Draw a picture that could accompany this poem in an **anthology**. Display your picture on a class bulletin board.
7. Write your own poem based on your last thoughts as you fall asleep at night or your first thoughts as you wake up in the morning.

The Michelle I Know

"What we've got—it's based on a little more than hair..."

ALISON LOHANS

BEFORE READING

Take a poll of the class using this question: When you are sick, do you want to be alone or do you want someone to be there with you?

Rob was late. And last night he'd gone to the after-game dance. With Vanessa.

Michelle turned over. The hospital bed was hard and confining. The entire back of her neck felt like one giant pillow crease. She rubbed it and as always, her fingers crept upward to explore the terrifying bleak landscape where her hair was supposed to be. She didn't have the energy to pound the pillow good and hard. Even if she did, she'd probably knock the intravenous needle out of place and then she'd have to lie there gritting her teeth while nurses poked and jabbed to set another IV.

It wasn't fair. Sometimes she felt so tired and sick it was even hard to lift the remote control for the TV.

Her clock radio said it was 7:27. Maybe Rob wasn't coming. She wasn't much to come to. Not any more. Even after the other kids quit showing up, he'd stuck it out. Once he'd even smuggled in his mom's poodle pup to break the monotony.

But now maybe he was having second thoughts.

All Michelle could see outside the fourth-storey window was cottony orange light dissolving into darkness. In the distance a siren screamed, drew nearer, then passed beneath her window. If she got up, she'd see blood-red lights flashing below and people hurrying into Emergency, all softened by the winter fog. Sometimes the fog got so thick it looked like you could walk right out the window and keep on going. Michelle's mouth quirked. In reality, it would be more like plunging down—gown flapping about her, IV monitor and pole and bottles all set to smash on the sidewalk. How much would it hurt, before . . .? But that might be a quick escape.

The guitar started playing again. Michelle relaxed a bit and fidgeted with her earrings. One of the holes in her left ear was kind of sore. She sighed and took out the tiny purple triangle, feeling for a safe spot on the bedside table. If her earlobe got infected, Dr. Warkentin would give her major heck.

She closed her eyes and tried to let the music wash away her frustration. It was total boredom, being in hospital for almost two months. Probably she was turning into a turnip. Or some kind of squash. No wonder Rob wasn't here. Vegetables weren't the greatest company. At least the music made everything more bearable. This was the third day. Or was it only the second? Time got pretty blurry, cut off from her normal life.

The soft scuff of rubber soles on carpet, the faintest swish of clothing told her that Brenda, the evening nurse, had come in. "Hi, kiddo," came the cheery voice. "Anything I can do for you?"

Eyes still shut, Michelle shook her head. She'd had it with hospitals. With routines. Needles in her arms. Chemotherapy that left her feeling like something a pulp mill spat out.

Brenda's voice prodded at her. "Your friend's late."

Michelle looked dully at the young nurse. "I don't think he's coming."

"Oh hush!" Briskly the older girl straightened the untouched pile of magazines left by the occupational therapist.

"I bet —"

"Watch out for my earring." Michelle tensed, then heard the predictable *thkk* sound of a tiny object hitting the carpet.

"Sorry." Brenda stooped. "I'll put it in your top drawer, okay? Now. Your friend. I bet the fog's keeping him. When I went out at supper it was like walking through whipped cream."

Michelle smiled faintly and waited while Brenda took her pulse and temperature, then checked the drip from her iv bottle.

Brenda patted her hand. "Cheer up. Doctor says your blood counts are super. You're on your way to remission, kid, and you know what that means."

"Yeah," she said sourly. "I get to go home and wait six months before I have enough hair to do anything with." It would be heaven to go home, though. It seemed ages since she'd been *someone*, with thick dark hair that swished against her cheeks. Who had lots of friends, and clothes that fit right. Who felt like the world was hers.

Now it was safest not to hope.

Brenda tossed her straw-coloured braid over her shoulder, then placed her hands in her uniform pockets. "You'll feel lots better once you're home. But you may not want to leave us. . . ." The nurse's voice lowered. "You've got an admirer right here in our midst, and *he* thinks you're gorgeous."

"Yeah, right. Tell me another one." Michelle shifted and the iv pole rattled.

"Honest. It sure isn't me." Brenda indicated her comfortably padded waistline. "If I ever get a boyfriend I'll know I'm dreaming."

"At least you've got hair." What she really meant was that Brenda had a face that was . . . friendly. The kind that was sure to draw people to her—but it would sound pretty sucky to say it out loud.

"So have you," Brenda countered. "Where is it, stuffed in the drawer with your washbasin?"

To be exact, the wig was stuffed in the drawer *under* the washbasin. Mom bought it when her hair first started thinning. It was awful. The colour was right, but that was all. Any way you looked at it, it was fake hair — like what you'd see on a Barbie doll.

Michelle glared at her skinny arms, mottled with bruises and needle scars. "It's gross," she muttered. "It's too hot. And prickly. Who cares, anyhow, with a death sentence hanging over your head?"

Brenda swished across the room to get a handful of clean straws from the cabinet. "Cases like yours go into remission for years now, Michelle," she said firmly. The way she said it, it sounded like she knew exactly how it felt to lie there at 3 A.M., scared cold, and faking sleep as the night shift crept in with flashlights to check the IV and write on the chart. "We had the cutest little guy in here once — he never came back, so we all started thinking maybe he didn't make it. But Doctor says she sees him every now and then, skateboarding and riding his bike like a maniac."

Michelle fell silent. In the hallway came the clatter of rolling wheels. Sour-faced Mrs. Begbie paused in the doorway, leaning heavily on her IV pole, her own bald head covered by a turquoise hat with wild feathers. "Nurse," she wheezed, "can you get someone to bring my pain shot?"

Brenda glanced at her watch. "I'll go check on it for you, Mrs. B."

Bored, Michelle flicked the TV switch. But that drowned out the guitar. She flicked it off and the screen went blank. Just like she felt. Visiting hours were almost over. Rob wasn't coming.

Suddenly Brenda was back. "C'mon — I'll take you to see Claude. Your admirer. Keep your friend guessing a little, huh?"

Michelle inspected the cool clear tubing that fed sugar water and, sometimes, chemo into her arm. "I don't feel like it."

"C'mon, go for it! Put on your wig — you can model it for Dr. Hernandez. He's at the nursing station."

Michelle groaned, then sat up because there was nothing better to do. But she left the wig in the drawer. "This Claude. Is he bald like me?"

"Right on. And he thinks you're gorgeous."

"Oh sure." Wearily Michelle swung her legs over the edge of the bed and let Brenda put slippers on for her. Her knees were bony. And the skimpy hospital gown was too much — even a mannequin would drop dead wearing it. She slid one arm into the hot-pink dressing gown Brenda held ready, but even that looked gimpy with one sleeve dangling because of the IV.

"Glamour!" Brenda's eyes teased her.

"God. What'd you do with my mink, throw it down the laundry chute?"

"Yep." Brenda's strong arm came around Michelle's waist as she pushed up, grasping the IV pole. "And I'm afraid I've got some bad news. It shrank."

Dr. Hernandez, the young resident, looked up and waved as they inched down the hallway. Michelle waved back, then remembered. Rob hadn't come.

"And here's Claude."

Michelle took one look and wished she could turn and run. Except she was too tired.

Claude was old enough to be her father. His arms were bruised like her own. His bald head gleamed with shiny flesh. A guitar lay in his lap.

Dizzy with exhaustion, Michelle sank into a visitor's chair. Some admirer. What was he, a dirty old man? See if she ever listened to Brenda again!

"So you're Michelle."

"Yeah," she mumbled and looked away.

"We're all pretty proud of Claude," Brenda said. "He's been in and out of this place for eight years now, and each time he comes back, we learn something new."

Eight *years*? And she'd thought eight weeks was torture. "I can hear you in my room," Michelle said hesitantly, since they obviously expected her to talk. "It helps."

Light glowed in the man's dark eyes, and suddenly his face was beautiful. "I taught myself to play in this joint," he said. "Drove everybody nuts." His right hand, splinted to keep the IV needle in place, strummed the guitar with a caressing stroke. A flurry of notes scattered.

"You?" said Brenda. "Never."

Outside a train rumbled past. Michelle fell silent. Ironic how hospitals ended up in the noisiest parts of town. Ironic how she, once with everything going for her, had so quickly been thrust on a shelf, forgotten, and now by Rob too. Once cancer cells got their claws into you, none of the old rules applied. You were totally at the mercy of doctors and nurses. And the disease.

"It's not so easy, eh?" Claude's soft voice startled her.

Quickly she forced her face into a polite mask. No point in grasping for the sympathy of somebody just as sick — probably forty, and bald besides. Brenda had disappeared; she guessed it was either be polite and talk, or else try getting back on her own. "No," she said. There was a long pause. Claude's bound fingers gently plucked the guitar. "You've had leukemia for eight *years*?" she burst out.

"Eight years. A long time. It's been pretty hard on the family. But I'm lucky. Most patients my age don't last."

Michelle looked cautiously at Claude, whose shiny bald head had odd bumps and ridges just like hers, who lacked eyelashes and eyebrows. Just as she did. "Do you ever feel like —" She broke off, then barged ahead after a steadying breath: "Like sometimes you'd rather die than be poked by one more needle?"

Claude looked beyond her, out at the night sky. "Sometimes," he said at last. "But we were each given a life. You don't throw that out like garbage."

"I hate it!" Sudden tears trickled down Michelle's cheeks and she wiped at them furiously. "How I look. How I feel. I hate *everything!*" She sniffed hard, blew her nose, but couldn't stop.

"Yeah, it gets that way sometimes." Claude's fingers coaxed more notes out of the guitar, sending music spilling into the hallway. Michelle rested her cheek against the ridge of the bedside table. "I've been there," he went on. "But you know, we're all in this together."

"Not my friends," she said bitterly.

"You have to be strong inside," he said. "Don't waste yourself fighting the wrong things."

Michelle traced her fingertip along the hard tabletop. At least this man was better than sour Mrs. Begbie, or Mr. Morris who let himself be wheeled around like a big doll. This man had dignity. Did she?

"Michelle?" Brenda's voice penetrated. "I found this guy wandering around the hallway. Is he somebody you know?"

Rob! He stood there in the doorway, still bundled up in his jacket, his face tense.

With a great effort Michelle wiped her eyes. "Hi," she mumbled.

The music stopped. A warm hand rested on her shoulder. "Remember. You've got to fight it."

She managed a wan smile. "Yeah."

"Sorry I'm late," Rob said. "That fog's impossible. I practically had to get out and put my nose on the street just to see the lines."

"Your attention please." The cold voice of the intercom spoke with dismissive finality. "Visiting hours are now over."

"Shush!" Brenda waved her hand at the speaker in the ceiling. "Quick! To your room!"

Shakily Michelle stood up, leaning on her IV pole. Rob moved in to help her. He smelled like fresh air. Which meant she must smell like . . . the hospital. Sick. Grimly, she kept her legs moving and her grip tight on the pole; she'd already learned how hard it could be to get back up after a fall. But visiting hours were over, and now Rob would have to go. Her eyes blurred.

"Who was that guy?" Rob asked.

"He's been sick for eight years." She knew she was wobbly, but it felt as if Rob had just shuddered. Walking took so much of her energy that she couldn't say more. Her bed, freshly made up, looked like heaven. Wearily she sank onto it.

But Brenda was drawing the curtains around her. Rob was pulling up a chair. "She says I can stay half an hour if I promise to be good," he whispered.

Brenda winked and disappeared.

Suddenly Michelle didn't know what to say. Here was Rob, late because of the fog.

But his face was still tense and his eyes were guarded. "How was last night?" she mumbled.

"Okay," he said indifferently. "We won the game."

They were not on the same wavelength. Needing to be doing something, Michelle reached for her mirror and studied herself. Her shiny bald head, the bony ridges where her eyebrows had once been. She yanked the wig out of the drawer and pulled it on. Loose hairs caught in her right earring. Furtively she glanced at Rob. "Well?" she demanded. "Am I still ugly?"

Rob sighed.

Might as well forget it. Who wanted a bald girlfriend who couldn't do anything but cry? "I'm ugly compared to Vanessa." She couldn't help the waspish note that sliced into her voice.

"What's the deal about Vanessa?" Rob's fingers tensed as they dangled between his knees. "I only went for something to do. Vanessa's boring, okay? The whole stupid dance was boring. What else do you want to know, what we —"

"Sorry." She felt heat creeping into her face. "When you were so late, I guess I thought. . . ." Out of the corner of her eye she watched him. His jaw was tight, but his green eyes were intent on her. "And then because I'm so ugly and everything, I thought . . . Oh forget it!" She pulled the wig off and threw it. It landed on her IV bottle and dangled there rakishly.

Michelle bit her lip. It looked so awful she nearly cried — to think she'd hoped Rob might like her better with the wig on. But it didn't look just awful, it looked — *awful*. So awful that . . . A giggle escaped.

Suddenly Rob lurched to his feet. He bowed to the IV pole. "Allow me, madam, may I have this dance?"

Michelle laughed out loud.

Rob grinned.

Michelle clapped a hand over her mouth, trying to keep her voice down, for suddenly she couldn't stop laughing. But she couldn't let herself get carried away. It was all very well for noble Rob to come to the hospital every day to see poor Michelle, who was so sick with leukemia, *but* . . .

"You shouldn't feel like you have to come here all the time," she mumbled. "It's no fun for you. I mean, you've been fantastic, really fantastic, but I don't want you to start hating me because I'm such a . . ." She swallowed hard.

Rob had to be set free. It wasn't fair to expect him to be the knight in shining armour. She had to have the strength to let him go.

"Michelle." His voice was quiet; solemnly he lifted a few strands of hair from the wig, rubbing them between his thumb and fingertips. "What we've got — it's based on a little more than hair, you know?"

She hiccupped, hardly daring to believe what she was hearing. She had to change gears, fast. Deliberately, she rubbed her hand over her bald head. "Well, at least this never gets tangled." She gulped in a deep breath. "How do you think it would look with flowers painted on it?"

Miraculously, Rob was still there. He was even laughing, and his incredible, world-stopping grin was dawning in his eyes. For the first time in months, Michelle felt a real smile swelling inside.

"Now *that's* the Michelle I know," Rob murmured. He leaned closer.

After Reading

RESPONDING

1. a) In your notebook, explain how you feel about the **character** of Michelle at various points in this **story** from the beginning to the end. Use examples from this story in your explanation.
   b) Discuss your reactions with a classmate.

UNDERSTANDING

2. With a partner, using the set of questions for finding **theme**, write a statement of the theme of this story. (See The Reference Shelf, pages 249–250.) Compare your statement with that of another partnership.

3. a) Make a list of all the things, large and small, that bother Michelle. Order your list from the things that bother her most to those that bother her least.
   b) As a class, discuss your lists, focusing on the content and order of each of your lists.
   c) Put yourself in Michelle's place. In a paragraph, explain why some small things may bother her as much as or more than the larger things.
4. The wig in the story is a symbol. Explain what it stands for and how Michelle's attitude toward the wig changes in the story.

THINKING ABOUT LANGUAGE

5. Make a list of the vocabulary in this story associated with hospitals and with Michelle's illness. Look up words that you do not know in a dictionary, and record their meaning.
6. a) In the first paragraph, there are two sentence errors. Identify each error. Explain why the writer would use these sentence errors on purpose.
   b) Correct the errors and compare the effectiveness of the new sentences with that of the originals.

EXTENDING

7. a) Choose one of the following characters from this story: Brenda, the nurse; Claude; or Michelle. Write a two-minute **speech** that one of them might deliver to people your age. Select a topic you think would fit the character, making sure there is enough information in the story to help you know what to say.
   b) With a partner who is using the same character, exchange and read each other's speech. Answer the following questions: What is the **topic**? Is the topic one that the character would talk about? Is enough information given in the story? Is the information interesting to people your age? How could the speech be improved?
   c) Revise your speech on the basis of your partner's comments.
   d) Rehearse and record your speech on audiotape to present to the class.

Marriage Is a Private Affair

"How could he shut his door against them?"

CHINUA ACHEBE

BEFORE READING

In a small group, discuss the appropriate role of parents in the selection of marriage partners for their children. Consider the following roles: the parents choose the marriage partner (arranged marriage); the young man asks his girlfriend's father for her hand in marriage; the parents accept or reject their son or daughter's choice; the parents are informed of their child's decision to marry. Be prepared to present the main ideas of your discussion to the class.

"Have you written to your dad yet?" asked Nene one afternoon as she sat with Nnaemeka in her room at 16 Kasanga Street, Lagos.

"No. I've been thinking about it. I think it's better to tell him when I get home on leave!"

"But why? Your leave is such a long way off yet — six whole weeks. He should be let into our happiness now."

Nnaemeka was silent for a while, and then began very slowly as if he groped for his words: "I wish I were sure it would be happiness to him."

"Of course it must," replied Nene, a little surprised. "Why shouldn't it?"

"You have lived in Lagos all your life, and you know very little about people in remote parts of the country."

"That's what you always say. But I don't believe anybody will be so unlike other people that they will be unhappy when their sons are engaged to marry."

"Yes. They are most unhappy if the engagement is not arranged by them. In our case it's worse — you are not even an Ibo."

This was said so seriously and so bluntly that Nene could not find speech immediately. In the cosmopolitan atmosphere of the city it had always seemed to her something of a joke that a person's tribe could determine whom he married.

At last she said, "You don't really mean that he will object to your marrying me simply on that account? I had always thought you Ibos were kindly disposed to other people."

"So we are. But when it comes to marriage, well, it's not quite so simple. And this," he added, "is not peculiar to the Ibos. If your father were alive and lived in the heart of Ibibio-land he would be exactly like my father."

"I don't know. But anyway, as your father is so fond of you, I'm sure he will forgive you soon enough. Come on then, be a good boy and send him a nice lovely letter..."

"It would not be wise to break the news to him by writing. A letter will bring it upon him with a shock. I'm quite sure about that."

"All right, honey, suit yourself. You know your father."

As Nnaemeka walked home that evening he turned over in his mind different ways of overcoming his father's opposition, especially now that he had gone and found a girl for him. He had thought of showing his letter to Nene but decided on second thoughts not to, at least for the moment. He read it again when he got home and couldn't help smiling to himself. He remembered Ugoye quite well, an Amazon of a girl who used to beat up all the boys, himself included, on the way to the stream, a complete dunce at school.

"I have found a girl who will suit you admirably — Ugoye Nweke, the eldest daughter of our neighbour, Jacob Nweke. She has a proper Christian upbringing. When she stopped schooling some years ago her father (a man of sound judgement) sent her to live in the house of a pastor where she has received all the training a wife could need. Her Sunday School teacher has told me that she reads her Bible very fluently. I hope we shall begin negotiations when you come home in December."

On the second evening of his return from Lagos Nnaemeka sat with his father under a cassia tree. This was the old man's retreat where he went to read his Bible when the parching December sun had set and a fresh, reviving wind blew on the leaves.

"Father," began Nnaemeka suddenly, "I have come to ask for forgiveness."

"Forgiveness? For what, my son?" he asked in amazement.

"It's about this marriage question."

"Which marriage question?"

"I can't—we must—I mean it is impossible for me to marry Nweke's daughter."

"Impossible? Why?" asked his father.

"I don't love her."

"Nobody said you did. Why should you?" he asked.

"Marriage today is different..."

"Look here, my son," interrupted his father, "nothing is different. What one looks for in a wife are a good character and a Christian background."

Nnaemeka saw there was no hope along the present line of argument.

"Moreover," he said," I am engaged to marry another girl who has all of Ugoye's good qualities, and who..."

His father did not believe his ears. "What did you say?" he asked slowly and disconcertingly.

"She is a good Christian," his son went on, "and a teacher in a Girls' School in Lagos."

"Teacher, did you say? If you consider that a qualification for a good wife I should like to point out to you, Emeka, that no Christian woman should teach. St. Paul in his letter to the Corinthians says that women should keep silence." He rose slowly from his seat and paced forwards and backwards. This was his pet subject, and he condemned vehemently those church leaders who encouraged women to teach in their schools. After he had spent his emotion on a long homily he at last came back to his son's engagement, in a seemingly milder tone.

"Whose daughter is she, anyway?"

"She is Nene Atang."

"What!" All the mildness was gone again. "Did you say Neneataga, what does that mean?"

"Nene Atang from Calabar. She is the only girl I can marry." This was a very rash reply and Nnaemeka expected the storm to burst. But it did not. His father merely walked away into his room. This was most unexpected and perplexed Nnaemeka. His father's silence was infinitely more menacing than a flood of threatening speech. That night the old man did not eat.

When he sent for Nnaemeka a day later he applied all possible ways of dissuasion. But the young man's heart was hardened, and his father eventually gave him up as lost.

"I owe it to you, my son, as a duty to show you what is right and what is wrong. Whoever put this idea into your head might as well have cut your throat. It is Satan's work." He waved his son away.

"You will change your mind, Father, when you know Nene."

"I shall never see her," was the reply. From that night the father scarcely spoke to his son. He did not, however, cease hoping that he would realize how serious was the danger he was heading for. Day and night he put him in his prayers.

Nnaemeka, for his own part, was very deeply affected by his father's grief. But he kept hoping that it would pass away. If it had occurred to him that never in the history of his people had a man married a woman who spoke a different tongue, he might have been less optimistic. "It has never been heard," was the verdict of an old man speaking a few weeks later. In that short sentence he spoke for all his people. This man had come with others to commiserate with Okeke when news went round about his son's behaviour. By that time the son had gone back to Lagos.

"It has never been heard," said the old man again with a sad shake of his head.

"What did Our Lord say?" asked another gentlemen. "Sons shall rise against their Fathers; it is there in the Holy Book."

"It is the beginning of the end," said another.

The discussion thus tending to become theological, Madubogwu, a highly practical man, brought it down once more to the ordinary level.

"Have you thought of consulting a native doctor about your son?" he asked Nnaemeka's father.

"He isn't sick," was the reply.

"What is he then? The boy's mind is diseased and only a good herbalist can bring him back to his right senses. The medicine he requires is *Amalile*, the same that women apply with success to recapture their husbands' straying affection."

"Madubogwu is right," said another gentleman. "This thing calls for medicine."

"I shall not call in a native doctor." Nnaemeka's father was known to be obstinately ahead of his more superstitious neighbours in these matters. "I will not be another Mrs. Ochuba. If my son wants to kill himself then let him do it with his own hands. It is not for me to help him."

"But it was her fault," said Madubogwu. "She ought to have gone to an honest herbalist. She was a clever woman, nevertheless."

"She was a wicked murderess," said Jonathan who rarely argued with his neighbours because, he often said, they were incapable of reasoning. "The medicine was prepared for her husband, it was his name they called in its preparation and I am sure it would have been perfectly beneficial to him. It was wicked to put it into the herbalist's food, and say you were only trying it out."

Six months later, Nnaemeka was showing his young wife a short letter from his father:

It amazes me that you could be so unfeeling as to send me your wedding picture. I would have sent it back. But on further thought I decided just to cut off your wife and send it back to you because I have nothing to do with her. How I wish that I had nothing to do with you either."

When Nene read through this letter and looked at the mutilated picture her eyes filled with tears, and she began to sob.

"Don't cry, my darling," said her husband. "He is essentially good-natured and will one day look more kindly on our marriage." But years passed and that one day did not come.

For eight years, Okeke would have nothing to do with his son, Nnaemeka. Only three times (when Nnaemeka asked to come home and spend his leave) did he write to him.

"I can't have you in my house," he replied on one occasion. "It can be of no interest to me where or how you spend your leave — or your life, for that matter."

The prejudice against Nnaemeka's marriage was not confined to his little village.

In Lagos, especially among his people who worked there, it showed itself in a different way. Their women, when they met at the village meeting, were not hostile to Nene. Rather, they paid her such excessive deference as to make her feel she was not one of them. But as time went on, Nene gradually broke through some of this prejudice and even began to make friends among them. Slowly and grudgingly they began to admit that she kept her home much better than most of them.

The story eventually got to the village in the heart of the Ibo country that Nnaemeka and his young wife were a most happy couple. But his father was one of the few people in the village who knew nothing about this. He always displayed so much temper whenever his son's name was mentioned that everyone avoided it in his presence. By a tremendous effort of will he had succeeded in pushing his son to the back of his mind. The strain had nearly killed him but he had persevered, and won.

Then one day he received a letter from Nene, and in spite of himself he began to glance through it perfunctorily until all of a sudden the expression on his face changed and he began to read more carefully.

"*…Our two sons, from the day they learnt that they have a grandfather, have insisted on being taken to him. I find it impossible to tell them that you will not see them. I implore you to allow Nnaemeka to bring them home for a short time during his leave next month. I shall remain here in Lagos…*"

The old man at once felt the resolution he had built up over so many years falling in. He was telling himself that he must not give in. He tried to steel his heart against all emotional appeals. It was a re-enactment of that other struggle. He leaned against a window and looked out. The sky was overcast with heavy black clouds and a high wind began to blow filling the air with dust and dry leaves. It was one of those rare occasions when even Nature takes a hand in a human fight. Very soon it began to rain, the first rain of the year. It came down in large sharp drops and was accompanied by the lightning and thunder which mark a change of season.

Okeke was trying hard not to think of his two grandsons. But he knew he was now fighting a losing battle. He tried to hum a favourite hymn but the pattering of large rain drops on the roof broke up the tune. His mind immediately returned to the children. How could he shut his door against them? By a curious mental process he imagined them standing, sad and forsaken, under the harsh angry weather — shut out from his house.

That night he hardly slept, from remorse — and a vague fear that he might die without making it up to them.

After Reading

RESPONDING

1. Identify the **character** in this **story** that you admire most. In a paragraph, use details from the story to support your choice.

UNDERSTANDING

2. Write a **report** contrasting the two views of marriage described in this story. Use subtitles such as "Courtship" and "Role of the Wife" to organize your report.
3. Write Okeke's return letter to Nene after she asks him to see his grandchildren.
4. Look up the meaning of the literary term **pathetic fallacy.** Explain how the writer has used pathetic fallacy in this story.
5. List the traditional religious and cultural attitudes toward marriage described in this story. Write an **essay** explaining whether these attitudes tend to promote the stability of society and marriages, or personal happiness.

THINKING ABOUT LANGUAGE

6. Select five effective adverbs used in this story. Analyze each in a chart like the one below.

EFFECTIVE ADVERB	WORD THE ADVERB MODIFIES	PART OF SPEECH OF THE WORD THE ADVERB MODIFIES	WHY THE ADVERB IS EFFECTIVE

EXTENDING

7. Write a continuation of this story. In a small group, have a "read-around" of each of your continuations.
8. Using print and/or electronic sources, research the country of Nigeria or the Ibo culture, and present your findings in an oral report to the class.
9. With a partner, write a film **script** for all or part of this story. If time permits, videotape your script and present the videotaped version to the class.

EXCERPT FROM *Leaving Home*

"Just seventeen... and already the burdens
of a man on his t'in little shoulders."

DAVID FRENCH

BEFORE READING

As a class, discuss the following question: Before a young person leaves home, what does he or she
have to think about and consider?

Scene

The play is set in Toronto on an early
November day in the late fifties.

Act One

*The lights come up on a working-class house in
Toronto. The stage is divided into three playing
areas: kitchen, dining room and living room. In
addition there is a hallway leading into the living
room. Two bedroom doors lead off the hallway, as
well as the front door which is offstage.*

*The kitchen contains a fridge, a stove, cup-
boards over the sink for everyday dishes, and a
small drop-leaf table with two wooden chairs,
one at either end. A plastic garbage receptacle
stands beside the stove. A hockey calendar hangs
on a wall, and a kitchen prayer.*

*The dining room is furnished simply with an
oak table and chairs. There is an oak cabinet
containing the good dishes and silverware.
Perhaps a family portrait hangs on the wall — a
photo taken when the sons were much younger.*

*The living room contains a chesterfield and
an armchair, a TV, a record player and a
fireplace. On the mantle rests a photo album
and a silver-framed photo of the two sons —
then small boys — astride a pinto pony. On
one wall hangs a mirror. On another, a
seascape. There is also a small table with a
telephone on it.*

*It is around five-thirty on a Friday after-
noon, and Mary Mercer, aged fifty, stands
before the mirror in the living room, admiring
her brand new dress and fixed hair. As she
preens, the front door opens and in walk her
two sons, Ben, eighteen, and Bill, seventeen.
Each carries a box from a formal rental shop
and schoolbooks.*

Mary: Did you bump into your father?
Ben: No, we just missed him, Mom. He's
already picked up his tux. He's probably at
the Oakwood. *(He opens the fridge and helps
himself to a beer.)*

Mary: Get your big nose out of the fridge. And put down that beer. You'll spoil your appetite.

Ben: No, I won't. (*He searches for a bottle opener in a drawer.*)

Mary: And don't contradict me. What other bad habits you learned lately?

Ben: (*teasing*) Don't be such a grouch. You sound like Dad. (*He sits at the table and opens his beer.*)

Mary: Yes, well just because you're in university now, don't t'ink you can raid the fridge any time you likes.

Bill crosses the kitchen and throws his black binder and books in the garbage receptacle.

Mary: What's that for? (*Bill exits into his bedroom and she calls after him.*) It's not the end of the world, my son. (*pause*) Tell you the truth, Ben. We always figured you'd be the one to land in trouble, if anyone did. I don't mean that as an insult. You're more . . . I don't know . . . like your father.

Ben: I am?

Music from Bill's room.

Mary: (*calling, exasperated*) Billy, do you have to have that so loud? (*Bill turns down his record player. To Ben*) I'm glad your graduation went okay last night. How was Billy? Was he glad he went?

Ben: Well, he wasn't upset, if that's what you mean.

Mary: (*slight pause*) Ben, how come you not to ask your father?

Ben: What do you mean?

Bill: (*off*) Mom, will you pack my suitcase? I can't get everything in.

Mary: (*calling*) I can't now, Billy. Later.

Ben: I want to talk to you, Mom. It's important.

Mary: I want to talk to you, too.

Bill: (*Comes out of bedroom, crosses to kitchen.*) Mom, here's the deposit on my locker. I cleaned it out and threw away all my old gym clothes. (*He helps himself to an apple from the fridge.*)

Mary: Didn't you just hear me tell your brother to stay out of there? I might as well talk to the sink. Well, you can t'row away your old school clothes — that's your affair — but take those books out of the garbage. Go on. You never knows. They might come in handy sometime.

Bill: How? (*He takes the books out, then sits at the table with Ben.*)

Mary: Well, you can always go to night school and get your senior matric, once the baby arrives and Kathy's back to work. . . . Poor child. I talked to her on the phone this morning. She's still upset, and I don't blame her. I'd be hurt myself if my own mother was too drunk to show up to my shower.

Bill: (*a slight ray of hope*) Maybe she won't show up tonight.

Mary: (*Glances anxiously at the kitchen clock and turns to check the fish and potatoes.*) Look at the time. I just wish to goodness he had more t'ought, your father. The supper'll dry up if he don't hurry. He might pick up a phone and mention when he'll be home. Not a grain of t'ought in his head. And I wouldn't put it past him to forget his tux in the beer parlour. (*Finally she turns and looks at her two sons, disappointed.*) And look at the two of you. Too busy with your mouths to give your mother a second glance. I could stand here till my legs dropped off before either of you would notice my dress.

Ben: It's beautiful, Mom.

Mary: That the truth?

Bill: Would we lie to you, Mom?

Mary: Just so long as I don't look foolish next to Minnie. She can afford to dress up — Willard left her well off when he died.

Ben: Don't worry about the money. Dad won't mind.

Mary: Well, it's not every day your own son gets married, is it? (*to Bill as she puts on large apron*) It's just that I don't want Minnie Jackson looking all decked out like the *Queen Mary* and me the tug that dragged her in. You understands, don't you, Ben?

Ben: Sure.

Bill: I understand too, Mom.

Mary: I know you do, Billy. I know you do. (*She opens a tin of peaches and fills five dessert dishes.*) Minnie used to go with your father. Did you know that, Billy? Years and years ago.

Bill: No kidding?

Ben: (*at the same time*) Really?

Mary: True as God is in Heaven. Minnie was awful sweet on Dad, too. She t'ought the world of him.

Bill: (*incredulously*) Dad?

Mary: Don't act so surprised. Your father was quite a one with the girls.

Ben: No kidding?

Mary: He could have had his pick of any number of girls. (*to Bill*) You ask Minnie sometime. Of course, in those days I was going with Jeremy McKenzie, who later became a Queen's Counsel in St. John's. I must have mentioned him.

The boys exchange smiles.

Ben: I think you have, Mom.

Bill: A hundred times.

Mary: (*gently indignant — to Bill*) And that I haven't!

Bill: She has too. Hasn't she, Ben?

Mary: Never you mind, Ben. (*to Bill*) And instead of sitting around gabbing so much you'd better go change your clothes. Kathy'll soon be here. (*as Bill crosses to his bedroom*) Is the rehearsal still at eight?

Bill: We're supposed to meet Father Douglas at the church at five to. I just hope Dad's not too drunk. (*He exits.*)

Mary: (*Studies Ben a moment.*) Look at yourself. A cigarette in one hand, a bottle of beer in the other, at your age! You didn't learn any of your bad habits from me, I can tell you. (*pause*) Ben, don't be in such a hurry to grow up. (*She sits across from him.*) Whatever you do, don't be in such a hurry. Look at your poor young brother. His whole life ruined. Oh, I could weep a bellyful when I t'inks of it. Just seventeen, not old enough to sprout whiskers on his chin, and already the burdens of a man on his t'in little shoulders. Your poor father hasn't slept a full night since this happened. Did you know that? He had such high hopes for Billy. He wanted you both to go to college and not have to work as hard as he's had to all his life. And now look. You have more sense than that, Ben. Don't let life trap you.

Bill enters. He has changed his pants and is buttoning a clean white shirt. Mary goes into the dining room and begins to remove the tablecloth from the dining room table.

Bill: Mom, what about Dad? He won't start picking on the priest, will he? You know how he likes to argue.

Mary: He won't say a word, my son. You needn't worry. Worry more about Minnie showing up.

Bill: What if he's drunk?

Mary: He won't be. Your father knows better than to sound off in church. Oh, and another t'ing — he wants you to polish his shoes for tonight. They're in the bedroom. The polish is on your dresser. You needn't be too fussy.

Ben: I'll do his shoes, Mom. Billy's all dressed.

Mary: No, no, Ben, that's all right. He asked Billy to.

Bill: What did Ben do this time?

Mary: He didn't do anyt'ing.

Bill: He must have.

Mary: Is it too much trouble to polish your father's shoes, after all he does for you? If you won't do it, I'll do it myself.

Bill: (*indignantly*) How come when Dad's mad at Ben, I get all the dirty jobs? Jeez! Will I be glad to get out of here! (*Rolling up his shirt sleeves he exits into his bedroom.*)

Mary takes a clean white linen tablecloth from a drawer in the cabinet and covers the table. During the following scene she sets five places with her good glasses, silverware and plates.

Ben: (*slight pause*) Billy's right, isn't he? What'd I do, Mom?

Mary: Take it up with your father. I'm tired of being the middle man.

Ben: Is it because of last night? (*slight pause*) It is, isn't it?

Mary: He t'inks you didn't want him there, Ben. He t'inks you're ashamed of him.

Ben: He wouldn't have gone, Mom. That's the only reason I never invited him.

Mary: He would have went, last night.

Ben: (*angrily*) He's never even been to one lousy Parents' Night in thirteen years. Not one! And he calls me contrary!

Mary: You listen to me. Your father never got past Grade T'ree. He was yanked out of school and made to work. In those days, back home, he was lucky to get that much and don't kid yourself.

Ben: Yeah? So?

Mary: So? So he's afraid to. He's afraid of sticking out. Is that so hard to understand? Is it?

Ben: What're you getting angry about? All I said was —

Mary: You say he don't take an interest, but he was proud enough to show off your report cards all those years. I suppose with you that don't count for much.

Ben: All right. But he never goes anywhere without you, Mom, and last night you were here at the shower.

Mary: Last night was different, Ben, and you ought to know that. It was your high school graduation. He would have went with me or without me. If you'd only asked him.

A truck horn blasts twice.

There he is now in the driveway. Whatever happens, don't fall for his old tricks. He'll be looking for a fight, and doing his best to find any excuse. (*calling*) Billy, you hear that? Don't complain about the shoes, once your father comes!

Ben: (*urgently*) Mom, there's something I want to tell you before Dad comes in.

Mary: Sure, my son. Go ahead. I'm listening. What's on your mind?

Ben: Well . . .

Mary: (*smiling*) Come on. It can't be that bad.

Ben: (*slight pause*) I want to move out, Mom.

Mary: (*almost inaudibly*). . . What?

Ben: I said I want to move out.

Mary: (*softly, as she sets the cutlery*) I heard you. (*pause*) What for?

Ben: I just think it's time. I'll be nineteen soon. (*pause*) I'm moving in with Billy and Kathy and help pay the rent. (*pause*) I won't be far away. I'll see you on weekends. (*Mary nods.*) Mom?

Mary: (*absently*) What?

Ben: Will you tell Dad? (*slight pause*) Mom? Did you hear me?

Mary: I heard you. He'll be upset, I can tell you. By rights you ought to tell him yourself.

Ben: If I do, we'll just get in a big fight and you know it. He'll take it better, coming from you.

The front door opens and Jacob Mercer enters whistling 'I's the b'y.' He is fifty, though he looks older. He is dressed in a peaked cap, carpenter's overalls, thick-soled workboots, and a lumberjack shirt over a T-shirt. Under one arm he carries his black lunchpail.

Mary: Your suit! I knowed it!

Jacob: Don't get in an uproar, now. I left it sitting on the front seat of the truck. (*He looks at Ben, then back to Mary.*) Is Billy home?

Mary: He's in the bedroom, polishing your shoes.

Jacob: (*Crosses to the bedroom door.*) Billy, my son, come out a moment.

Bill enters, carrying a shoe brush.

Put down the brush and go out in my truck and bring me back the tux on the seat.

Bill: What's wrong with Ben? He's not doing anything.

Jacob: Don't ask questions. That's a good boy. I'd ask your brother, but he always has a good excuse.

Ben: I'll go get it. (*He starts for the front door.*)

Jacob: (*calling after Ben*) Oh, it's too late to make up now. The damage is done.

Mary: Don't talk nonsense, Jacob.

Jacob: (*a last thrust*) And aside from that — I wouldn't want you dirtying your nice clean hands in your father's dirty old truck!

The front door closes on his last words. Bill returns to his room. Jacob sets his lunchpail and his cap on the dining room table.

Jacob: Did he get his diploma?

Mary: Yes. It's in the bedroom.

Jacob: (*Breaks into a smile and lifts his cap.*) And will you gaze on Mary over there. When I stepped in the door, I thought the Queen had dropped in for tea.

Mary: You didn't even notice.

Jacob: Come here, my dear, and give Jacob a kiss.

Mary: (*She darts behind the table, laughing.*) I'll give Jacob a swift boot in the rear end with my pointed toe.

Jacob grabs her, rubs his rough cheek against hers.

You'll take the skin off! Jake! You're far too rough! And watch my new dress! Don't rip it.

Jacob releases her and breaks into a little jig as he sings.

I's the b'y that builds the boat
And I's the b'y that sails her,
I's the b'y that catches the fish
And takes 'em home to Lizer.

After Reading

RESPONDING

1. Choose one of the **characters** from the excerpt. Make a list of his or her characteristics. In a paragraph, discuss what you like or dislike about this character and why.

UNDERSTANDING

2. Reread the description of the stage set and make point-form notes on what can be learned about the family by looking at the set's various parts.

3. With a partner, make notes on the relationships between the following people: Billy and Ben; Ben and his mother; Ben and his father; Billy and his father. Make sure your notes refer to specific comments made or actions taken by the characters.

4. Describe the functions of the **scene** up to the point Jacob is introduced. Create your description using the following subtitles: Introducing Characters, Developing Characters, Creating **Suspense**, Introducing **Conflict**.

THINKING ABOUT LANGUAGE

5. The playwright has given Mary Mercer an accent. Identify where the accent could be from, and explain why being from that place might be important to our understanding of the character.

EXTENDING

6. With a partner, rewrite the scene that takes place when Jacob Mercer gets home. Focus the scene on Mary and Jacob, *or* Ben and Jacob, *or* Billy and Jacob. You may introduce one new character (Minnie or Kathy) if you wish to. Be prepared to read your scene aloud.

Love Like the Ocean:
EXCERPT FROM *Monkey Beach*

"Such a lovely day. Late summer. Warm.
Look at the pretty, fluffy clouds."

EDEN ROBINSON

BEFORE READING

Recall a time when you were afraid for somebody's safety. Write a journal entry about what happened and how you felt.

Six crows sit in our greengage tree. Half-awake, I hear them speak to me in Haisla.

La'es, they say, *La'es, La'es*.

I push myself out of bed and go to the open window, but they launch themselves upward, cawing. Morning light slants over the mountains behind the reserve. A breeze coming down the channel makes my curtains flap limply. Ripples sparkle in the shallows as a seal bobs its dark head.

La'es—Go down to the bottom of the ocean. The word means something else, but I can't remember what. I had too much coffee last night after the Coast Guard called with the news about Jimmy. People pressed cups and cups of it into my hands. Must have fallen asleep fourish. On the nightstand, the clock-face has a badly painted Elvis caught in mid-gyrate. Jimmy found it at a garage sale and gave it to me last year for my birthday—that and a card that said, "Hap B-day, sis! How does it feel to be almost two decades old? Rock on,

Grandma!" The Elvis clock says the time is seven-thirty, but it's either an hour ahead or an hour behind. We always joke that it's on Indian time.

I go to my dresser and pull out my first cigarette of the day, then return to the window and smoke. An orange cat pauses at the shoreline, alert. It flicks its tail back and forth, then bounds up the beach and into a tangle of bushes near our neighbour's house. The crows are tiny black dots against a faded denim sky. In the distance, I hear a speedboat. For the last week, I have been dreaming about the ocean—lapping softly against the hull of a boat, hissing as it rolls gravel up a beach, ocean swells hammering the shore, lifting off the rocks in an ethereal spray before the waves make a grumbling retreat.

Such a lovely day. Late summer. Warm. Look at the pretty, fluffy clouds. Weather reports are all favourable for the area where his seiner[1] went missing. Jimmy's a good swimmer. Everyone says this like a mantra that will keep him safe. No one's as optimistic about his skipper, Josh, a hefty good-time guy who is very popular for his generosity at bars and parties. He is also heavily in debt and has had a bad fishing season. Earlier this summer two of his crew quit, bitterly complaining to their relatives that he didn't pay them all they were due. They came by last night to show their support. One of my cousins said they've been spreading rumours that Josh might have sunk his *Queen of the North* for the insurance and that Jimmy's inexperience on the water would make him a perfect scapegoat. They were whispering to other visitors last night, but Aunt Edith glared at them until they took the hint and left.

I stub out my cigarette and take the steps two at a time to the kitchen. My father's at the table, smoking. His ashtray is overflowing. He glances at me, eyes bloodshot and red-rimmed.

"Did you hear the crows earlier?" I say. When he doesn't answer, I find myself babbling. "They were talking to me. They said *la'es*. It's probably—"

"Clearly a sign, Lisa," my mother has come up behind me and grips my shoulders, "that you need Prozac." She steers me to a chair and pushes me down.

Dad's old VHF is tuned to the emergency channel. Normally, we have the radio turned to CFTK. He likes it loud, and the morning soft rock usually rackets through the house. As we sit in silence, I watch his cigarette burn down in the ashtray. Mom smoothes her hair. She keeps touching it. They both have that glazed, drawn look of people who haven't slept. I have this urge to turn on some music. If they had found the seiner, someone would phone us.

"Pan, pan, pan,"[2] a woman's voice crackles over the VHF. "All stations, this is Prince Rupert Coast Guard." She repeats everything three times, I don't know why. "We have an overdue vessel." She goes on to describe a gillnetter that should have been in Prince Rupert four days ago. Mom and dad tense expectantly even though this has nothing to do with Jimmy.

At any given moment, there are two thousand storms at sea.

…

Find a map of British Columbia. Point to the middle of the coast. Beneath Alaska, find the Queen Charlotte Islands. Drag your finger across the map, across the Hecate Strait to the coast and you should be able to see a large island hugging the coast. This is Princess Royal Island, and it is famous for its kermode bears, which are black bears that are usually white. Princess Royal Island is the western edge of traditional Haisla territory. *Ka-tee-doux Gitk'a'ata*, the Tsimshians of Hartley Bay, live at the mouth of the Douglas Channel and surrounding areas just north of the island. During land claim talks, some of this territory is claimed by both the Haisla and the Tsimshian nations—this is called an overlap and is a sticky topic of discussion. But once you pass the head of the Douglas Channel, you are firmly in Haisla territory.

Early in the nineteenth century, Hudson's Bay traders used Tsimshian guides to show them around, which is when the names began to get confusing. "Kitamaat" is a Tsimshian word that means people of falling snow, and it was their name for the main Haisla village. So when

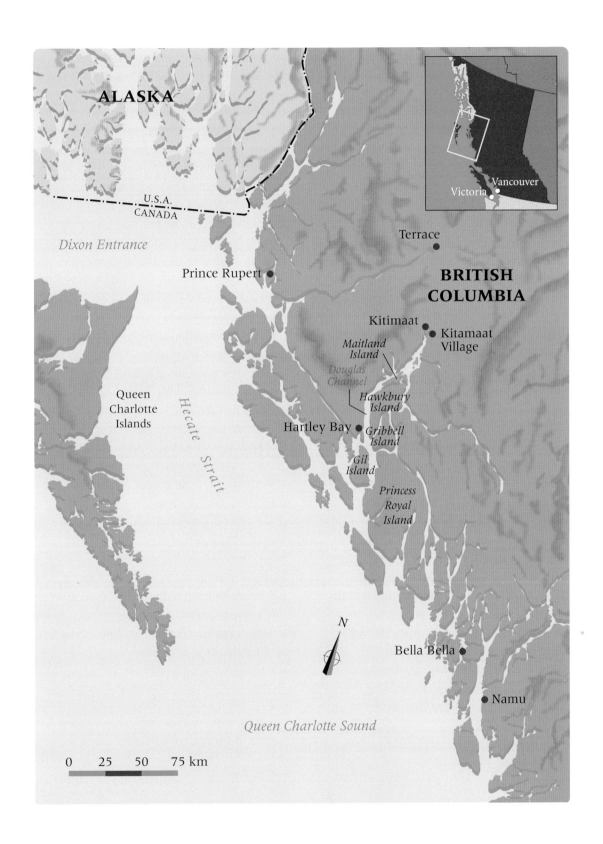

ALASKA

U.S.A.
CANADA

Dixon Entrance

Prince Rupert

Terrace

BRITISH
COLUMBIA

Kitimaat

Kitamaat
Village

Maitland
Island

Douglas
Channel

Queen
Charlotte
Islands

Hecate Strait

Hawkbury
Island

Hartley Bay

Gribbell
Island

Gil
Island

Princess
Royal
Island

N

Bella Bella

Namu

Queen Charlotte Sound

0   25   50   75 km

Victoria Vancouver

the Hudson's Bay traders asked their guides, "Hey, what's that village called?" the Tsimshian guides said, "Oh, that's Kitamaat." The name got stuck on to the official records and the village has been called Kitamaat ever since, even though it should really be called Haisla. There are about four or five different spellings of Kitamaat in the historical writings, but the Haisla decided on Kitamaat. To add to the confusion, when Alcan Aluminum moved into the area in the 1950s, it built a "city of the future" for its workers and named it Kitimat too, but spelled it differently.

If your finger is on Prince Rupert or Terrace, you are too far north. If you are pointing to Bella Coola or Ocean Falls, you are too far south. If you are pointing in the right place, you should have your finger on the western shore of Princess Royal Island. To get to Kitamaat, run your finger northeast, right up to the Douglas Channel, a 140-kilometre-long deep-sea channel, to its mouth. You should pass Gil Island, Princess Royal Island, Gribbell Island, Hawkesbury Island, Maitland Island and finally Costi Island. Near the head of the Douglas, you'll find Kitamaat Village, with its seven hundred Haisla people tucked in between the mountains and the ocean. At the end of the village is our house. Our kitchen looks onto the water. Somewhere in the seas between here and Namu—a six-hour boat ride south of Kitamaat—my brother is lost.

My mother answered the phone when the Coast Guard called. I took the phone from her hands when she started crying. A man told me there had been no radio contact since Saturday, two days earlier. The man said he'd like to ask me a few questions. I gave him all the information I could—that Jimmy had phoned us from Bella Bella on Friday. He told us that 36 hours' notice had been given for a Sunday opening for sockeye salmon in Area 8. Josh had been planning to move the seiner closer to his favourite Area 8 fishing point. No, I didn't know where that point was. Jimmy had said that since it was a boring sit-and-wait kind of job, the crew was splitting up. The three senior fishermen in Josh's crew were staying in Bella Bella and taking a speedboat to join the *Queen* early Sunday. Jimmy had the least seniority so he had to go with Josh.

The man told me that Josh had called his crew in Bella Bella to say the engine was acting up so he was stopping over in Namu. When the crew arrived at the Area 8 fishing site, they couldn't find the *Queen of the North*. They searched all afternoon. No one in the fishing fleet reported seeing the *Queen*. No one knew if she'd gone down or if she'd just broken down and was holed up somewhere. Area 8 was large, the man said. There had been no mayday, but he didn't say if this was a good or a bad thing. Did I know of anything else that could be helpful? No, I said. It wasn't really a lie. What I knew couldn't be particularly useful now.

---

1 A boat on which a large net, with sinkers on one edge and floats on the other, called a seine, is used to catch fish.
2 The international call for assistance in a non-life-threatening situation.

After Reading

RESPONDING

1. In your notebook, draw or write a response to the **atmosphere** or **mood** of the first three paragraphs.

UNDERSTANDING

2. This excerpt is part of the beginning of the novel, in which we learn about the major **characters**, the **setting**, and the **conflict**. In a group of three, make notes on these aspects of this opening section. Share your notes with each other so that all members of the group have the same information.
3. With a partner, record at least three predictions about what is going to happen in this novel. Make sure your predictions make sense on the basis of what you have read, and make sure they are all different. Be prepared to put your predictions on the board.
4. With a partner, discuss why you think the author spent so much time telling the reader where she lived. What does this information add to this excerpt?
5. Explain how the writer has created **suspense** in the last four lines of the final paragraph.
6. Even though you have read just a brief excerpt from the novel, explain why the writer called this chapter "Love Like the Ocean."

THINKING ABOUT LANGUAGE

7. Make a list of the technical language from this excerpt that is associated with fishing. **Define** any unfamiliar words.

EXTENDING

8. Write a business letter from the Coast Guard to Lisa's family, giving details you have about the disappearance of the *Queen of the North* and Lisa's brother. Compare your letter with that of a partner, looking closely at the facts from the excerpt, the **tone** of the letter, the set-up of the letter, and the letter's organization.

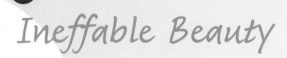

Ineffable Beauty

JAMES STRECKER

BEFORE READING

1. Look up the meaning of "ineffable." With the class, predict what this **poem** is going to be about.

2. As a class, read the poem aloud.

To create
the pigment of

roses

for your cheek,
living rabbits   5
were

tortured
in a lab; their

eyes were
burned away.   10

I have no word
to compare

your skin

to petals.

After Reading

RESPONDING

1. a) With a partner, discuss your reactions to this **poem**. How does it make you feel? How has the poet made you feel this way? Should poets write about these kinds of subjects?

   b) Individually, write a **journal** entry about your reactions to this poem.

UNDERSTANDING

2. Describe the **narrator's tone**. Explain how the poet has achieved this tone both through words and through the way the poem looks.

3. The poet uses contrast effectively in the first nine lines of this poem. Show how he has used contrast and why it is effectively used.

4. Explain what the narrator means when he or she has "no word to compare your skin to petals."

THINKING ABOUT LANGUAGE

5. The title of the poem is ironic because the words mean something quite different in the **context** of the poem. Explain their **irony** and how the effect is created.

EXTENDING

6. a) Using print, human, and electronic resources, find out some facts about testing cosmetics on animals.

   b) Write a letter to a real cosmetics company (e.g., The Body Shop) either congratulating them for not using animals in cosmetic testing or requesting that they continue to use animals. Be sure the content and **tone** of your letter is suitable for the **audience**.

   c) Have a partner give you suggestions for revisions based on the content of your letter, on how you have included information from your research, on the organization, and on the tone of your writing.

7. a) With a partner, create a print advertisement that supports a ban on testing cosmetics on animals. Refer to "The Pitch" in The Reference Shelf (pages 304–305).

   b) Write an explanation of your advertisement in which you identify its audience and purpose, and discuss the choices you made in the design to create both **implicit** and **explicit meanings**.

   c) As a class, and with the help of your teacher, create an evaluation sheet to assess each advertisement.

Naht

DANIELLE LAGAH

BEFORE READING

As a class, discuss the following question: Are there any situations in which animal euthanasia is acceptable? Make notes on the class discussion.

Jeet (Brother):

All season we saved
the new puppies and old
sick dogs too
Piara and me, we lifted them
over the mud wall   5
when the police came feeding
their handfuls of sweet lardu
stuffed with poison

The village will be overrun with mange
they said, *these dogs will steal*   10
the bread from babies
and my auntie said it too
shaking her finger at us
from over her washing

but we lifted them   15
over the mud wall
felt their furred bellies
hearts beating in our hands before
we let them drop
into the wide fields of wheat   20
and called out *Run Run*
Run

After Reading

RESPONDING

1. Whose side are you on when you read this **poem**? Write a paragraph in which you take a side, and support your beliefs.

UNDERSTANDING

2. In a brief paragraph, explain why the police wanted to feed the dogs poison.

3. With a partner, make a list of what we can infer about the location of this poem. Support your inferences with evidence from the poem.

4. In this poem, the poet has created **suspense** at the end of almost every line. Using any four lines from the poem, show how the poet has created this suspense.

THINKING ABOUT LANGUAGE

5. a) Punctuate and capitalize the last **stanza**. Put your results on the blackboard.
   b) Underline each phrase with a "squiggly" line and each clause with a straight line.

EXTENDING

6. Choose one situation in which you think animal euthanasia is acceptable. Write a case study under the following headings: Problem/Issue; Background; Facts; Discussion; Alternative Courses of Action; Recommendations. (See The Reference Shelf, page 263.)

Picketing Supermarkets

TOM WAYMAN

BEFORE READING

In your notebook, describe a cause that is important enough to you that you would choose to demonstrate for or against it by marching in a public demonstration or writing a letter.

Because all this food is grown in the store
do not take the leaflet.
Cabbages, broccoli and tomatoes
are raised at night in the aisles.
Milk is brewed in the rear storage areas.   5
Beef produced in vats in the basement.
Do not take the leaflet.
Peanut butter and soft drinks
are made fresh each morning by store employees.
Our oranges and grapes   10
are so fine and round
that when held up to the lights they cast no shadow.
Do not take the leaflet.

And should you take one
do not believe it.   15
This chain of stores has no connection
with anyone growing food someplace else.
How could we have an effect on local farmers?
Do not believe it.

The sound here is Muzak, for your enjoyment.   20
It is not the sound of children crying.
There *is* a lady offering samples
to mark Canada Cheese Month.
There is no dark-skinned man with black hair beside her
wanting to show you the inside of a coffin.   25
You would not have to look if there was.
And there are no Nicaraguan heroes
in any way connected with the bananas.

Pay no attention to these people.
The manager is a citizen.   30
All this food is grown in the store.

After Reading

RESPONDING

1. In a sentence or two, explain why people are picketing and handing out leaflets at the super-market in this **poem**.

UNDERSTANDING

2. Find two examples of **irony** in this poem. If you are not sure what irony is, check its meaning in the **glossary**.
3. With a partner, create a leaflet that carries a message about one of the issues being protest-ed in this poem. Display your leaflet on the class bulletin board.

THINKING ABOUT LANGUAGE

4. Identify five words in this poem that contribute to the political message of the poem. For each word, explain its political **connotation** in the context of this poem.

EXTENDING

5. Research an issue in the news that some members of society are protesting about. Stage a **debate** in your class on this issue. You may need to do additional research to prepare arguments for the debate. (See The Reference Shelf, pages 278–279.)

6. With a partner, write a **dialogue** that occurs between a picketer at the supermarket and a shopper who wants to enter the store and buy groceries. Rehearse your dialogue, and present it to the class.

King Midas and the Golden Touch: A Traditional Greek Myth

"Midas would never be really happy until the whole world had become a vault filled with gold that he could call his own."

RETOLD BY ROBERT R. POTTER

BEFORE READING

If you could have any wish in the world, what would it be? In your notebook, write down the wish. Below it, draw two columns: one for the good things that would come from getting your wish and another for the not-so-good things that could result from getting it.

In the days of long ago, when this world of ours was both a younger and a stranger place, there lived a very rich king named Midas [MY-dus].

King Midas loved gold more than anything else in the world. He loved his kingdom only because of the gold in its hills, and he loved his crown only because it was made of solid gold. He saw gold in the morning sunlight, gold in the daytime flowers, and gold in the hair of the beautiful daughter he kissed on the head every night.

This little girl, Iris by name, was the only family that the rich King Midas had. Indeed, it would be hard to say which Midas loved more, his gold or his daughter. But one thing was sure. The more Midas loved his daughter, the more he wished to become the richest man on earth. "My darling," he often told his daughter, "when I die, I want you to have more gold than any man, woman, or child on the face of the earth."

Iris, however, had grown tired of gold, gold, and more gold. She had been named for the goddess of the rainbow, and she liked the blue of the sky, the green of the trees, or the red of the sunset fully as much as the yellow of gold. And while she loved her father dearly, she did get tired of looking at the long rows of buttercups, yellow roses, and sunflowers that grew in the palace garden. Iris could remember when the flowers had been of every color in the rainbow. But that had been before her father had become so interested in gold. It had been back in the days when the palace rang with singing and music.

Alas, the only music that pleased Midas now was the sound of one gold coin striking against another. The only flowers that pleased him were yellow flowers. He liked to think how much his garden would be worth if each of the many flowers were made of gold. In fact, Midas had so fallen in love with gold that he could hardly touch anything that was not made of the yellow metal.

Every morning after breakfast, Midas went down to a dark vault in the basement of his palace. It was here that he kept his gold. First he would carefully lock the door. Then he would take a box of gold coins, or a pail of gold dust, and bring it from a dark corner of the room into the one small sunbeam that fell from the one small window. Then he would count the coins in the box, or let the gold dust flow through his fingers into the pail. "O Midas," the rich king would say to himself, "what a happy man you are!"

Midas called himself a happy man, yet deep in his heart he knew that he was not quite so happy as he might be. The vault was small. Midas would never be really happy until the whole world had become a vault filled with gold that he could call his own.

One day, as Midas sat counting his money, a shadow suddenly fell across the single sunbeam in his vault. He looked up into a face that was young, handsome, and smiling. Midas couldn't help thinking that the stranger's smile had a kind of golden glow about it. Indeed, the whole room seemed to glow with the stranger's smile.

The king knew that he had carefully turned the key in the lock. No man but Midas himself had ever entered the underground vault. Who could the stranger be? And how had he got through the door? Again Midas looked at the stranger with the sunny smile.

Of course — this was a god! Midas was sure of it.

But what god could he be? What god could be as pleasant as the smiling stranger? And what god would have a reason to visit the rich King Midas?

"Bacchus [BAK-us]!" Midas said suddenly. "The god of happiness!"

The stranger nodded his head. "Friend Midas, you are a smart man," he said. "And a rich one. I have never seen so much gold in one place as you have piled up in this room."

"Yes, I have done pretty well," Midas agreed. "But when I think of all the gold in the world —"

"What!" cried Bacchus. "With all this gold, you are not the happiest man alive?"

Midas shook his head.

Bacchus sat down on a box of gold coins. "I find this strange, friend Midas," he said. "Tell me, just what would make you really happy?"

Midas thought for a minute. He had felt from the beginning that the stranger meant no harm, but instead had come to do him a favor. This was an important moment. Midas must not say the wrong thing. In his mind he piled golden mountain upon golden mountain, but even mountains were too small. At last he had a bright idea. It seemed fully as bright as the yellow metal he loved so much.

"I wish," said King Midas, "that everything I touch might be changed to gold."

"The golden touch!" Bacchus cried. "I said before that you were a smart man, King Midas." The god's smile grew very wide. It seemed to fill the room, like a bursting of the sun. "But are you quite sure that this will make you more happy than you are now?"

"Why not?" said Midas.

Bacchus smiled again. "And you will never be sorry you wanted it?"

"How could I?" asked the king. "I want nothing else to make me as happy as a man can be."

"Then it is as you wish," replied Bacchus. "At sunrise tomorrow, the golden touch will be yours."

Once more Bacchus smiled. This time his smile was so bright that Midas had to close his eyes. When he opened them, the god had disappeared. Only the small sunbeam remained to light the room.

That night Midas found it hard to fall asleep. His mind raced with thoughts of the golden touch that would be his in the morning. It was after midnight when he finally stopped tossing and turning.

The sun was high in the sky when Midas opened his eyes. The first thing he saw was a blanket woven of the brightest gold. He shook the sleep out of his head and looked again. This time he noticed his hand resting on the blanket, with the tips of his fingers touching the golden cloth.

The golden touch was his!

Midas jumped up with a shout of joy. He ran about the room, touching everything that happened to be in his way. He touched the foot of the bed, and a bed of gold gleamed before his eyes. He touched the dresser, and it too turned to gold. He touched the table — gold! The curtains — gold! The walls — bright gold! "O Midas," the king cried, "what a happy man you are! What a very happy man you are!"

As quickly as possible, Midas dressed himself in a robe of golden cloth. He was pleased to find that the cloth stayed as soft as it had ever been. From a pocket he took a handkerchief that Iris had embroidered for his last birthday. The handkerchief, too, was gold, with the girl's many-colored stitches now changed to bright yellow.

Somehow or other, this last change did not quite please King Midas. For an instant he wished that he held the same handkerchief that little Iris had given him.

But it wasn't important. Singing to himself, Midas opened a golden door and walked down a flight of golden stairs to breakfast. He wanted to surprise his daughter, so he was careful not to touch anything. Midas really loved the child, and he loved her so much the more now that such good luck had come his way.

By good fortune, the small bell Midas rang for his meals had long been made of gold. Iris would notice nothing strange except the gold robe, for Midas was careful not to place his hands on the table in front of him, or on the chair in which he sat. At length an attendant appeared with a golden tray. On the tray was the king's usual breakfast: a fresh orange, two pieces of buttered toast, and a large cup of steaming coffee. The servant told Midas that Iris had eaten hours before, and was now playing in the garden. Midas ordered that she be called.

Then the king turned to his meal. It was by now the middle of the morning, and the sight of the food made him hungry. But when he picked up the orange — of course!

"What!" said Midas, as he looked at the golden orange in his hand. "Now, this is a problem."

Very carefully, Midas reached out and touched one of the pieces of toast. At once it turned to gold. Only the butter still looked real. The coffee cup, too, and the coffee in it, became gold at the king's touch.

"I don't quite see," Midas thought, "how I am to get any breakfast."

Breakfast! Why, he would never be able to eat again! Already he was very hungry. By dinner time he would be starving. The poorest man in the kingdom, who sat down to the poorest supper, would be better off than he.

Moving quickly, Midas picked up the good piece of toast, rushed it to his mouth and tried to swallow it in a hurry. But the golden touch was too quick for him. The hot metal burned his lips and tongue. Midas cried out in pain and jumped up from the table.

At this moment, Iris entered from the garden. She found her father, dressed in a strange robe of golden cloth, dancing around the room like a wild man. Suddenly he stopped and looked at her. Iris watched two big teardrops work their way down her father's face. For a moment she tried to find out what was the matter with him. Then, with her heart full of love, she ran forward and threw her arms around her father's waist.

"My darling, darling daughter!" cried Midas.

But the girl made no answer.

Alas, what had the golden touch done now! It took Midas a moment to free himself of the metal arms around his body. He could not make himself look at the golden statue of what had once been his very own daughter. With a loud roar, he left the room and sped down to the only place he could be alone — his underground vault. He sat down on a box of gold and covered his face with his hands.

How long he sat there not even Midas could have said. With his eyes shut, he thought of all the times he had told Iris that she was worth her weight in gold. But now, now he felt differently. He wished that he were the poorest man in the whole wide world, if only the loss of his riches might bring the rosy color back to his daughter's cheeks.

A sudden change in the light made Midas open his eyes. There in front of him stood Bacchus. The god still had a sunny smile on his face.

"Well, friend Midas," said Bacchus, "how do you like the golden touch?"

Midas shook his head. "I am the most unhappy of men."

Bacchus laughed. "Let us see, then. Which of these two things do you really think is worth the most — the gift of the golden touch, or your own daughter Iris, as warm and loving as she was yesterday?"

"My daughter!" cried Midas. "My daughter! I would not have given the smallest dimple in her chin for the power to change this whole earth into a solid lump of gold!"

For the first time, the smile left the god's face. "Yesterday," said Bacchus, "I said you were smart. But today I say you are wise. Now I will tell you how you can lose the golden touch. Wash yourself in the river that runs next to the palace garden. Wait!" The god poured a pail of gold dust out onto the floor. "Take this pail. Bring back some water, and sprinkle it over anything that your greed has changed to gold."

Midas lost no time. He raced to the river and jumped in. Then he sped back to the palace, in such a hurry that he didn't notice that he no longer wore a golden robe. He poured the whole pail of water over the golden statue of his daughter.

"Father!" cried Iris. "Look! See how my dress is all wet!"

The girl could remember nothing that had happened since she had thrown her arms around her father's waist.

And Midas was wise enough not to tell her. For he knew now that there was something better than all the gold in the world. This was the beating of one small and tender heart that truly loved him.

After Reading

RESPONDING

1. As a class, discuss the lesson we are supposed to learn from this myth.

UNDERSTANDING

2. Explain how the writer of this myth builds **suspense** once King Midas has the golden touch.
3. In a small group, discuss how this myth could be applied to modern society. Who would Midas represent? Who would the daughter represent? What would the "golden touch" be? Be prepared to share your ideas with the class.
4. Bacchus says to Midas, "I said you were smart. But today, I say you are wise." Interpret what Bacchus means.

THINKING ABOUT LANGUAGE

5. a) Look at the **dialogue** in this myth. From these examples and on the basis of your personal knowledge, write rules for the correct punctuation of dialogue.
   b) As a class, check that you have the rules correct and that your list covers all the rules.
   c) Individually, write the dialogue that might have occurred between Midas and his daughter if he had chosen to tell her what had happened.

EXTENDING

6. Look back at the writing you did for the "Before Reading" activity. Having read "Midas and the Golden Touch," consider how you would change your own wish. Revise your wish, thinking about what it might mean to you, your friends, your family, and society.

7. a) With a partner, write the script for the opening **scene** of a film version of a modern Midas story. In this scene, introduce the two main **characters** and the **conflict**. Use "Medicine Woman" (pages 133–138) as a model for script writing.
   b) Exchange your completed scene with another partnership. Assess how well the other partnership has fulfilled the content requirements and how well they have created interest in the story.
   c) Revise your scene on the basis of the comments you received. Rehearse the scene, and present it to your classmates.

There Will Come Soft Rains

"Smoke and silence. A great quantity of smoke."

RAY BRADBURY

BEFORE READING

In your notebook, write a paragraph describing how the world would change if human beings disappeared completely. Be prepared to present your ideas to the class.

In the living room the voice-clock sang, *Tick-tock, seven o'clock, time to get up, time to get up, seven o'clock!* as if it were afraid that nobody would. The morning house lay empty. The clock ticked on, repeating and repeating its sounds into the emptiness. *Seven-nine, breakfast time, seven-nine!*

In the kitchen the breakfast stove gave a hissing sigh and ejected from its warm interior eight pieces of perfectly browned toast, eight eggs sunny side up, sixteen slices of bacon, two coffees, and two glasses of milk.

"Today is August 4, 2026," said a second voice from the kitchen ceiling, "in the city of Allendale, California." It repeated the date three times for memory's sake. "Today is Mr. Featherstone's birthday. Today is the anniversary of Tilita's marriage. Insurance is payable, as are the water, gas, and light bills."

Somewhere in the walls, relays clicked, memory tapes glided under electric eyes.

Eight-one, tick-tock, eight-one o'clock, off to school, off to work, run, run, eight-one! But no doors slammed, no carpets took the soft tread of rubber heels. It was raining outside. The weather box on the front door sang quietly: "Rain, rain, go away: rubbers, raincoats for today. . . ." And the rain tapped on the empty house, echoing.

Outside, the garage chimed and lifted its door to reveal the waiting car. After a long wait the door swung down again.

At eight-thirty the eggs were shriveled and the toast was like stone. An aluminum wedge scraped them into the sink, where hot water whirled them down to a metal throat which digested and flushed them away to the distant sea. The dirty dishes were dropped into a hot washer and emerged twinkling dry.

Nine-fifteen, sang the clock, *time to clean*.

Out of the warrens in the wall, tiny robot mice darted. The rooms were acrawl with the small cleaning animals, all rubber and metal. They thudded against chairs, whirling their mustached runners, kneading the rug nap, sucking gently at hidden dust.

Then, like mysterious invaders, they popped into their burrows. Their pink electric eyes faded. The house was clean.

Ten o'clock. The sun came out from behind the rain. The house stood alone in a city of rubble and ashes. This was the one house left standing. At night the ruined city gave off a radioactive glow which could be seen for miles.

Ten-fifteen. The garden sprinklers whirled up in golden founts, filling the soft morning air with scatterings of brightness. The water pelted windowpanes, running down the charred west side where the house had been burned evenly free of its white paint. The entire west face of the house was black, save for five places. Here the silhouette in paint of a man mowing a lawn. Here, as in a photograph, a woman bent to pick flowers. Still farther over, their images burned on wood in one titanic instant, a small boy, hands flung into the air; higher up, the image of a thrown ball; and opposite him a girl, hands raised to catch a ball which never came down.

The five spots of paint — the man, the woman, the children, the ball — remained. The rest was a thin charcoaled layer.

The gentle sprinkler rain filled the garden with falling light.

Until this day, how well the house had kept its peace. How carefully it had inquired, "Who goes there? What's the password?" and, getting no answer from lonely foxes and whining cats, it had shut up its windows and drawn shades in an old-maidenly preoccupation with self-protection which bordered on a mechanical paranoia.

It quivered at each sound, the house did. If a sparrow brushed a window, the shade snapped up. The bird, startled, flew off! No, not even a bird must touch the house!

The house was an altar with ten thousand attendants, big, small, servicing, attending, in choirs. But the gods had gone away, and the ritual of the religion continued senselessly, uselessly.

Twelve noon.

A dog whined, shivering, on the front porch.

The front door recognized the dog voice and opened. The dog, once huge and fleshy, but now gone to bone and covered with sores, moved in and through the house tracking mud. Behind it whirred angry mice, angry at having to pick up mud, angry at inconvenience.

For not a leaf fragment blew under the door but what the wall panels flipped open and the copper scrap rats flashed swiftly out. The offending dust, hair, or paper, seized in miniature steel jaws, was raced back to the burrows. There, down tubes which fed into the cellar, it was dropped into the sighing vent of an incinerator which sat like evil Baal in a dark corner.

The dog ran upstairs, hysterically yelping to each door, at last realizing, as the house realized, that only silence was here.

It sniffed the air and scratched the kitchen door. Behind the door, the stove was making pancakes which filled the house with a rich baked odor and the scent of maple syrup.

The dog frothed at the mouth, lying at the door, sniffing, its eyes turned to fire. It ran wildly in circles, biting at its tail, spun in a frenzy, and died. It lay in the parlor for an hour.

Two o'clock, sang a voice.

Delicately sensing decay at last, the regiments of mice hummed out as softly as blown gray leaves in an electrical wind.

Two-fifteen.

The dog was gone.

In the cellar, the incinerator glowed suddenly and a whirl of sparks leaped up the chimney.

Two-thirty-five.

Bridge tables sprouted from patio walls. Playing cards fluttered onto pads in a shower of pips. Martinis manifested on an oaken bench with egg-salad sandwiches. Music played.

But the tables were silent and the cards untouched.

At four o'clock the tables folded like great butterflies back through the paneled walls.

Four-thirty.

The nursery walls glowed.

Animals took shape: yellow giraffes, blue lions, pink antelopes, lilac panthers cavorting in crystal substance. The walls were glass. They looked out upon color and fantasy. Hidden films clocked through well-oiled sprockets, and the walls lived. The nursery floor was woven to resemble a crisp cereal meadow. Over this ran

aluminum roaches and iron crickets, and in the hot still air butterflies of delicate red tissue wavered among the sharp aroma of animal spoors! There was the sound like a great matted yellow hive of bees within a dark bellows, the lazy bumble of a purring lion. And there was the patter of okapi feet and the murmur of a fresh jungle rain, like other hoofs, falling upon the summer-starched grass. Now the walls dissolved into distances of parched weed, mile on mile, and warm endless sky. The animals drew away into thorn brakes and water holes.

It was the children's hour.

Five o'clock. The bath filled with clear hot water.

Six, seven, eight o'clock. The dinner dishes manipulated like magic tricks, and in the study a *click.* In the metal stand opposite the hearth where a fire now blazed up warmly, a cigar popped out, half an inch of soft gray ash on it, smoking, waiting.

Nine o'clock. The beds warmed their hidden circuits, for nights were cool here.

Nine-five. A voice spoke from the study ceiling: "Mrs. McClellan, which poem would you like this evening?"

The house was silent.

The voice said at last, "Since you express no preference, I shall select a poem at random." Quiet music rose to back the voice. "Sara Teasdale. As I recall, your favorite. . .

There will come soft rains and the smell of the ground,

And swallows circling with their shim-
   mering sound;

And frogs in the pools singing at night,
And wild plum trees in tremulous white;

Robins will wear their feathery fire
Whistling their whims on a low fence-wire;

And not one will know of the war, not one
Will care at last when it is done.

Not one would mind, neither bird nor tree
If mankind perished utterly;

And Spring herself, when she woke at
   dawn,
Would scarcely know that we were gone."

The fire burned on the stone hearth and
the cigar fell away into a mound of quiet
ash on its tray. The empty chairs faced
each other between the silent walls, and
the music played.

At ten o'clock the house began to die.
    The wind blew. A falling tree bough
crashed through the kitchen window.
Cleaning solvent, bottled, shattered over
the stove. The room was ablaze in an
instant!
    "Fire!" screamed a voice. The house
lights flashed, water pumps shot water
from the ceilings. But the solvent spread
on the linoleum, licking, eating, under the
kitchen door, while the voices took it up
on chorus: "Fire, fire, fire!"
    The house tried to save itself. Doors
sprang tightly shut, but the windows were
broken by the heat and the wind blew and
sucked upon the fire.

The house gave ground as the fire in ten
billion angry sparks moved with flaming
ease from room to room and then up the
stairs. While scurrying water rats squeaked
from the walls, pistoled their water, and
ran for more. And the wall sprays let down
showers of mechanical rain.
    But too late. Somewhere, sighing, a
pump shrugged to a stop. The quenching
rain ceased. The reserve water supply
which had filled baths and washed dishes
for many quiet days was gone.
    The fire crackled up the stairs. It fed
upon Picassos and Matisses in the upper
halls, like delicacies, baking off the oily
flesh, tenderly crisping the canvases into
black shavings.
    Now the fire lay in beds, stood in win-
dows, changed the colors of drapes!
    And then, reinforcements.
    From attic trap doors, blind robot faces
peered down with faucet mouths gushing
green chemical.
    The fire backed off, as even an elephant
must at the sight of a dead snake. Now
there were twenty snakes whipping over
the floor, killing the fire with a clear cold
venom of green froth.
    But the fire was clever. It had sent flame
outside the house, up through the attic to
the pumps there. An explosion! The attic
brain which directed the pumps was shattered into bronze shrapnel on the beams.
    The fire rushed back into every closet
and felt of the clothes hung there.
    The house shuddered, oak bone on
bone, its bared skeleton cringing from the
heat, its wire, its nerves revealed as if a
surgeon had torn the skin off to let the red
veins and capillaries quiver in the scalded
air. "Help, help! Fire! Run, run!" Heat

snapped mirrors like the first brittle winter ice. And the voices wailed "Fire, fire, run, run," like a tragic nursery rhyme, a dozen voices, high, low, like children dying in a forest, alone, alone. And the voices fading as the wires popped their sheathings like hot chestnuts. One, two, three, four, five voices died.

In the nursery the jungle burned. Blue lions roared, purple giraffes bounded off. The panthers ran in circles, changing color, and ten million animals, running before the fire, vanished off toward a distant steaming river. . . .

Ten more voices died. In the last instant under the fire avalanche, other choruses, oblivious, could be heard announcing the time, playing music, cutting the lawn by remote-control mower, or setting an umbrella frantically out and in the slamming and opening front door, a thousand things happening, like a clock shop when each clock strikes the hour insanely before or after the other, a scene of maniac confusion, yet unity; singing, screaming, a few last cleaning mice darting bravely out to carry the horrid ashes away! And one voice, with sublime disregard for the situation, read poetry aloud in the fiery study, until all the film spools burned, until all the wires withered and the circuits cracked.

The fire burst the house and let it slam flat down, puffing out skirts of spark and smoke.

In the kitchen, an instant before the rain of fire and timber, the stove could be seen making breakfasts at a psychopathic rate, ten dozen eggs, six loaves of toast, twenty dozen bacon strips, which, eaten by fire, started the stove working again, hysterically hissing!

The crash. The attic smashing into kitchen and parlor. The parlor into cellar, cellar into subcellar. Deep freeze, armchair, film tapes, circuits, beds, and all like skeletons thrown in a cluttered mound deep under.

Smoke and silence. A great quantity of smoke.

Dawn showed faintly in the east. Among the ruins, one wall stood alone. Within the wall, a last voice said, over and over again and again, even as the sun rose to shine upon the heaped rubble and steam: "Today is August 5, 2026, today is August 5, 2026, today is . . ."

After Reading

RESPONDING

1. "The five spots of paint—the man, the woman, the children, the ball—remained. The rest was a thin charcoal layer." Explain the significance of this **image** in relationship to the events in this **story**.

UNDERSTANDING

2. On the basis of the description of the house in this story, describe what can be inferred about the lifestyle and values of the people who lived in it.
3. Reread the **poem** by Sara Teasdale that appears in this story. With a partner, answer the following questions:
   a) What is the relationship of this poem to the story?
   b) What is the **rhyme scheme** of the poem?
   c) Why is it **ironic** that this poem was a favourite of Mrs. McClellan?
   Be prepared to present your answers to the class.
4. Find examples of **personification** in the last section of this story. Explain why this device is appropriate to the story.

THINKING ABOUT LANGUAGE

5. Explain why the story ends with three ellipsis dots. Explain at least one other purpose of ellipsis dots in written work. (See The Reference Shelf, page 237.)

6. Give one reason why the word "favourite" is spelled one way in this story and another way in the activities in this textbook.

EXTENDING

7. This story was written during the Cold War. Explain whether the story is as relevant to readers today as it was at that time. Look up the meaning of the term "Cold War" in a dictionary or encyclopedia if you are not sure what it means.

8. With a partner, brainstorm possible calamities that could result in the annihilation of humans. Which would make the best premise for a news story or film with a similar **theme** to the one in this story? Be prepared to present your ideas to the class.

UNIT 3

\> Media

A Major in Television and A Minor in Knowledge

"The media do not *reflect* reality but *create* it."

DAVID SUZUKI

BEFORE READING

As a class, discuss what people did for entertainment before television was invented. Can we, or do we go back to those forms of entertainment today? Why or why not?

When I was five years old, my parents never worried that I was watching too much television, because there wasn't any.

One day in the late forties, the boy next door declined my invitation to go to the movies because his family was saving up to buy a television set. I laughed at his silly dream.

However, by the fifties, our neighbors' prescience was proven and I visited them to gaze in envy and awe at the black and white shadows flitting through a dense screen of electronic "snow."

The entire history of television has taken place during my life, and it is an appropriate symbol for technologies — the automobile, the telephone, nuclear power, the pill, computers — that have transformed our lives.

Television spread with lightning speed and plays a prominent role in our perceptions.

It is said the average Canadian watches six to eight hours a day, while in most cities cable makes more than twenty channels accessible almost around the clock. Dishes capture signals directly from satellites and provide an extensive menu of choices. Television is the major way people learn about the world. It shapes their ideas and values from infancy. Yet we seldom ask what the long-term effects of television have been on society.

Television is a medium of the *visual*. Pictures *can* be worth a thousand words. The ability to juxtapose images, speed up or slow down, or explore otherwise inaccessible phenomena or events cannot be matched by any other medium. Thus, TV is most powerful when it brings pictures of prehistoric coelocanths, a sprouting seed or a fetus *in utero*. But far too often its potential is wasted on the sensational or trivial.

The dependence on visual images imposes serious constraints on TV programs, and this can be seen in comparison with radio. The entire range of ideas and discoveries in science, for example, can be explored on radio, which requires the listener's imagination. The scope is considerably narrower with television, so that areas such as mathematics, geology, molecular biology and astronomy, to name a few, are seldom covered.

The media do not *reflect* reality but *create* it. And because television has become the dominant medium, it is important to be aware of this. Decisions on the priorities of programming and the subjects of news reports are made by people at various levels of production. Because everyone looks at the world through the lenses of his or her own heredity and experience, those decisions will be expressions of the socio-economic, ethnic, religious, and psychological backgrounds of the people making them.

Other considerations also determine whether an event is ever reported — whether there is a camera crew available, the time of day, ambient light, facilities for editing raw footage, the number of other reports on the news schedule.

And how are reports presented? Entire events involving perhaps dozens of speakers may be encapsulated in a twenty-second report. In thirty minutes, we are presented with news of the entire world packaged in segments ranging from fifteen to 120 seconds. An "in-depth" report refers to a two- to four-minute piece. (Any savvy politician knows the value of a short, snappy answer and the best time to call a press conference.)

Even documentaries must compete for the attention and then the memory of viewers watching programs in blocks of time during which they are confronted with a numbing array of choices and interspersed commercials. What is ultimately retained from an evening of television viewing may be snippets whose source is unclear. As host of "The Nature of Things" on CBC television, I am frequently given credit for reports that were broadcast on other shows.

Television is a powerful invention whose potential to entertain, inform and educate is too often squandered in the interest of profit, glibness and conformity. For viewers who use the technology selectively and sparingly, it can fulfil much of its promise. But what kind of minds and society have been created as a result of this technology? We have to ask this question and seek serious answers.

After Reading

RESPONDING

1. Write an **opinion piece** on one important point that Suzuki makes in this essay.

UNDERSTANDING

2. a) With a partner, find the **thesis** of this essay.

   b) Using the thesis you have found, make an outline of this essay in your notebooks.

3. **Summarize** Suzuki's argument for the reason why mathematics, geology, and so on (eighth paragraph, on pages 188–189) are rarely covered on television.

4. Explain how television "creates reality" for the viewers (ninth and tenth paragraph, on page 189).

THINKING ABOUT LANGUAGE

5. The sixth paragraph starts with a sentence in the passive voice. Why it is appropriate to use passive voice in this case?

EXTENDING

6. a) In a small group, listen to the news on a variety of radio stations. If possible, include an all-news station, the CBC, a pop music station, a country music station, and an easy-listening "adult" station. Choose the same time of day for each member of the group to listen to the stations, so that you can compare the news broadcasts. If you can, tape-record the broadcasts. If not, take notes on the following things:

   • What stories were in the news
   • What stories were excluded from the news
   • The order in which the stories appeared in the news
   • The length of each story
   • The details included about the top story

   Make point-form notes comparing the news broadcasts as presented by the stations in each category. Were the reports **biased** or slanted? In your notebook, explain the similarities and differences by considering the **audiences** and the purposes of the news broadcasts.

   b) Find other classmates who listened to the same news report you did. As a group, discuss your notes and add to your information. Prepare a report to present to the class on the news broadcasts on one of the stations.

   c) As members of the audience, ask each group questions about what they have heard and their interpretation of it.

Reflections Dental

PHYLLIS MCGINLEY

BEFORE READING

As a class, discuss the work of orthodontists. Consider the services orthodontists provide, the demand for their services, and whether orthodontics is a career with a future.

How pure, how beautiful, how fine
Do teeth on television shine!
No flutist flutes, no dancer twirls,
But comes equipped with matching pearls.
Gleeful announcers all are born   5
With sets like rows of hybrid corn.
Clowns, critics, clergy, commentators,
Ventriloquists and roller skaters,
M.C.s who beat their palms together,
The girl who diagrams the weather,   10
The crooner crooning for his supper —
All flash white treasures, lower and upper.
With miles of smiles the airwaves teem,
And each an orthodontist's dream.

'Twould please my eye as gold a miser's —   15
One charmer with uncapped incisors.

After Reading

RESPONDING

1. This **poem** was written about 50 years ago. With a partner, discuss whether the ideas expressed in it are still true today. Be prepared to present your conclusion to the class.

UNDERSTANDING

2. In a single sentence, state the main idea in this poem.
3. Identify the **rhyme scheme** of this poem. Explain the relationship between the rhyme scheme and the **tone** of the poem.

THINKING ABOUT LANGUAGE

4. Make a list of all the words in this poem that are used as synonyms for teeth. Identify which words are true synonyms and which are **metaphors**.

EXTENDING

5. Write a personal **opinion essay** explaining whether society places too much emphasis on physical appearances. With a partner, take your essay through the writing process, focusing on tone, the use and effectiveness of supporting evidence, and organization.
6. Research the range of jobs available in dentistry. For each, identify the kind of education required. Create an informational **brochure**, with illustrations, to present your findings.

Those Gap Kids Ads Are Not Alright

"...those creepy new Gap Kids ads..."

RACHEL GIESE

BEFORE READING

In your notebooks, write a synonym and a **definition** for each of these words: manifesto (noun), egregious (adjective), archness (noun), ubiquitous (adjective), deleterious (adjective), rampant (adjective), precocious (adjective), shilling (verb).

It isn't easy being a member of the under-13 set these days.

On one side, they're targets of the new "child-free" lobby, a growing group of non-parents, mainly American, who resent benefits like parental work leave, child-care tax credits and subsidized day care and who feel put out by crying toddlers and public breast-feeding.

They've even got a manifesto of sorts in journalist Elinor Burkett's new book *The Baby Boon: How Family-Friendly America Cheats The Childless*. But for many, it goes beyond fair tax breaks and into the realm of out-and-out child-hating. One New Yorker has launched a very public campaign to ban children at her local Starbucks, while others regularly deride kids as "scrogs," "crib lizards" and "ankle biters."

On the other side, children are the target of the advertising industry, an even more powerful (and dangerous) group that just adores them — or at least adores their naïveté, desire to fit in and buying power.

The most egregious example of late is those creepy new Gap Kids ads, one with a bunch of young girls in a faux rock band, the other with young boys dancing, both groups singing the Kinks song "You Really Got Me," cannily appealing both to kids with the cool clothes and their parents with the retro song.

Though the kids in the ads aren't wearing anything more suggestive than T-shirts and cargo pants, there's something pornographic about the spots. It's the druggy way the kids sing and their knowing, beyond ironic, attitude. They're mini-versions of the models in last year's "Everyone In Vests" Gap campaign, joy-lessly singing Madonna's "Dress You Up

In My Love." That kind of archness is too grown-up for kids, almost grotesque. It seems even more inappropriate than overtly sexual behaviour.

And that's just the tip of the marketing iceberg. Pokemania will soon be giving way to a glut of Harry Potter merchandise. Back-to-school shopping means more weirdly adult clothing ads, like the Guess campaign with its vinyl python print pants for preteens and a style pictorial in *The New York Times Magazine* a few weeks back involving 8-year-olds decked out in designer fashions.

As the direct buying power of 4- to 12-year-olds has grown — in the U.S. it's up from $2.9 billion in 1978 to $24 billion in 1998 — so has advertising and marketing aimed at young consumers, with child behaviour specialists helping to shape the most effective messages. Advertising directed toward kids has become so ubiquitous and sophisticated that a group of concerned activists is currently lobbying the American Psychological Association to start disciplining its members who work as consultants and researchers for corporations that target children.

According to *Salon* magazine, these activists (many of whom are psychologists themselves) are worried that child-oriented marketing has reached "epidemic levels. . . . It is an enormous onslaught that constitutes arguably the largest single psychological project ever undertaken . . . promoting and assisting the commercial exploitation and manipulation of children."

Cigarette ads aimed at kids are an obvious example of the danger of child-oriented marketing. It's a little harder to pinpoint the actual deleterious effects of other forms of marketing, such as the commercials on the Youth News Network broadcast into classrooms, or whatever Disney movie/action figure/lunch box is currently in vogue.

But it's not impossible to see the kind of impact marketing has on kids. Advertising has invaded all of children's "safe spaces" like schools and playgrounds, limiting opportunities to establish children's culture outside of commercial forces. Too much heavily marketed crappy junk food and time spent inactive, watching television, has led to an epidemic of child obesity.

Children's imaginations and verbal skills are eroding — the August issue of *Harper's* notes that in 1945 the average child between 6 and 14 had a vocabulary of 25,000 words, compared with 10,000 today. Marketing and rampant consumption foster greed and provide kids with even more fodder for feelings of inadequacy and alienation.

With their bored, precocious zombie children dancing in too-expensive outfits, shilling mass-produced clothes and singing lyrics that are over their heads, those Gap ads are an unintentional indictment of themselves, an example of all that's ugly about child-oriented marketing. Those aren't kids at play, getting messy and having fun — they're child labourers, future anorexics and marketing execs. And you can just imagine those kid actors screaming at their agents on cellphones, the kind of spoiled, overindulged kids that child-free activists just love to hate.

After Reading

RESPONDING

1. Write a response to the following question or discuss the question as a class: What places, if anywhere, should be "child-free" zones? (For our purpose, a child will be defined as anyone 18 years of age or younger.) Provide clear reasons for your opinion.

UNDERSTANDING

2. a) Working with a partner, record the writer's **thesis** and the points that she uses to support her thesis.
   b) Divide the **article** into an introduction, body, and conclusion by writing down the sentence that starts each part.
3. Look closely at the fifth and sixth paragraphs (on page 193). In your own words, explain why the writer thinks that the Gap advertisements aimed at young teenagers are inappropriate.
4. a) *Salon* magazine calls child-oriented advertising a "psychological project." Explain what is meant by this term. Who is involved in the "project," according to the magazine?
   b) Think back to the advertisements that were on television and in magazines when you were younger. In a **journal**, write about whether or not you think the advertisers took advantage of your need to fit in and be part of the world around you. In a small group, discuss your journal responses. Then, as a class, discuss the **topic**.

THINKING ABOUT LANGUAGE

5. Describe the **tone** of this article. Explain how its vocabulary and the structures and lengths of its sentences create this tone.
6. Examine the third sentence of the sixth paragraph. Write down the three words that use apostrophes in this sentence. For each word, explain why the apostrophe is used. Discuss your answers with the class.

EXTENDING

7. a) Watch several after-school television shows or look through a magazine aimed at young teens. Make a list of five advertisements that target the young teen **audience**. If possible, videotape the ads. If you are using a magazine, cut out the ads (if the magazine is yours) or photocopy them (if the magazine is not yours). For each ad, make notes on the following:
   • The product being advertised
   • The models: their clothing, their attitudes, what they are doing in the advertisement

- The messages, both **implicit** and **explicit**, in the advertisement
- Whether or not the advertisement focuses on fitting in

b) In a small group, discuss your findings. Jot down any similarities you found among the ads your group members chose.

c) Individually, choose one of the advertisers. Find out where you can mail or e-mail letters to that company. Write a letter to the head of advertising, telling that person about your findings and about how you feel about the company's ad.

d) Take your letter through the writing process, having your partners focus on the letter's content, **tone**, and format. When the group's letters have been revised and edited, send them, keeping a copy of each letter for display in the classroom. If you get responses from the advertisers, post the responses.

Zits

JERRY SCOTT AND
JIM BORGMAN

BEFORE READING

1. As a class, **define** average.
2. In point form, describe an "average" teenager in your peer group.

After Reading

RESPONDING

1. Respond to these questions: Is it good enough to be "aggressively average"? What happens if you are not average?

UNDERSTANDING

2. a) Comic strips and cartoons often carry a social message. Write down the message that you think Jerry Scott and Jim Borgman are conveying in their comic strip. State whether or not you agree with their message, and why.
   b) Compare the message you found in this comic strip with a partner's interpretation of the message. Discuss whether or not each of you agreed with the cartoonists' messages.
   c) What makes people understand things differently? Discuss this as a class.
3. Examine each frame of the comic strip. Make a list of the techniques that the cartoonists have used in each frame to make the visual part of the cartoon humorous. (See The Reference Shelf, pages 298–299.)

THINKING ABOUT LANGUAGE

4. a) Look at the adjectives used to describe Jeremy's hair, clothes, and personality. Show how these words emphasize the "averageness" that Jeremy is aiming at.
   b) The figure of speech used to describe the effect when two opposite words are combined to created an **image** (e.g., "explosive silence") is called an *oxymoron*. Look at the adverbs that describe the adjectives in each of the first three frames. Explain why they could be considered oxymorons and why they are effective in helping get the message across.

EXTENDING

5. a) In a small group, record the everyday influences on you and other teenagers. Include specific influences in your home, school, job, community, and the media.
   b) Select a television program or a movie targeted at people your age (no two groups can choose the same show or movie). Describe what is considered "average" in the portrayal of the **characters** that are your age. Include all aspects of the characters' lives (such as home, school, job, and community).
   c) Using audio-visual support, create an interactive presentation (including everyone in your group) on your findings about your television program or movie. Rehearse your presentation.
   d) As a class, create an assessment form for this project and use it to assess the class presentations.

Lettering Techniques

JUDY TATCHELL AND
CAROL VARLEY

BEFORE READING

In a small group, discuss your experiences with reading instructions and "how-to" books. Make lists of helpful and unhelpful features in these books. Be prepared to report on your discussion to the class.

The following techniques help you to keep your letters the same size and in a straight line. You can use them with all kinds of lettering. They will help you make the styles in this book look smart and professional.

KEEPING LETTERS EVEN

You can keep your letters level and even by drawing faint pencil rules, called guidelines.

Unless you want very thin or very fat-looking letters, the distance between the guidelines should be between three and nine times the thickest part of your letter.

Three times the thickest part of the letter.

Nine times the thickest part of the letter.

Guidelines too far apart for thickness of the letter: letter looks very thin.

Guidelines too close for thickness of the letter: letter looks very fat.

MOVING THE MIDDLE

You can also draw a guideline to position the strokes across the middles of some letters. Moving this guideline up or down changes the look of the letters, as shown.

ABOUT PENCILS

Pencils are described by how hard or soft their leads are. The usual range is from 7B (softest) to 6H (hardest). A medium pencil is called HB. A 2B, an HB and a 2H are enough to start with.

A hard pencil makes a thin, greyish line. A soft pencil makes a thicker, blacker line which is easily smudged.

Hard pencils are useful for drawing faint guidelines. A softer pencil is probably better for sketching letter shapes.

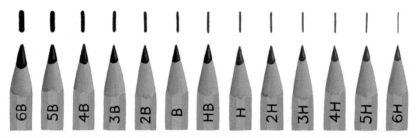

SMALL LETTERS

Small letters are just over half as tall as capitals. Small letter sticks (ascenders) and tails (descenders) extend above and below the guidelines by about the same amount. You can vary this for different effects, though.

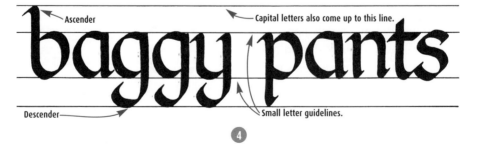

Ascender

Capital letters also come up to this line.

Descender

Small letter guidelines.

4

FLOWING LETTERS

You can use an italic nib to do this flowing, joined-up style.

Try using just one guideline through the middle of the letters. It keeps them level but not absolutely even, so they look less rigid.

SPACING TIPS

Leave a space the size of a capital "E" between words made up of capital letters.

PPY EBIR

Leave the space of a small "n" between words made up of small letters.

cenupon nantim

ABOUT ITALIC PENS

For some of the styles in this book, you will need a square-nibbed, or italic, pen. This gives a variety of thick and thin lines….

To test whether you are holding the pen nib at the right angle, draw a cross. Both strokes should be the same thickness.

You can put different italic nibs on a dip pen and use them with a bottle of ink.

You can buy felt pens with broad, flat italic-shaped ends from art shops

5

Making Posters

The most important thing about lettering on a poster is that it catches people's attention and is easy to read from a distance.

MATERIALS

The size of the paper you use for a poster depends on how far away you want the poster to be seen from.

Poster for a notice board.

A poster to go outside needs to be much bigger.

The lettering on a poster needs space around it. This will help the message to stand out. Make sure that the paper you choose is big enough for this.

Poster paper comes in different colours

You can buy different kinds of paper from art shops. If your poster is going outside where it might get wet, buy a harder, less absorbent type of paper.

Use poster paint or gouache that does not run in the wet.

DESIGNING A POSTER

First, write down what you want to say. Keep it simple.

Then divide the message up and number the parts in order of importance. You need to make the most important words stand out.

Finally, choose a suitable style for the message and illustration.

DROP SHADOWS

To do a drop shadow, draw a letter. Then copy the outline a bit to the side, and above or below the letter shape. Fill in the shadow with a darker shade.

(14)

POSTER TIPS

★ Use strong shapes and colours.

★ Don't use too many lettering styles and sizes on a poster or it will look confusing. Two or three different sorts is probably enough.

★ Attract people with a strong image and one main bit of writing. They will come closer to read the rest.

PRACTISING BIG LETTERS

Practise big letters on old news-paper or large sheets of scrap paper. Do bold, wide sweeps of your hand.

GIANT-SIZED POSTERS

Billboard posters are made up of several sections. You could make a huge poster yourself, out of several sheets joined together.

15

HOW TO DRAW
Lettering

JUDY TATCHELL AND CAROL VARLEY

Consultant: Graham Peet

Designed by
Nigel Reece and Richard Johnson

Illustrated by Fiona Brown and Guy Smith

Hand Lettering by David Young

Additional illustrations by
Chris Smedley and Robin Lawrie

CONTENTS

Index

3-D letters, 11, 17, 27

alphabets to copy,
    30–31
Art Nouveau style, 9
    alphabet, 31
atmospheric lettering,
    6-7

bindings, 29
bubble letters, 16

calligraphy, 22–23
captions, 29
centring letters, 13
comic strip lettering,
    12–13
computer style, 7
construction lines, 10,
    11
copperplate, 23
copying letters, 2
correcting mistakes, 27
crayons, 2, 20

distorting letters, 15
drop shadows, 14

enlarging letters, 15, 27
envelope, making an, 7

fabric, lettering, on,
    21–22
flourishes, 23
frame style, 12

gothic
    alphabet, 30
    style, 8, 20

graffiti styles, 16–17
graphology, 23
grid, 15, 19, 21
guidelines, 2, 4, 5, 10,
    11

handwriting, 22–23
historical styles, 8–9

illumination, 6, 20
italic, 22–23
    alphabet, 31
    nib, 5, 8, 22

justification, 18

layout, 19, 28
letter
    capital, 5, 8, 9, 10,
        26
    designs, 25
    shapes, 25
    solid, 11
    small, 5, 8, 9, 26
logo, 24

magazines, 7, 18–19, 20
marker pens, 16
monograms, 25
multiple copies, 27

newspapers, 7, 15,
    18–19

paint, 14, 20, 24
paper, 14, 15, 28
paste-up, 19
pencil, 4
    hard, 4, 20
    soft, 4
    twin-pointed, 22

pen
    felt-tip, 2, 16, 20
    gold, 20
    italic, 5, 8, 22
    silver, 20
perspective, 10
photocopying, 6, 18,
    19, 27
posters, 2, 14–15
preliminaries, 28
presentation, 28
printing, 24–25
projects, 2, 28
protest messages, 17, 21

reducing letters, 15, 27
roman
    alphabet, 30
    calligraphy, 22

signature, 16, 23
sound effects, 12, 13
speech bubbles, 12, 13
spray paint, 16, 17
stencilling, 26–27

T-shirts, 2, 21
tag, 16
techniques, 3–5, 10–11
titles, 12, 18, 28

vanishing point, 10, 11

wildstyle, 17
word processor, 18

32

After Reading

RESPONDING

RESPONDING

1. With a partner, discuss the comprehensiveness and organization of the information in this excerpt from a book. Make a list of any **topics** you feel have been left out. On the basis of the book's contents page and the index, determine whether the book seems to be well organized. Be prepared to present your conclusions to the class.

UNDERSTANDING

2. Using both the contents page and the index on pages 204–205 of this text, list the topics covered on pages 22 and 23 of the book this excerpt is taken from. In a paragraph, explain what kind of information you would expect to find on those pages.
3. Identify information in this selection that would be helpful even if you were to use a computer to create a poster.
4. With a partner, identify groups of people who would be likely to buy a book like this. Discuss why this selection has been chosen for inclusion in a Grade 11 English textbook. Be prepared to present your ideas to the class.

 ## THINKING ABOUT LANGUAGE

5. Another name for small letters and capital letters is lower-case and upper-case letters. Explain why a writer should or should not use these styles interchangeably or for variety in a selection such as this.
6. Explain the reason for the hyphen as it is used in the following words in this selection: "fat-looking letters," "joined-up style," and "giant-sized posters." Write the grammar rule that explains this use of the hyphen.

EXTENDING

7. With a partner, analyze a poster in your school, keeping in mind the information and advice presented in this selection. Present your analysis of the poster to your class.
8. a) Create a poster for your classroom about a common spelling or grammatical error. Use information from this excerpt to make your poster eye-catching and effective.
   b) As a class, develop an evaluation form to assess the effectiveness of the poster.

Head Game

"Some shampoo claims are just a lot of lather."

CONSUMER REPORTS

BEFORE READING

With your class, discuss shampoos. Do you buy shampoo, or do you ask your parents or guardians to buy a certain product? What do you want from a shampoo? Are there products that you would like to try? Why? Do you have favourite shampoo commercials?

All shampoos clean hair. You've probably guessed that already, and we've been saying it for years. To gain a share of the crowded, $6 billion hair-care market, manufacturers embellish what is essentially detergent with a few extra ingredients and a basketful of adjectives: volumizing, clarifying, hydrating, revitalizing, moisturizing, texturizing, replenishing, and glossing, for starters. Do shampoos deliver what their adjectives claim? Not necessarily.

For this report, we focused on the promises for which many people are now buying shampoo. We tested 57 products that make one of four popular claims: to condition dry or damaged hair, retain color, add volume, or remove the buildup of styling products ("clarify," in hair-ese). Within each claim category, we also tested nine "normal" products for comparison (they're marked with a red dot in the charts beginning on page 208), and we paired a few shampoos with their same-brand conditioners, to see how results might change. We included three Head & Shoulders dandruff shampoos (but didn't test how well they controlled dandruff).

We washed some 1,700 ponytails made up of hair appropriate for each claim — hair that was harmed by bleaching; dyed; fine; or gelled, moussed, and sprayed. After the tresses were shampooed (and conditioned in some cases), then blow-dried, trained sensory panelists and a consultant judged how well each product did its advertised job. Did damaged tresses become shiny, smooth, and easier to comb? Did dyed tresses keep their color? Did fine, limp tresses become fuller? Did tresses made stiff by styling products feel and look clean?

The consultant and trained panelists also judged ease of combing and detangling for all categories. The panelists judged flyaway hair, for all categories; color fading, for color-retention products; and volume, for shampoos that claimed to add it.

Our test tresses were of straight hair, but the results we found with regard to fading color and concealing damage should apply to most hair. Curlier hair may need extra conditioning …

FOR DRY OR DAMAGED HAIR

> **Claim: Replenishes damaged hair.** > **Reality: Shampoo alone usually can't do the job.**
"Moisturizing" is the word of choice among products for damaged or dry hair, but merely adding moisture to hair would make it limp or frizzy and wouldn't improve damage. What dry, rough, dull hair needs is a coating, to smooth its outer cuticle, and emollients, to make hair fibers more flexible and resilient. Those are functions best handled by a conditioner, not a stand-alone shampoo.

> **Moderately Effective**

21¢ **Finesse** Plus Moisturizing Shampoo Plus Conditioner for dry or coarse hair

> **Slightly Effective**

25 cents and under:[*]

9¢ **Suave** Moisturizing, for dry or damaged hair

11¢ **Suave** Thermal Formula for normal to damaged hair

11¢ **Suave** Shampoo Plus Conditioner Healthy Shine with Pro-Vitamins Moisturizing Formula for dry or damaged hair

12¢ **Suave** Shampoo Plus Conditioner Healthy Shine with Pro-Vitamins Regular Formula for normal hair •

14¢ **Suave** Professionals Biobasics

21¢ **Finesse** Moisturizing, dry or coarse hair

22¢ **Vidal Sassoon** Ultra Care Shampoo & Conditioning Rinse All-in-One Texturizing Formula D[1]

22¢ **Vidal Sassoon** Texturizing Formula D for dry or damaged hair[1]

23¢ **L'Oreal** HydraVIVE Shampoo & Conditioner 2 in 1 for dry hair

23¢ **Thermasilk** Heat Activated Regular for normal hair •

23¢ **Thermasilk** Heat Activated Moisturizing for dry or damaged hair[1]

26 to 50 cents:

26¢ **Head & Shoulders** Dandruff for normal hair •

26¢ **Head & Shoulders** Dandruff Dry Scalp for normal or dry hair

26¢ **Pantene** Pro-V Ultra V Moisturizing for dry, damaged hair[1]

26¢ **Pantene** Pro-V Ultra V Shampoo Plus Conditioner for normal hair •

26¢ **Pantene** Pro-V Ultra V Shampoo Plus Conditioner Moisturizing for dry, damaged hair

26¢ **Pert Plus** Shampoo Plus Conditioner Deep Moisturizing

27¢ **Pert Plus** Shampoo Plus Conditioner Simply Cleanse & Condition •

27¢ **Clairol** Herbal Essences Moisture Balancing for normal hair •

27¢ **L'Oreal** HydraVIVE Daily Moisture for dry damaged hair

28¢ **Clairol** Herbal Essences Replenisher for colored, permed, dry, damaged hair

34¢ **Infusium 23** Moisturizing for normal to dry hair

43¢ **Neutrogena** Clean replenishing for dry, damaged hair

50 cents and over:

50¢ **Biolage** Normalizing • (salon)

65¢ **Nexxus** Therappe Moisturizing (salon)

74¢ **Redken** All Soft (salon)

> **Less Effective**

7¢ **Suave** Balsam & Protein •

7¢ **White Rain** Classic Care Moisturizing Formula

14¢ **Suave** Professionals Humectant

28¢ **Pantene** Pro-V Ultra V for normal hair[1] •

35¢ **Frizz-Ease** Corrective Shampoo and Shiner Conditioning Glossing Formula

59¢ **Biolage** Hydrating (salon)

> **Top Choices for Combing or Detangling**

Finesse Plus Moisturizing Shampoo Plus Conditioner
L'Oreal HydraVIVE Daily Moisture for dry damaged hair
Redken All Soft (salon)
Suave Shampoo Plus Conditioner Healthy Shine with Pro-Vitamins Moisturizing Formula for dry or damaged hair
Thermasilk Heat Activated Regular for normal hair •
Thermasilk Heat Activated Moisturizing for dry or damaged hair[1]
Finesse Moisturizing for dry or coarse hair

---

[*] Prices are per fluid ounce.

[1] Formulation changed after our tests.

FOR COLOUR-TREATED HAIR

> Claim: Prevents color from fading. > Reality: Wear a hat.

Color-treated hair can suffer may insults: repeated washing and exposure to sun and chlorine, among others. Washing can remove some color; the sun's rays can degrade the color you've dyed in. Shampoos and shampoo-conditioner combinations formulated for color-treated hair promise to reduce fading by cleaning hair gently or protecting it with sunscreen. **Revlon ColorStay Stay Brunette** claims further that it "seals the hair shaft to lock in color" in the first week after coloring. Perhaps, but **Revlon ColorStay Stay Brunette** was only slightly effective in our two tests on gray tresses colored brown. We tested each shampoo by washing some tresses 14 times and exposing others to intense ultraviolet light.

No product — with a claim or without — was excellent at holding hair color. **L'Oreal ColorVIVE Gentle Shampoo for color-treated or high-lighted hair** was best, but not by much. Don't assume a conditioner will help hold your color. We found that using conditioners with their sister shampoos actually made color fade more in four out of six cases.

> **Moderately Effective**

27¢ **L'Oreal** ColorVIVE Gentle for color-treated or highlighted hair

> **Slightly Effective**

25 cents and under:

7¢ **Suave** Balsam & Protein •

12¢ **Suave** Shampoo Plus Conditioner Healthy Shine with Pro-Vitamins Regular Formula for normal hair •

23¢ **Aussie** Color Mate

23¢ **Thermasilk** Heat Activated Revitalizing Color Care Formula[1]

23¢ **Thermasilk** Heat Activated Regular for normal hair •

26 to 50 cents:

26¢ **Head & Shoulders** Dandruff for normal hair •

26¢ **Pantene** Pro-V Ultra V Shampoo Plus Conditioner for normal hair •

26¢ **Pert Plus** Shampoo Plus Conditioner Simply Cleanse & Condition •

27¢ **Clairol** Herbal Essences Moisture Balancing for normal hair •

28¢ **Pantene** Pro-V Ultra V for normal hair[1] •

30¢ **Revlon** ColorStay Stay Brunette

35¢ **Pantene** Pro-V Color Gentle Cleansing[1]

50 cents and over:

50¢ **Biolage** Normalizing • (salon)

56¢ **Biolage** Color Care (salon)

74¢ **Redken** Color Extend for color-treated hair (salon)

> **Top Choices for Combing or Detangling**

Thermasilk Heat Activated Revitalizing Color Care Formula[1]
Pantene Pro-V Ultra Color Gentle Cleansing[1]

> **For Controlling Flyaway Hair**

Pantene Pro-V Ultra V for normal hair[1] •
Suave Balsam & Protein •

---

[1] Formulation changed after our tests.

FOR FINE OR LIMP HAIR

> **Claim: Builds fullness.** > **Reality: None makes hair much fuller; a normal shampoo can do as much as one that makes a claim.**

Fine or limp hair has no backbone. Among other things, it lacks the rigidity that enables thick or coarse hair shafts to stand apart from one another, creating a fuller look. Shampoos can make the shaft a bit more rigid by coating it with a polymer or by removing natural oils that tend to make hair limp. **Nexxus Diametress Hair Thickening Shampoo** uses another approach: It claims to make the hair shaft thicker. We measured hair strands' thickness after washing, and didn't find any difference. In fact, when we shampooed tresses of fine, limp hair, we found the volumizing products did no better at creating volume than those designed for normal hair. Our tests of six shampoo-conditioner pairs showed that another "normal" shampoo, **Suave Balsam & Protein**, when used with its sister conditioner, performed as well as the front-runner.

> **Moderately Effective**

26¢ **Pantene** Pro-V Ultra V Shampoo Plus Conditioner for normal hair •

> **Slightly Effective**

25 cents and under:

7¢ **Alberto VO5** Extra Body

7¢ **Suave** Balsam & Protein •

9¢ **Suave** Extra Body

12¢ **Suave** Shampoo Plus Conditioner Healthy Shine with Pro-Vitamins Regular Formula for normal hair •

23¢ **Finesse** Bodifying for fine or thin hair

23¢ **Thermasilk** Heat Activated Regular for normal hair •

23¢ **Thermasilk** Heat Activated Volumizing for fine or thin hair[1]

26 to 50 cents:

26¢ **Head & Shoulders** Dandruff for fine or oily hair

26¢ **Pantene** Pro-V Ultra V Extra Body for fine hair[1]

26¢ **Pert Plus** Shampoo Plus Conditioner Simply Cleanse & Condition •

27¢ **Clairol** Herbal Essences Moisture Balancing for normal hair •

27¢ **L'Oreal** BodyVIVE Thickening plus Ceramide-R & Protein thin/extra fine

28¢ **Clairol** Herbal Essences Extra Body for fine/limp hair

28¢ **Pantene** Pro-V Ultra V for normal hair[1] •

42¢ **Neutrogena** Clean Volumizing for fine, thin hair

50 cents and over:

65¢ **Amplify** Volumizing (salon)

74¢ **Redken** Headstrong Volume (salon)

$1.33 **Nexxus** Diametress Hair Thickening (salon)

> **Less Effective**

7¢ **White Rain** Classic Care Extra Body

26¢ **Head & Shoulders** Dandruff for normal hair •

26¢ **Pantene** Pro-V Ultra V Shampoo Plus Conditioner Extra Body for fine hair

26¢ **Pert Plus** Shampoo Plus Conditioner Extra Body

33¢ **Thicker Fuller Hair** Revitalizing (Cleanse)

50¢ **Biolage** Normalizing • (salon)

68¢ **Physique** Amplifying

> **Top Choices for Combing or Detangling**

Pantene Pro-V Ultra V Shampoo Plus Conditioner for normal hair•

Thermasilk Heat Activated Regular for normal hair •

Pert Plus Shampoo Plus Conditioner Simply Cleanse & Condition •

Thermasilk Heat Activated Volumizing for fine or thin hair[1]

> **For Controlling Flyaway Hair**

Finesse Bodifying for fine or thin hair

• These shampoos are for "normal" hair, and make no claims for use on damaged, color-treated, or fine or limp hair. They were included for comparison's sake.

[1] Formulation changed after our tests.

After Reading

RESPONDING

1. Read the **article**, and think about the results of the tests. In your notebook, write your initial reactions to this article.

UNDERSTANDING

2. Explain whether it is fair to compare shampoos made for normal hair with specialty shampoos.
3. Create a graph to represent the information listed in the "For Dry or Damaged Hair" section.
4. Reread the section "For Fine or Limp Hair." **Summarize** this section in approximately 50 words.
5. Look at the **layout** of this article. With a partner, make a list of the techniques the designer has used to make important information easy to locate and read.

THINKING ABOUT LANGUAGE

6. Reread the first five paragraphs of this article. Find an example and explain the use of each of the following: colon, parentheses, quotation marks, italics, dash.

EXTENDING

7. a) Read the "The Pitch" in The Reference Shelf, pages 304–305. In a small group, find three print advertisements for shampoo, each claiming to do something special for your hair. For each, make notes on the attention-getting techniques, product claims, and added-value claims. Create a visual display of your research, and present your findings to the class.

   b) Individually, write a letter of complaint to the advertisers or to the product manufacturers about their product claims, using this article as support for your complaint.

   c) Have a partner read your letter for content, organization, layout, and **tone**. Revise the letter as necessary, and send the letter to the company or advertiser.

The Big Story

"He came back safe and sound."

GEORGE LOVERIDGE

BEFORE READING

With a partner, brainstorm a list of events in people's lives that are deemed newsworthy and are reported in the local newspaper or on local newscasts. Do you feel that the media ever report stories about individuals that infringe on those people's privacy? Be prepared to present a **summary** of your ideas to the class.

Ernie Gibson wanted to be a newspaper reporter. After he finished school, he got a job on a small-town newspaper. Most of the time he worked in the *News* office, reading proof and checking facts. Sometimes he wrote about women's club meetings or high-school activities. Once in a while he handled routine police cases. His boss, a man named Truelove, covered everything that was interesting. Only if Truelove quit or dropped dead, Ernie said to himself, would he ever get a chance to show what he could do with a real story.

One morning Ernie was on his way back to the office with some notes he had taken about a dog show. The big story that day was a robbery in a supermarket. But Truelove was covering that.

It was hot and still early so Ernie decided to stop in at the Half Moon for a cup of coffee.

As soon as he entered the coffee shop, the counterman said, "Hear about the drowning?"

"No. When?"

"Just now. Over at Willow Lake. Officer Trask was here and he got a call. He didn't even finish his coffee."

"Thanks," Ernie said.

He ran to his car and backed it quickly into the road. It took him less than ten minutes to drive to the lake, and he spent the time hoping and praying that Truelove hadn't heard the news.

In a meadow near the lake Ernie spotted a state police car. He went bumping across the field and parked beside it. Then he saw Officer Trask down by the bank, staring out into the water. Near him was a small pile of clothing.

"Who is it?" Ernie asked.

"Don't know for sure," Trask said. "A kid heard someone yell for help and found this pile of clothes. We're bringing a boat to look for the body."

"Any identification on the clothes?"

"An Army I.D. card — for a John Vollmer. There's a letter addressed to him, too. In the back pocket."

Ernie copied down the name and address — John Vollmer, 44 Cargill Street. "When will the boat get here?"

"Here it comes now," Trask said.

The small boat was lifted off the trailer and launched quickly. One man rowed and another pulled grappling hooks through the water. Except for the ripples caused by the oars and the hooks, the lake was smooth and still.

"No telling how far out he was," Trask said.

Ernie nodded and watched for a few minutes. Then he said, "I'm going to check something."

"Okay."

Ernie drove to Cargill Street and found John Vollmer's house. When he rang the bell, a tall, gray-haired man came to the door.

"Does John Vollmer live here?" Ernie asked.

"Yes," the man said.

"Is he here?"

"Not now."

"Are you his father?"

"Yes."

"I'm from the *News*," Ernie said. "I wanted to get a little information about him. Maybe you can help."

A stout woman came up behind the man. "What's the matter?" she asked.

"Why, nothing I know of," the man told her; then he turned back questioningly to Ernie.

"I heard your son was home," Ernie said. "We have a column in the *News* about servicemen, and I thought maybe I could write something about him."

"Yes, I see that column," the man said. "Come on in."

Ernie went into the front room, which was small and crowded with furniture. He stepped around a low table and saw a picture of a young man in an Army uniform. The television set in the corner was on, and the woman went over to it and turned down the volume.

"Have a seat," she said. "Johnny just got home from overseas. Just yesterday it was. He was over there more than a year, and I thought he'd never come back."

The father smiled. "It's tough on mothers. On fathers, too. Have some coffee, young man? We've got some on the stove."

"No, thanks," said Ernie. "Was he wounded?"

"Not a scratch, thank God," the woman said. "He came back safe and sound."

A pretty girl, about eighteen, came into the room. The woman smiled and said, "This is Johnny's sister — Margie. This young man is from the *News*. He's going to put something in the paper about Johnny."

"Why don't you turn off the TV, Mother?" the girl asked. "Then maybe he can hear better."

"I turned it down. Does it bother you, Mr. ——?"

"Gibson, my name is. No. It doesn't bother me."

"All the time Johnny was gone, I didn't watch TV much," the woman explained. "I said to myself, 'What if something was happening to him and I was watching a show and enjoying myself?' You know what I mean? But now he's back and I watch it again."

Ernie nodded. Then he began asking all the questions he could think of: "When is John's birthday? Where did he go to school? How were his grades? Did he ever win any athletic awards? Does he have a girlfriend?"

Ernie took notes on the answers, but all the time he was writing he was also listening nervously for the ring of the telephone or a knock on the door.

"Sure you won't have a cup of coffee?" the father asked again.

"No, thanks."

"Maybe he'd like some ginger ale," said Margie.

"Would you, Mr. Gibson?"

"No, nothing. Thanks very much. Where is John now?"

"He went out," the mother said. "He got home just yesterday, and then this morning he decided he had to go out."

The father smiled. "Women. You can't please them. What's he want to sit around the house with us old people for?"

Margie said, "Johnny thought he might go over to Willow Lake for a swim. He used to swim there when he was a kid. He was going to do that or maybe look up some of his friends."

Ernie pointed to the picture of the soldier on the table. "Is that John? Could I borrow it?"

"Yes, but you'll be careful with it, won't you?" the mother said. "That's my best picture of Johnny."

"Nothing will happen to it."

"Will you promise to bring it back?"

"Of course."

"He's a good boy," the woman said. "You can put that in your story. He never forgets his mother. It was my birthday when he was over there, but he didn't forget. He sent his sister here some money to get me a present."

Ernie got up and took the picture from the table. "I'll return it," he said.

The father and mother stood up, too, and the father said, "When's this story going to be in the paper?"

"Probably this afternoon."

"Soon as that? You work fast, you fellows, don't you? I'll have to get a couple of extra copies. I'll send one to his grandmother."

Ernie said good-by.

"Come again," the mother said. "And be sure to bring my picture back."

"Yes," the father said. "Come back. I bet Johnny would like to meet you. Say, will this cost anything — to have the story in the paper?"

"No. Oh, no. Thanks. See you again." Ernie hurried down the steps and got into his car and drove back to Willow Lake.

About a dozen people were gathered on the bank of the lake. A doctor was trying to revive the body of a young man in blue swimming trunks. There was a cut on the young man's leg, probably from the grappling hook.

Ernie went up to the state trooper. "Can they help him?"

"No chance. Been in too long."

"Is it Vollmer?"

"Yeah," said Trask. "He's still wearing his Army dog tags."

Ernie nodded; then he looked around and saw a house on the other side of the meadow. He ran across the field and knocked on the front door.

A woman opened it and said, "Yes?"

Ernie gave his name and business and asked permission to use the telephone.

"Trouble at the lake?" she asked.

"I'm afraid so."

The woman let him in and showed him where the telephone was.

Ernie called the newspaper office and started reading his notes to the rewrite man at the news desk. He spoke quickly and professionally, spelling out the name — "Vollmer. 'V' as in 'vinegar,' 'o' as in 'olive,' . . ."

Then he added, "I've got a picture of him. I'll bring it in. Leave space for it."

Ernie thanked the woman and went back to his car. As he drove away, he passed an ambulance heading for the lake.

He stopped for a quick lunch and then went back to the *News* office. After he turned in the picture of John Vollmer, Ernie leaned back in his chair, put his hands in his pockets, and propped his feet on his desk.

Around three o'clock Truelove came in with the afternoon *News*. "Well, you're on the front page with the story of the drowned soldier. You might have let me know about it. It's good work but —"

Ernie said, "Thanks." He put the newspaper on his desk but didn't look at it.

"And here," Truelove said. He pulled a brown envelope out of his pocket. "Here's the dead guy's picture. Someone said you wanted it back."

Ernie took the envelope and stared at it for a minute; then slowly he got to his feet. "I've got to go out," he told Truelove. "I'll be back soon."

Once again Ernie drove to Cargill Street. This time he pulled up behind a police car that was parked in front of the Vollmer house.

Ernie ran up the steps and dropped the picture of John Vollmer into the mailbox near the front door. Then he walked back to his car and after a little while — not knowing what else to do — he drove away.

After Reading

RESPONDING

1. In your notebook, describe your feelings just after you finished reading this story.

UNDERSTANDING

2. In your notebook, write a few paragraphs explaining whether Ernie Gibson is a good reporter. Find reasons in the story to support your position. Include an introductory and concluding sentence. Have a classmate read your writing and give you suggestions for revision.

3. Write a letter to the editor of the *News* from a member of John Vollmer's family the day after they found out about the drowning and read Ernie Gibson's **article** in the newspaper.

4. a) Write a **memo** from Truelove, the editor of the *News*, to Ernie Gibson, reporter, inviting him to a meeting to discuss a complaint that Truelove received regarding the John Vollmer story.

   b) As a class, discuss the **tone** of some of the memos written by the members of the class.

THINKING ABOUT LANGUAGE

5. In your notebook, copy sentences from this story that illustrate the following: a simple sentence, a complex sentence, and a compound sentence. In each case, explain why the sentence you chose is an example of that sentence structure.

EXTENDING

6. As a class, identify familiar news reporters from print, radio, and television. With a partner, assess the effectiveness of one of the reporters, considering such points as the kind of stories reported on, the thoroughness of the information presented, and the reporter's writing or speaking style. Be prepared to present your assessment to the class.

7. With a partner, write five principles that you think should be included in a code of ethics for news reporters. Post your points on the bulletin board, and be prepared to explain why you think they are important.

Getting Down to the Wireless

"...wireless technology isn't welcome in school."   JAMES CARELESS

BEFORE READING

As a class, create a reasonable policy for the students' use of pagers and cell phones in your school. Try to take into account the convenience of these technologies, as well as their ability to disrupt. Remember that the policy you create may need to include exceptions to general rules.

No doubt about it, wireless technology is this fall's hot fashion accessory for kids returning to class.

Depending on their — and your — budget, students can tote everything from a simple pager that only receives phone numbers to a keyboard-equipped RIM BlackBerry 957 that not only sends and receives e-mail, but can also surf the Web.

And speaking of the Web, there are also PCS phones that can do this task, as well as the more mundane chore of good ol' fashioned phone calls.

Just how popular are these devices with students? Well, Motorola recently lent staff and students at a school in Palm Beach County, Florida, 30 new PageWriter T900s — a cassette-tape-sized pager that can send and receive e-mail using a tiny keyboard and a text-only flip-up screen.

The result? "Among the students we saw phenomenal call rates," says Jim Page,

Motorola's vice-president of business development. They made an average of 60 to 70 calls a day each. Mind you, Motorola was paying the bills.

And the staff were supposed to give back the pagers but became so addicted to wireless e-mail, "we allowed them to retain them."

Closer to home, 56 per cent of 1,000 Canadians over 18 recently surveyed by Decima Research believe pagers are useful for those aged 12–16, and 75 per cent approved of them for the over-16 crowd.

The reason: parents want to be able to keep in touch, whether it's to find out where their children are, or just tell them to pick up some milk on the way home.

Carriers are cashing in on the demand for wireless pagers and cellphones.

Bell Mobility will launch a $99 Back-to-School all-inclusive pager special that includes the pager itself, the activation fee and six months of airtime.

The $99 price tag is "a very strong price point with the student population," says Liz Scott, Bell Mobility's associate director of consumer paging acquisitions. "Research has also indicated that they like the bundled 'grab and go' concept."

Meanwhile, cheap PCS phones abound in Canada. Over at Fido, for instance, you can buy a Nokia 5190 PCS handset for $50 after rebate.

After you pay the $48 activation fee, you can buy airtime for as little as 10 cents a minute. And that's not the only good deal available in mobile phones. All of Canada's five carriers — Rogers AT&T, Bell Mobility, Telus Mobility, Clearnet, and Fido (Microcell) — offer similarly affordable PCS packages.

Is there a fly in this ointment? Well, actually there are two.

The first is the sheer task of deciding how much wireless technology your kids need, and don't need. The second is the Toronto District School Board's opposition to wireless devices, which are not allowed to be used on school property.

This said, the board does acknowledge that students on their way out of the building may use cellphones, [Gail] Nyberg [chair of the school board] says.

"We also make exceptions in emergencies, such as when a student is waiting for a transplant, and the hospital gives them a pager to keep them posted about available donor organs."

Otherwise, wireless technology isn't welcome in school.

As for what to buy, there are ways to decide whether or not your 12-year-old actually needs Rogers AT&T's new Web-browsing RIM BlackBerry 957 pager — as low as $28 per month on a two-year contract, plus $25–$50 airtime costs per month.

Your child will likely want a pager or mobile phone because "it's cool" or because "everyone else has one."

But you might ask yourself why they need one. For instance, if you just want to send short messages to your kids, then a traditional one-way pager is fine.

But if it's instant contact you want, then a mobile phone is your best choice.

The reason: two-way pagers like the RIM BlackBerry and Motorola's PageWriter do send and receive e-mail. However, these messages don't always get to the other person within minutes. In fact, sometimes they can be delayed for hours.

If you decide on a phone, you'll have to decide whether to buy a PCS-only handset, or a more expensive dual-mode PCS/cellular model.

Here's the rule of thumb: If your child is only going to use it in Toronto, you can get away with a cheap PCS-only digital phone. But if you want their phone to work in the country, then you'll need a dual-mode handset.

As for airtime packages, it's usually cheaper to sign up for regular service, in order to get lower per-minute rates.

However, the advantage of buying your airtime beforehand — using prepaid cards — is that it stops your child from racking up bills to the South Pole out of boredom. Once they've used up the airtime you've paid for, the phone simply stops working.

When it comes to surfing the Web on a phone or pager, unless your children need to keep on top of the stock market, or are willing to pay for this feature themselves, there's no reason to buy them a Web-enabled phone.

After Reading

RESPONDING

1. In your notebook, list a few characteristics you associate with students who carry pagers or cell phones. Compare your list with that of a partner. Be prepared to present ideas from your discussion to the class.
2. Explain whether the title of this **article** is appropriate and/or effective.

UNDERSTANDING

3. In a paragraph, explain one reason why Canadians, in the survey described in the seventh paragraph (on page 217), gave a higher rate of approval to the use of pagers by teenagers over 16 than by those 16 or younger.
4. Complete a chart comparing at least four of the products discussed in this **article**.

DEVICE	FEATURES	ADVANTAGES	DISADVANTAGES
One-way pagers			
Two-way pagers			

THINKING ABOUT LANGUAGE

5. a) With a partner, assess the balance between technical and everyday words and language in this article. How much technical knowledge does the reader need to understand the article? Write a shorter version of this article so that it is suitable for a reader with either more or less technical knowledge than that expected by the original.
   b) With a partner, revise your article, focusing on its **voice, diction,** and level of language. (See The Reference Shelf, pages 231–232.) Be prepared to submit your final draft.

EXTENDING

6. Write a letter to the chair of the Toronto District School Board explaining why you agree or disagree with the board's policy on pagers and cell phones as described in this article. Take your letter through the writing process in preparation for publication.

UNIT 4

> The Reference Shelf

The English Language

Note: For a more detailed discussion of grammar, punctuation, research, and writing, and for additional examples and exercises, students and teachers should refer to *The Harcourt Writer's Handbook* (Toronto: Harcourt Canada, 1999).

PARTS OF SPEECH

A **noun** names a person, place, or thing. Nouns are commonly classed as **common** (desk, chair), **proper** (Canada, Maria), **collective** (herd, class), **concrete** (pen, paper), and **abstract** (anger, honesty).

A **pronoun** takes the place of a noun. Pronouns agree with their antecedents (the words to which pronouns refer) in number and gender but take the case of the role they play in a sentence. Pronouns can be classed as **possessive** (my, her, your) or **relative** (that, which, who, whom, whose).

An **adjective** describes a noun or pronoun. Adjectives can be **positive** (good, fast, beautiful), **comparative** (better, faster, more beautiful), or **superlative** (best, fastest, most beautiful).

An **adverb** describes the how, when, or where of a verb, adjective, or other adverb. Examples:
He will talk proudly. (how) He will talk tomorrow. (when) He will talk here. (where)

A **verb** identifies the action or state of being in a sentence. Verbs can be classed as transitive, intransitive, and linking or copula.

Transitive verbs express an action toward an object (person or thing). Example:
Jason *wrote* the essay. (The action "wrote" is directed toward "essay.")

Intransitive verbs express action or tell something about the subject without directing the action toward a receiver (object). Example:
Mary *played* for fifteen minutes. (The action "played" is not directed toward an object or receiver.)

Copula verbs link or connect the subject with a noun, pronoun, or adjective in the predicate of a sentence. They express a state of being or becoming, rather than an action. Examples:

Juanita *is* a good student. (Juanita = good student)

Pierre Trudeau *remained* popular even after he retired from political life. (Pierre Trudeau = popular)

The baby *seemed* happy and contented. (baby = happy, contented)

A **verb tense** tells when the action occurs. The three most commonly used tenses in English are **present, past**, and **future**. Do not change needlessly from one tense to another. When writing about events that take place in the present, use verbs in the present tense. Similarly, when writing about events that occurred in the past, use verbs in the past tense.

Verb voice can be active or passive. **Active voice** expresses an action that is done by its subject. Example:

Mary *baked* the cake. (The subject "Mary" performs the action "baked.")

Passive voice expresses an action that is done by its subject. Example:

The cake *was baked* by Mary. (The subject "cake" receives the action "was baked.")

The passive voice is also used when the doer of the action is unknown or not important to the context. Example:

An announcement *was made* over the P.A. system. (The doer of the action is unknown.)

The active voice tends to be more direct, hard-hitting, and forceful; however, the passive voice is often used effectively to create an objective tone and clarity in reports, manuals, and scholarly essays.

Some Specific Verb Forms

An **infinitive** is a verb form preceded by the preposition "to." It can be used as a noun, adjective, or adverb. Examples:

To know her is *to love* her. (Both "to know" and "to love" are infinitives. As nouns, they act respectively as subject and subjective completion of the copula verb "is." As verbs, they express action or emotion and have an object "her.")

The cat *to adopt* is the tabby. ("To adopt" is an infinitive. As an adjective, it modifies the noun "cat.")

Ready *to go*, we loaded the car. ("To go" is an infinitive. As an adverb, it modifies the adjective "ready.")

A **gerund** is a verb form usually ending in "ing." Gerunds are verb forms used as nouns. Like other nouns, they can be modified by an adjective. Like other verbs, they can also be modified by adverbs. Example:

Floating lazily in the pool is my favourite summer pastime. ("Floating" is a gerund. As a noun, it is the subject of the predicate verb "is"; as a verb, it is modified by the adverb "lazily.")

A **participle** is a verb form. It can be in the present tense (ending in "ing") or in the past tense (often ending in "d" or "ed"). Participles are used as adjectives. Like other adjectives and verbs, they can be modified by an adverb. Examples:

Looking at the camera, Samantha smiled. ("Looking" is a present participle. As an adjective, it modifies "Samantha," the noun subject of the sentence; as a verb, it has an object, the prepositional phrase "at the camera.")

Freshly *baked* cookies are delicious. ("Baked" is a past participle. As an adjective, it modifies the noun "cookies"; as a verb, it is modified by the adverb "Freshly.")

Infinitive phrases include the infinitive form of a verb and its object or modifier. They can be used as nouns, adjectives, or adverbs. Examples:

To research your topic thoroughly is important. (In this sentence, "To research your topic thoroughly" acts as the noun subject of the verb "is." Within the infinitive phrase, "To research" has an object, the noun "topic," and is modified by the adverb "thoroughly.")

She is the player *to watch in the next game.* (Here, "to watch in the next game" acts as an adjective modifying the noun "player." Within the infinitive phrase, the prepositional phrase "in the next game" acts as an adverb modifying the infinitive "to watch.")

At noon, Rama went to the kitchen *to make himself a sandwich.* (Here, the infinitive phrase "to make himself a sandwich" is used as an adverb modifying the verb "went." Within the infinitive phrase, the infinitive "to make" has both a direct object, "sandwich," and an indirect object, "himself.")

Gerund phrases include the gerund form of a verb and its object or modifier and are used as nouns. Examples:

The gentle pattering was as welcome as the rain that caused it. (The gerund phrase "The gentle pattering" acts as a noun because it is the subject of the verb "was." Within the gerund phrase, "gentle" is an adjective modifying the noun part of the gerund "pattering.")

I feared *skiing down the mountain alone.* (The gerund phrase is used as the object of the verb "feared." The gerund "skiing" is modified by the adverb phrase "down the mountain" and by the adverb "alone.")

Participial phrases include the participle form of a verb (ending in "ing") and its object or modifier. They are used as adjectives. Example:

Seeing the cat, the dog barked loudly. (The participial phrase "Seeing the cat" acts as an adjective modifying "dog," the noun subject of the sentence. Within the participial phrase, "cat" acts as an object of the verb part of the participle "Seeing.")

Conjunctions

A **conjunction** is a word that joins words or groups of words used in the same way. Common conjunctions are *and, but, or, so, for, when.* A conjunction can also be a group of words: *as though, except that, in order that, so that, not only…but also.*

Conjunctions can be divided into two classes: **coordinating** and **subordinating**.

CONJUNCTION TYPE	DESCRIPTION	EXAMPLES
coordinating	combines words or groups of words used in the same way (principal clauses)	and, but, nor, or, so I was hungry *so* I ate the sandwich. He wasn't angry *or* sad. She lost the match, *but* she didn't feel disappointed.
subordinating	combines a main idea (principal clause) and a secondary or less important idea (subordinate clause)	although, if, provided that, whenever, because, unless, while, though *Whenever* she can't sleep, she reads a book.

Other common parts of speech include **prepositions** and **interjections**.

OTHER PARTS OF SPEECH	DESCRIPTION	EXAMPLES
preposition	relates a noun or pronoun to some other words in the sentence	at, behind, by, in, into, near, of, on, to, through, under, with
interjection	refers to a word or words that express emotion or thought, but are not essential to the sentence	alas, hey, oh dear, oops, ouch, well, wow

Words need to be joined together to make sense. Joined together, they are called sentences. It is easy to recognize a sentence: it begins with a capital letter, it ends with a period (or other end punctuation), and it contains at least one verb.

Sentences come in a variety of forms. Some sentences are simple; some are complex. All sentences have a **subject** and a **predicate**. Sentences may also include such elements as an **object**, a **subjective completion**, **prepositional** and **participial phrases**, and **principal** and **subordinate clauses**.

SENTENCE PART	DESCRIPTION	EXAMPLES
subject	indicates who or what performs the action of the predicate	*Marie* was furious. Her *brother* spilled coffee all over her new dress.
predicate	indicates what is said about the subject; the key word in the predicate is the verb	Sita *is* clever. The cat *slept* on the couch.
object	receives the action of a transitive verb	The banging of the door startled *the dog.*
subjective completion	describes the subject after a linking or copula verb	Sandy Wong is the *owner.* Jack looks *sad.*
prepositional phrase	begins with a preposition followed by a noun or pronoun (the object of the preposition) and any adjectives modifying that object	The man *in the car* is Josh's brother.
prepositional adjective phrase	modifies a noun or pronoun	The members *of the union* want to negotiate. (The adjective phrase "of the union" modifies the noun "members.") None *of us* had money. (The adjective phrase "of us" modifies the pronoun "none.")

(continued)

(continued)

SENTENCE PART	DESCRIPTION	EXAMPLES
prepositional adverb phrase	modifies a verb, adjective, or adverb	She asked *for water.* (The adverb phrase "for water" modifies the verb "asked.") Paul is good *at physics* but better *at geography.* Is the water warm enough *for swimming*? (The adverb phrase "for swimming" modifies the adverb "enough.")
principal clause (independent clause)	refers to the main idea and makes sense on its own	*She did not go home.*
subordinate clause (dependent clause)	refers to the secondary idea and does not make sense on its own	She did not go home *because she had choir practice.*

Types of Subordinate Clauses

Adjective clauses are subordinate clauses used to modify a noun or pronoun. Examples:

This is the woman *who stole my bag.* ("Who stole my bag" is an adjective clause modifying the noun "woman.")

Social psychology, *which is a field of psychology*, explores the effects of people on people. "Which is a field of psychology" is an adjective clause modifying "social psychology." (Note: Clauses that provide additional rather than essential information to the sentence are set off by commas.)

Adverb clauses are subordinate clauses used to modify a verb, adjective, or adverb. Examples:

After she read the letter, she tore it. ("After she read the letter" is an adverb clause modifying the verb "tore.")

Her singing voice is clearer *than it ever was.* ("Than it ever was" is an adverb clause modifying the adjective "clearer.")

Noun clauses are subordinate clauses used as a noun. Examples:

Mary thought *that this ruling was unfair to the team.* ("That this ruling was unfair to the team" is a noun clause acting as the object of the verb "thought.")

Whoever baked this cake certainly likes raisins and walnuts. ("Whoever baked this cake" is a noun clause and the subject of the sentence.)

ACTIVITY

Draw a table like this:

Principal Clause	Subordinate Adjective, Adverb, or Noun Clause

Look at these sentences. Decide which are the principal and subordinate clauses, and enter them into the appropriate columns of your table.

a) While he was walking along the beach, Ahmed found many interesting shells.

b) The man, who appeared to be in his fifties, was hit by the red car.

c) The match was called off because of rain.

d) Even though she was ill, she went to school.

e) If the bus arrives late, we will miss the opening ceremony.

f) Everyone was sad that Sue was leaving.

SENTENCE VARIETY

In order to create variety in your writing, you need to know about different sentence types, and orders.

SENTENCE VARIETY	DESCRIPTION	EXAMPLES
Type of Sentence by Purpose:		
assertive	makes statements	The band is making an announcement today.
interrogative	asks questions	Where is my book?
imperative	makes commands	Go away.
exclamatory	expresses emphatic or emotional utterances	Oh, be quiet!
Type of Sentence Structure:		
simple	has one principal clause with a subject and predicate	Mary is the best player.
compound	has two or more principal clauses, which need connecting words	Mei Lin felt sad, but Suk Ying was happy to be leaving.
complex	has one principal clause and one or more subordinate clauses, which need a connecting word to relate the subordinate clause(s) to the principal clause	I was late because I missed the appointment and had to wait an hour before the doctor was free.
compound-complex	contains two principal clauses and at least one subordinate clause. This is the most unwieldy and difficult sentence structure to use correctly. However, the ability to combine ideas and subordinate some of the ideas is a skill that demonstrates a sophisticated control of language and ideas, and it allows for subtle and precise emphasis on certain ideas in a piece of writing.	The doctor treated the cancer that threatened the man's life, and the dentist treated the toothache that caused the man great pain. ("The doctor treated the cancer" and "the dentist treated the toothache" are both principal clauses; "that threatened his life" and "that caused him great pain" are both adjectival subordinate clauses, modifying the nouns "cancer" and "toothache," respectively.)

(continued)

(continued)

SENTENCE VARIETY	DESCRIPTION	EXAMPLES
Sentence Order:		
natural	places the subject before the predicate	The birds flew away.
inverted	places the predicate before the subject	Behind the social persona lurked an evil mind.
split	places part of the predicate before the subject (or between the subject and the verb) for emphasis or effect	When we least expect it to, life often surprises us with good fortune.

SENTENCE ERRORS

Writers often make errors. The following table lists some common sentence errors and shows how they can be corrected.

SENTENCE ERROR	DESCRIPTION	EXAMPLES	HOW TO FIX IT
fragment	a group of words, punctuated as a sentence that lacks either a subject or a complete verb	Desperately running to catch the bus. The rhythmic pattern in the poem "Catalogue."	Maya was desperately running to catch the bus. The rhythmic pattern in the poem "Catalogue" creates the effect of movement.
run-on	too many complete sentences or thoughts joined together as a single sentence	I got a lot of work done today I finished the reading and I went to the library and I started my assignment but I didn't fill in the chart because I couldn't find it.	I got a lot of work done today. I finished the reading, and I went to the library. I started my assignment, but I didn't fill in the chart because I couldn't find it.

(continued)

(continued)

SENTENCE ERROR	DESCRIPTION	EXAMPLES	HOW TO FIX IT
comma splice	a comma is used to separate two main clauses or two complete thoughts that are not connected by a connecting word	I liked the story by Ray Bradbury, it deals with the destructiveness of war.	I liked the story by Ray Bradbury. It deals with the destructiveness of war.
subject–verb disagreement	the rule that singular subjects take singular verbs and plural subjects take plural verbs is broken	Jean and Maxine is starting a business. The distance between the two bus stops are two kilometres.	Jean and Maxine *are* starting a business. The distance between the two bus stops *is* two kilometres.
pronoun–antecedent disagreement	pronouns do not agree with their antecedents in gender (masculine, feminine, or neuter), number (singular or plural), or person (first person, second person, or third person)	Everyone must do their part. One of the women had lost their job.	Everyone must do *his or her* part. One of the women had lost *her* job.

LANGUAGE AND STYLE

Formal and Informal Language

When you are writing, you need to decide the appropriate level of language to use. The language of a report or set of instructions, for example, needs to be clear and helpful to the reader, and dialogue in a film needs to be appropriate to the character speaking.

Levels of Language

Slang is very informal (and often quickly outmoded) vocabulary and language patterns used by particular groups or in special informal contexts. It is usually not appropriate to use slang in formal written work, but it is often used in fiction to show character and create mood.

A **colloquialism** is also an informal, conversational expression that is often inappropriate to use in formal written work. Many dictionaries will tell you whether an expression is considered slang or colloquial.

Jargon is specialized vocabulary used by a profession, trade, or group. It must be used carefully in oral and written work because it can all too easily obscure meaning or mislead or exclude non-specialists.

Good writing uses simple, clear language — called Plain Language (see below) — and avoids the use of slang, colloquialisms, and jargon.

Dialect is a local version of a language, with its own vocabulary and sentence structure.

We use **Standard Canadian English** in our schools. This is the oral and written English used by a broad range of Canadian society (including government, medicine, law, science, business, and the media). Standard Canadian English follows accepted rules and practices of grammar, usage, spelling, and punctuation.

Style

Using Variety for Rhetorical Effect

In fiction and poetry, writers use different words that refer to the same person, place, or thing to explore shades of meaning. Similarly, in advertisements, poetry, and fiction, spelling and grammar are sometimes used incorrectly to catch the reader's interest or to make a point. For instance, "night" appears as "nite" on some signs and posters. In the excerpt from the play *Leaving Home*, Mary's character largely speaks in ungrammatical English to reflect the fact that she has received minimal education. For example: "I just wish to goodness he had more t'ought, your father. The supper'll dry up if he don't hurry" (page 156).

Plain Language Style

When to Use a Plain Language Style

Plain Language Style is used when the clear and accurate communication of information is the main goal of the writing. This is especially important in media such as reports, instructions, recipes, warnings, and policies.

In reports and instructions (e.g., see the instructions for "Setting Up a Printer," pages 42–44), writers try to use the same word consistently to refer to the same person, place, or thing so that the reader does not become confused. The consistent use of the same word for the same thing in reports and instructions is one of the aspects of a Plain Language Style.

Some rules of using a Plain Language Style:
- Use words that your reader is likely to know. Keep technical words and jargon to a minimum. Provide a definition of any word the reader is not likely to be familiar with.
- Omit unnecessary words.
- Organize the information you are communicating in a logical manner.
- Use parallel structures in a list of instructions to make them easier to follow.
- Use a clear layout, icons, and illustrations to make your document clear and easy to read.

You can find out more about "Plain Language Style" by using the phrase to create an Internet search.

SPELLING

Good spelling is important to communicate ideas and information clearly and accurately. Incorrect spelling will distract your reader from the ideas you are expressing. In some cases, it may even confuse the reader about what is being referred to or said.

Following is a list of common sources of spelling errors in people's writing:
- differences in American and Canadian spelling (e.g., *color* is American; *colour* is Canadian)
- new and unfamiliar technical, business, and literary terms
- names that have different spellings (Mckay, MacKay, etc.)
- homophones (there, their, and they're)
- frequently confused words (accept, except)
- correct placement of apostrophes (do'nt for don't)

How to Improve Your Spelling*

One way to improve your spelling is to look for spelling patterns. There are three common sets of spelling patterns in English:

---

* Excerpted from Lynn Archer, Cathy Costello, and Debbie Harvey, *Reading and Writing for Success* (Toronto: Harcourt Brace & Company, Canada, 1997), pages 225-226.

- **Sound Patterns:** Look for words, or parts of words, that sound alike: **sh**ip, **sh**ore, **sh**ampoo; br**ead**, h**ead**.
- **Meaning Patterns:** Look for words that share similar or related meanings: **tw**o, **tw**ice, **tw**ins; **visi**ble, **visi**on, **vis**ual. These are sometimes called word families.
- **Function Patterns:** Look for words that are the same part of speech. For example, you add -**ed** to most verbs to make the past tense, no matter how the ending is pronounced: load**ed**, call**ed**, jump**ed**.

If there is a word that you always have trouble spelling, see if it fits a spelling pattern that will help you remember the correct spelling.

TECHNOLOGY TIP

Computer spell checkers have made it easier to pick up obvious spelling errors that may slip by when you proofread your writing. But a spell checker does not know when you have used **there** instead of **their**, or **right** instead of **write**.

Keep a list of the words you misspell. Look them up in a dictionary and write them correctly in an alphabetical list. Then use your list for reference when you are writing. If you put a check mark beside a word in your list each time you find that you have spelled it correctly without looking it up, you will have a record of how your spelling is improving.

Make up your own memory aids. Sentences, poems, or phrases about spelling patterns and odd ways of pronouncing words can help you remember how to spell difficult words. Try this memory aid:

"**i** before **e** except after **c** or when sounded like **a** as in **neighbour** and **weigh**."
Common exceptions: **neither, height, weird, either, seize, ancient, foreign, leisure, forfeit**.

If you are not sure how to spell a word, follow these steps.

1. Think about the way the word looks. Write it down the way you think it might be spelled. If it does not look right, try again.
2. Look up your best version of the word in the dictionary. Some sounds can be spelled in more than one way. If you cannot find a word in a dictionary, there may be a different way to spell one of the sounds in the word. See the following chart:

Sound (consonants)	Different Spellings
f	**f**ish, **ph**ysical
sk	**sk**ip, **sc**are, **sch**ool
s	**s**oft, **c**ivil, **ps**ychology
sh	**sh**ip, **ch**ef
k	**k**ick, **c**andy, **ch**emistry, **qu**iche
r	**r**oof, **wr**inkle
n	**n**ow, **kn**ife, **gn**ome, **pn**eumonia, **mn**emonic

Sound (vowels)	Different Spellings
a (as in c**a**ve)	tr**a**ce, tr**ai**n, d**ay**
e (as in m**e**)	th**e**se, t**ea**m, s**ee**, k**ey**
o (as in g**o**)	b**o**ne, c**oa**t, t**oe**, l**ow**

3. When you have found the word in the dictionary, check the pronunciation and read the definitions. Knowing more about the word may help you remember it.

4. Practise spelling the word: look at it spelled correctly, and then cover the word and write it down. Check to see if you spelled it correctly.

PUNCTUATION

End stops such as the **period** (.), the **question mark** (?), and the **exclamation mark** (!) are used to end a sentence. Other punctuation marks (**commas**, **dashes**, and so on) perform different functions.

A **comma** (,) is used after an introductory word, phrase, or clause; to separate items in a list; after the introduction to direct speech; and to make the meaning of the sentence clear.

A **dash** (—) is used before or around a definition or clarification of a word, phrase, or idea. For example:

In a democracy, a premise of jurisprudence—the science or philosophy of law—is that everyone is equal before the law.

A **colon** (:) is used to introduce a list, an example, a quotation, or an explanation. The colon is also used in dramatic dialogue to indicate that a character begins speaking.

A **semicolon** (;) is used to join principal or independent clauses in a sentence. This use is sometimes referred to as a "soft" period. It is used in this way with some transitional words and phrases. Examples:

Patty likes to act; her sister gets stage fright. (The semicolon here replaces a period because the two ideas are very closely connected.)

Rajiiv felt shy; however, he soon made some new friends. (There are several transitional words and phrases like "however" that usually require a semicolon when used.)

Alana, Eric, and Tina voted for Kelly; Claude, Francine, and Alison voted for Helga. (The use of commas in the two principal clauses makes the semicolon useful for clarity.)

The semicolon is also used between items in a series when the items themselves contain commas. Example:

My painting class will meet on Monday, October 16; Tuesday, October 24; Monday, October 31; and Friday, November 1.

A **hyphen** (-) is used to combine words or parts of words to form an expression that needs to be seen as one word. Examples:

ex-ballplayer, run-on sentence

Quotation marks (" ") are used to indicate direct speech and the titles of short poems, stories, and articles. **Direct speech** requires quotation marks; **indirect speech** does not. Examples:

Direct: "Do you have a loonie?" Dad asked. "I need one for the parking meter."

Indirect: My dad asked me for a loonie for the parking meter.

Italics or <u>underlining</u> are used to indicate the titles of books, full-length plays, newspapers, and magazines. Example:

We read an article called "Pampered Teens Don't Have It Bad" in *The Toronto Star.*

Parentheses ( ) are used around a word, phrase, or idea that could be left out without destroying the sense of the writing. These words, phrases, or ideas are sometimes called "parenthetical." They are also used around references and notes inserted into a text. Examples:

My favourite drink is chocolate milk (real chocolate, real milk).

Many British novelists have dealt with the theme of social inequities (see Austen, Dickens).

Ellipsis dots (...) are used by writers to show that part of a quotation has been left out or to indicate a pause in dialogue. Examples:

The prime minister, who was in China at the time, said the report was nonsense.

with ellipses becomes

The prime minister...said the report was nonsense.

"Tell you the truth, Ben. We always figured you'd be the one to land in trouble, if anyone did. I don't mean that as an insult. You're more ... like your father" (from *Leaving Home*, page 156).

Reading and Researching

READING STRATEGIES

Backgrounds of Readers and Writers Influence the Interpretation and Meaning of Texts

With some texts (e.g., a bus schedule), every reader will get the same information and understanding. With most texts, however, readers will not get exactly the same meaning because of differences in personal experiences and prior knowledge. For instance, a student who has had similar experiences of fear will understand "The Best Kind of Fear" by J. William Knowles (page 22) in a different way than will a student without that experience. Readers' personal experiences and prior knowledge affect their understanding of and preferences for texts. Because class and group discussions of texts draw on a wide range of experience and knowledge, they can help to refine your comprehension of what you have read.

Similarly, each writer writes from his or her own personal experience and knowledge. Shakespeare could not write about airplanes because they were not part of his experience. An author's view of people, emotions, and values will reflect his or her own experience and knowledge. For this reason, it is always important that you read critically in order to evaluate the information and ideas in a text. In some cases, you may alter your ideas in light of new information in a text; in other cases, you may disagree with a text because it does not seem valid in light of your experience.

Using Prior Knowledge and Experiences

You can bring prior knowledge and experiences from your own life, from personal reading, and from your previous studies to help create both interest in and understanding of what you read. You might bring previous knowledge about

- the subject of the piece
- the issues in the piece
- the author
- the author's style and themes
- the setting (both time and place)
- subject-specific information (science, mathematics, history, geography, another language, technology, art, music, drama)
- vocabulary

Predicting

Predicting is a skill that makes you think ahead before you read. Whether or not your predictions are correct doesn't matter as much as the interaction you are having with the text. Once again, this kind of activity can increase your interest in what might, at first, seem to be a boring text.

Before Reading

- Use the title to predict the content of the text and its purpose.
- Look at any illustrations or graphical elements to establish possible events (fiction) or points the writer is making (non-fiction).
- Read a summary or cover blurb to predict what might happen, who is involved (fiction), or the writer's point of view (non-fiction).
- Use the vocabulary in the first few lines to predict the author's style, the time in which the piece is set, the difficulty of the piece (fiction and non-fiction), or the specific subject matter to be discussed (non-fiction).
- Read the first one or two paragraphs to predict the narrator's tone, the initial problem in the story, something about the characters (fiction), the audience for whom it was written (fiction and non-fiction), and the thesis or point of view (non-fiction).

During Reading

- Predict what decisions the characters will make (fiction).
- Forecast how the setting might change and the effect this could have on the action (fiction).
- Try to foresee changes in the direction of the plot (fiction).
- Predict what arguments or details a writer might use to support important points (non-fiction).

After Reading

Questioning can help you create and maintain interest in what you are reading. Wondering on paper (which is really what questions are) also helps you decide what you need and want to know. You can use questions at any time before, during, or after your reading to help you predict.

Questions are useful to help you recall, restate, reflect on, and analyze what you have read.

Questions to help you recall might include the 5Ws and 1H: who, what, where, when, why, and how (the same questions that are used for creating a news report).

To restate, try using one of the following to start your question:
How could I
- rephrase?
- reword?
- explain?
- illustrate?

To help you reflect, think about some of the following question starters:
- What would happen if...?
- What would I have done...?
- What else could have happened...?
- If I could choose one part that makes me feel ... what would it be?
- Which character do I most identify with?
- I wonder if the writer...?
- How is this like...?

You could use some of the following questions to help you analyze:
- What evidence do I have that...?
- What conclusions can I draw...?
- What reasons are there for...?
- What can I infer from...?
- What arguments can I select...?
- How do I know that...?
- What proofs do I have that...?
- What do I need to find out about...?

Understanding Strategies Used in Writing Prose and Poetry

Writers are often asked, "Did you mean to...?" Yes, writers do think of symbols, image patterns, metaphors, irony, contrasts, and a host of other things when they write. Some start their work with an image or symbol at the core; others bring it in as they draft and redraft their work.

For readers to draw out the greatest meaning from a text, it is important that they be aware of how writers use the tools of their trade and notice the writers' techniques and how their writing has been crafted.

Following are some tools that writers use for both prose and poetry:

- **Syntax** is the structure of a sentence or the way a sentence is put together.
- An **allusion** is a reference to a well-known character, place, or story or to another literary work. For example, "The young player threw the baseball with Herculean strength." The allusion is to the great strength of the Greek hero Heracles. (Note: Hercules is the Roman name for Heracles.)
- An **oxymoron** juxtaposes (places side by side) two opposites to create a vivid image. Examples: "crashing silence," "loving hate," "bittersweet."
- **Contrast** is used to show how two or more characters, objects, or ideas are different.
- **Hyperbole** is a fancy name for exaggeration. It can be used seriously to create in a reader's mind a picture "larger than life," or it can be used comically to make a reader laugh.
- **Understatement** is the opposite of hyperbole. It shows something as much less important than it is. The effect of understatement is often ironic or sarcastic.
- Three types of **irony** are verbal irony, dramatic irony, and situational irony. **Verbal irony** occurs when the real or intended meaning of a word, phrase, or sentence is different from what the speaker of that word, phrase, or sentence intended. A different kind of irony, occurring in fiction and drama, is **dramatic irony**. This takes place when the reader or viewer shares knowledge with the writer that a character does not have. The character will then say or do something that foreshadows what the audience knows will happen but that the character has no idea about. The character speaks more truly than he or she can possibly know. **Situational irony** occurs when what actually happens is different from what is expected by the reader or viewer.
- A **symbol** is an object, person, or action that is used to represent some other idea, principle, object, theme, or character. A country's flag is the symbol of

that country; each hockey team has its symbol on its jersey. Many names are symbolic. Many of those names are also allusions to famous people.

Reading Prose

Plot

Plot does not always drive a piece of fiction. A story may be character driven or thematically driven. No matter what drives a story, there is always some kind of plot, however thin.

Jack Hodgins, a famous Canadian novelist, identifies six things a plot-driven story must have:

- a main character (protagonist) we care about or are interested in
- knowledge that this character has a goal and a strong reason for achieving it
- obstacles that stand in the way of the character's goal
- a sense that each event is somehow the cause of the event that follows
- conflicts that intensify to the point where something has to break, which then causes the main character's life to turn a corner
- a resolution that allows the reader to feel the story has come to a satisfying end*

The ways writers approach story writing are as varied as the writers themselves. A writer may outline the whole story before it is written, or a writer may develop a story from an idea about a character, a theme, or a situation.

Setting versus Scene

The word **setting** is most often used by students to mean the place or time in which a story is set. Writers, however, often use the word to describe a writing technique, that is, "telling about" a story. The word **scene** means "showing" the story. Most writers agree that "showing" is more effective than "telling."

To "show" a story
- use description
- appeal to the five senses
- include dialogue
- include action

Example 1

Once there was a boy named Arthur. He lived a long time ago. He had a magic birth that he didn't know about, and he was raised by a kind old man. Arthur was responsible for his stepbrother's horse, sword, and lance. One day, right before a competition, Arthur forgot his stepbrother's sword. He didn't have time to go back home before his brother's event, but he had seen a

---

* Jack Hodgins, "Specialized Tool: Fiction," in *A Passion for Narrative* (Toronto: McClelland & Stewart, 1993), page 126.

sword sticking out of a stone, so he ran over and pulled it out. After that he became king because the person who could pull the sword from the stone was destined to become king.

Example 2

"Where is my sword, little brother?"

Arthur felt a great weight growing in his stomach. He thought quickly. "I must have left it on my horse, sir." But he knew he hadn't. He sighed loudly. Ever since he was a child, Arthur had been forgetful. His stepfather would always pat him on the back, smile, and say, "That's all right, Wart. Someday you'll remember all right."

But today, Arthur knew even his stepfather wouldn't be so kind. This was, after all, his stepbrother's one chance to prove his skills as a young knight. Arthur forced a smile and swallowed the lump in his throat. He felt his face flame; he tasted the biting acid of fear.

His brother spoke before Arthur could think any more. "I'm going to make sure my name is on the contestants' list, Arthur. When you have my sword, bring it to me in front of the striped tent"—he pointed—"over there."

As he watched his brother lead his horse toward the tent, Arthur remembered where he had seen a sword. Maybe he could borrow it just for the afternoon. He raced into the woods overlooking the fairgrounds. The sword was resting in a stone. Its hilt reflected the shafts of light shining through the trees. Arthur could smell success. He wiped the sweat from his palms, spat into them, and wrapped his small hands around the handle. He pulled, but the sword stuck. He tried again and thought he felt some movement. On the third try, the sword came out of the stone, so hard that Arthur landed—thwap!—on his rear.

ACTIVITIES

1. How does the second example above "show" the story rather than "tell about" it?
2. Look back at one of the stories you have read from this anthology. Examine the plot of the story using Jack Hodgins's six aspects of plot. When you have looked at each point, decide whether the story you have examined is plot driven. What aspects of a plot-driven story does it have? What is it missing?

Characters

As readers, how do we learn about **character?**
- the narrator tells us
- the main character tells us herself or himself
- other characters tell us
- the character's own behaviour tells us

What makes one character different from another?
- appearance
- speech (level of language, dialect, speech rhythms, pet words)
- action (physical reactions to things; body language; facial expressions; habits like a cough, throat clearing, giggling, talking constantly when nervous)
- thoughts and opinions

ACTIVITY

Choose one story you have read from this anthology. Make a four-column chart with headings: "What the narrator tells us," "What the character tells us," "What other characters tell us," "What the character's behaviour tells us." Fill in the chart for one main character in the story. (Note: You may not be able to find something for every column. If you can't fill in every column, explain why not.)

Narrative Point of View

There are five main **points of view** a writer can use in fiction.

NARRATOR	DESCRIPTION	COMMENTS
first person involved	the narrator is the main character in the story	• a very personal type of narration that makes the reader feel involved with the character who is telling the story • the reader should be clear about the amount of time that has passed between the events and the telling of them • the reader should be able to decide whether the narrator has changed or developed since the events took place

(continued)

NARRATOR	DESCRIPTION	COMMENTS
		• the reader must decide over the course of the story whether the narrator is trustworthy (whether everything he or she is saying is the truth)
first person observer	the narrator may be a minor character in the story and have some role to play in the plot, or he or she may be observing the action from a distance, unknown to the characters in the story	• the writer creates some distance between the reader and the events by using this type of narrator • the reader must question whether this narrator is telling the truth about the events as he or she saw them or was involved in them
third person omniscient	the narrator knows all, sees all, and tells all	• this type of narrator is the most reliable since he or she can see inside and tell us, the readers, about every character's thoughts
third person limited	the narrator tells the story from the perspective of one or two main characters, but does not tell the thoughts of anyone else	• this narrator has the same effect as the first person narrator since we feel very close to the character whose story is being told • at times we feel as if we are inside that character's head, but the narrator can also step back from the character or action • this narrator is less reliable as a source of total information than the omniscient narrator

(continued)

(continued)

NARRATOR	DESCRIPTION	COMMENTS
third person reporter	the narrator tells the facts, without going into any of the characters' heads	• the reader feels very distanced from this narrator as he or she cannot get into the heads of any of the characters and the reader can hear only what is being reported. This limits our understanding of motivations and emotions. • this narrator is only as reliable as his or her observations. Remember, he or she can't be in every place at one time, and so we might be missing some details.

Story Forms

There are many story forms. Some have become so popular that they are considered **genres**. Examples of genres are:

- science fiction
- fantasy
- detective fiction
- romance
- historical fiction

Some other story forms include:

- adventures
- parodies
- quests
- tall tales
- legends
- myths
- fairy tales
- fables
- parables
- sequels
- prequels
- humour
- choose-your-own-adventures

Reading Poetry

Types of Poetry

A **narrative** poem
- tells a story
- may take the form of a ballad
- is generally organized in stanzas with regular rhythm and **rhyme scheme**

A **lyric** poem
- conveys strong emotions and impressions

Although words to songs are called lyrics, lyric poetry is not necessarily set to music.

Used frequently by Shakespeare, **blank verse**
- has a regular rhythm pattern
- does not have a regular rhyme scheme

A **free verse** poem
- has very few restrictions
- has no set rhyme, rhythm pattern, or line length

A **sonnet**
- has 14 lines of iambic pentameter verse
- is either Petrarchan, Shakespearean, or modern

Petrarchan (or Italian) sonnets
- consist of an octave (eight lines of regular rhyme scheme) followed by a sestet (six lines of regular rhyme scheme, ending in a rhyming couplet)
- usually develop their idea or mood in the octave and change or comment upon it in the sestet
- have a typical rhyme scheme of abba, abba, cde, cde

Shakespearean (or English) sonnets
- consist of three quatrains (four-line stanzas with a regular rhyme scheme) followed by a rhyming couplet
- usually develop their idea or mood through the quatrains and change or summarize it in the rhyming couplet
- have a typical rhyme scheme of abab, cdcd, efef, gg

A **modern sonnet** may adapt and change the traditional structures or rhyme schemes.

The **haiku** and the **tanka** are two types of traditional Japanese poetry. Both have very specific forms, and both revolve around a strong image. The **haiku**
- consists of three unrhymed lines: five syllables in the first, seven syllables in the second, and five in the third
- has a final line that resonates with more than one level of meaning
- is often about nature and the passage of time

The **tanka**
- consists of five unrhymed lines with a total of 31 syllables
- has the following format: lines 1 and 3 have five syllables each; lines 2, 4, and 5 have seven syllables each
- is often about love

Concrete poetry is arranged in a shape that enhances or reflects the topic.

Imagistic poetry
- tends to be fairly short
- focuses on one or two central images

Haiku is a type of imagistic poetry (although it was invented long before the imagist writers popularized imagistic poetry).

Sound

Authors use many devices to manipulate the sounds of their writing. Here are some devices you should know. (Note: These are all elements of rhetoric; they are tools you can use not only when analyzing reading but also when you are doing your own writing.)

- Imitating an **accent** from a different culture can be an effective way to distinguish one character from another or to denote a feeling, mood, or culture. Be careful, though; overuse of an accent can make a character laughable or can perpetuate stereotypes.
- **Alliteration** is the repetition of the initial sound in a series of words (luscious lying lips). The words do not have to be in sequence but should be relatively close to each other to sustain an effect.
- **Assonance** is the internal rhyming of vowel sounds. ("When shall we three meet again?"—William Shakespeare)
- **Cacophony** is a mixture of harsh, discordant, or dissonant sounds. ("All day cars mooed and shrieked / Hollered and bellowed and wept"—James Reaney)
- Like assonance, **consonance** is internal rhyme or repetition, except using consonants, not vowels. ("The blood-dimmed tide is loosed"—Willliam Butler Yeats)
- **Dialect**, such as a patois, is an effective tool for characterization but, like accents, must be used sparingly to avoid stereotyping.
- When a line of poetry continues on to the next line without any end marks, it is called **enjambment**:

    And no one will know of the war, not one
    Will care at last when it is done.—Sara Teasdale

- **Euphony** is a blending of sounds to make a musical, lyrical sound.
- When words make or represent a sound, they are examples of **onomatopoeia** (e.g., boom, boff, bang, clang).

- An echo effect can be set up with the **repetition** of a word or series of words. If an entire stanza is repeated, it is called a **refrain** or **chorus**. (Watch that you don't overuse repetition; it can get tiresome and trite.)
- **Rhyme** is an obvious way of drawing attention to sound. End rhyme and internal rhyme are both effective ways to echo sounds.

Line Divisions

There are many reasons for dividing lines, other than rhythm and rhyme. When you are reading or writing a poem, consider these reasons for grouping words into a line:

- to contain a complete thought
- to set off a strong image
- to emphasize a word or phrase
- to complete a thought started in a previous line
- to use to advantage a grammatical structure (phrase or clause)
- to create irony or a reversal of expectation

ACTIVITY

Following is a poem that has been written in prose form. Work with a partner and divide the poem into lines and stanzas, thinking about rhythm, sound, content, and function. Compare your form of the poem with those of your classmates. Be ready to defend your line breaks.

"Jabberwocky"
Lewis Carroll

'Twas brillig, and the slithy toves did gyre and gimble in the wabe; all mimsy were the borogoves, and the mome raths outgrabe. "Beware the Jabberwock, my son! The jaws that bite, the claws that catch! Beware the Jubjub bird, and shun the frumious Bandersnatch!"

Close Reading of a Text

The demand for the analytical reading of texts increases as you progress through your schooling. It is important that you know how to read a text closely in order to discover details in it that you might miss in a cursory reading.

When reading literature, one of the most important concepts to establish is the **theme** of the piece. A theme is different from a **subject**. The subject is what the piece is about; the theme is what the author is saying about the subject. There may be more than one theme in a piece of writing.

You can use sets of questions (heuristics) such as the following to help you establish the theme:
• What is the text about?
• What is the author saying about that subject?
or
• Who wins?
• Who loses?
• What is won?
• What is lost?
• Whose side is the author on?

Examining the answers to these questions may help you to discover the meanings and ideas the author is conveying through his or her work.

Creating a Theme Statement

When creating your theme statement, put your ideas about the theme in complete sentences. A single word can often capture the subject of a piece of writing, but not the theme. Try starting your sentence with "The author is saying that...."

ACTIVITY

As a class, read one drama, poem, or short story in this textbook. Using one of the sets of questions above, come to an understanding of what the author is saying to his or her audience. In a small group, discuss your ideas about the theme and come to a consensus. Present your theme (and any differing opinions) to the class. Discuss the similarities among the themes that various groups have identified.

Additional Tools for Close Reading

Some elements appear in all types of literature. Much like the elements of design in visual arts, these elements are tools writers use to emphasize or develop the theme. Following is a list of these elements.

Figures of speech—including simile, metaphor, alliteration, and onomatopoeia

Rhetoric—imagery, word choice, sentence structure, and diction

Structure—the way the writing is put together

Prose
- chapters
- divisions within chapters
- sequence of events

Poetry
- stanzas
- typographical layout
- line divisions
- groups of stanzas (sometimes called "chapters," "books," or simply given numbers)

Drama
- acts
- scenes
- prologues and epilogues

Setting

Time
- era
- time of year
- time of day

Space
- real or fantasy world
- country or city
- dark or light
- enclosed or open space

Character
- what the character does and says, about himself or herself and others
- what others say about him or her
- how the character reacts to others and to a variety of situations
- what the narrator says about him or her
- his or her physical features and psychological makeup
- what motivates him or her

Perspective—the type of narration (in novels, short stories, and poems) and the way we see the action (in drama)

You can create your own heuristic by asking yourself, How does any single design element or combination of design elements help emphasize or develop the theme?

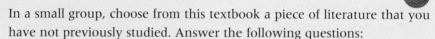

ACTIVITY

In a small group, choose from this textbook a piece of literature that you have not previously studied. Answer the following questions:
- Which one or two elements are the most evident in the author's work?
- How do these elements develop and change throughout the work?
- What pattern(s), if any, emerge(s)?
- How does each of these elements support or emphasize the theme of the writer's work?

Write a thesis about the work based on the theme and the elements you have identified.

BIAS

Detecting Bias

Unintentional bias is often present in written or media works. When you are reading or viewing these works, you can detect bias by watching for stereotypes, determining what interests are being served, and identifying the underlying assumptions and values behind the ideas and information presented.

Avoiding Bias

To avoid bias in your own work
- use inclusive language (e.g., firefighter instead of fireman)
- use current terminology (e.g., Aboriginal peoples rather than Indians)
- avoid stereotypes
- do not be afraid to identify the assumptions or values you bring to the work

RESEARCH STRATEGIES: GENERATING IDEAS

In ancient times, speakers would be given a topic on which they would be expected to speak convincingly without notes. One useful technique they all knew was called the **classical topoi**. These were simple questions the speakers asked themselves to help them first to think about their topics and then to generate and organize their ideas. These questions are

- What is it?
- What is it like?
- What is it unlike?
- Where did it come from?
- What can come of it?
- What has been said about it?

Before you visit the library or surf the Internet, figure out what you already know about your subject and what you need to know. Using the classical topoi, you can generate even more questions to help you narrow and refine your research focus.

WHAT IS IT?	WHERE DID IT COME FROM?
• Is it living or dead? • Is it animate or inanimate? • Is it animal, vegetable, mineral? • What does it look like? • How does it work? • Is it real or imagined? • Who or what uses it?	• Where or when did it happen? • Who or what made it? • How was it invented? • How long has it existed? • What causes it? • Is it still going on?
WHAT IS IT LIKE?	**WHAT CAN COME OF IT?**
• Is it a part of something bigger? • How is it the same as...? • Is there something similar that came before or comes after?	• Can it change? • Can it be changed? • Will it happen again? • How will it happen? • If it disappears, what will happen? • What happened as a result of it? • Was its effect positive or negative? • Would people welcome it again? • Would people try to prevent it?
WHAT IS IT UNLIKE?	**WHAT HAS BEEN SAID ABOUT IT?**
• Is it opposite to something? • How is it different from...? • Is it unique?	• Who said it? • What was said? • What statistics have been collected on it?

ACTIVITY

Choose one of the following topics and, using as many of the questions above (page 253) as you can, make a list of what you already know about the topic. Make another list of what you would like to find out. Organize your notes in a way that will be useful when you have to go back and reread them.

infatuation	perogies	Special Olympics	pow wow	Ottawa
generation gap	Scrabble	snowboarding	music videos	

The Good, the Bad, and the Misinformed

How to Find "Good" Information

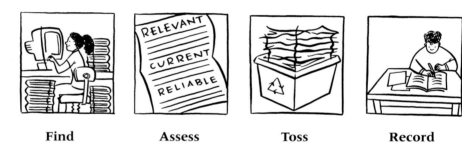

| Find | Assess | Toss | Record |

Find

Find the locations of possible information.

- Make a list of things you want to find out.
- Start with very general resources, such as dictionaries, encyclopedias, atlases, indexes (any or all of these could be electronic sources, depending on your library). Then move to more specific sources, such as books, magazines, periodicals, newspapers, CD-ROMs, non-print resources (videotapes, audiotapes, artwork, and so on), and other electronic resources.
- If using books, skim tables of contents and indexes to find out whether your topic is listed.
- Scan articles for titles, illustrations, subtitles, and captions that include references to your topic.
- Skim read to establish the amount and usefulness of the available information.
- Save resources that look as if they will have the information you need.

Assess

Assess the resources you have saved.

- Look for information that is verified in several sources. Assessing is particularly important for information that comes from the Internet.
- Decide whether the information is useful, given the topic you've chosen.
- Ask yourself whether the resource presents a complete view or a one-sided view of your topic.
- Search out information that is clear, understandable, and at a level appropriate for you.
- Check whether the information is up-to-date.

Toss

Begin to weed and toss out information.

- Discard information that can be found in only one source and for which you cannot find support anywhere else.
- If the author is not reliable, do not use his or her information. (Ask a librarian, teacher, or other experts if you don't know about the author's reliability.)
- Do not include anything that suggests racism, sexism, homophobia, or other forms of prejudice and bias.
- Discard information from old research or outdated sources.
- Do not include vague or overgeneralized information.
- Avoid personal opinion pieces that don't contain facts.

Record

Begin to record information.

- Record information in an organized way (on cue cards, in a special notebook, in an electronic file).
- Keep accurate records (including page numbers) of quotations you have used or ideas you have paraphrased.
- Put ideas in your own words to guarantee that you understand them, but be sure you document their source. *Do not plagiarize.*

RESEARCH DOCUMENTATION

To avoid *plagiarism* (using someone else's work and claiming it as your own), it is necessary to cite the sources of information and ideas in your work.

If you summarize or paraphrase someone else's ideas in your writing, do not use quotation marks around the reference, but do indicate the source of the idea, either in a parenthetical note following the reference or in a footnote or endnote.

If you use a direct quotation from someone else in your writing, integrate it into your text with an introductory sentence or phrase, and use quotation marks around the exact words of the person you are quoting. For example:

The Canadian Encyclopedia reports that Pierre Elliott Trudeau was born in...

We see Calpurnia's fear for Caesar's safety when she says, "You shall not stir out of your house today." (II, ii, 9)

The Canadian Human Rights Act gives each of us "an equal opportunity to work and live without discrimination."

If you need to change the punctuation of the original to suit the context in your own writing, put square brackets around any changes you made. For example:

Caesar responds that any harm that might come his way will dissipate "when they shall see [t]he face of Caesar." (The square brackets show that the "t" on "the" was a capital in the original because it started a new line of poetry.)

In general, quotations should be kept short and relevant. If your quotation goes on for several sentences, it is best double indented (from both margins) and single spaced. For example:

The exact language of the report in this section reads:

> The mayor's taskforce found that residents wanted frequent and reliable garbage pickup at least twice a week in the summer and once in the winter. The additional summer service was requested due to concerns about odours and animals.

If there is a grammar or spelling error in the original, the word "sic" in square brackets indicates that you are aware of the error but have left the original intact. For example:

The witness was quoted as saying, "I never seen [sic] the man before."

At the end of a research report, provide your reader with all the sources you consulted in preparing the report. Sources are listed on a final page titled Bibliography, Works Cited, or References. Following is the format for a few typical sources. (Note: If you don't have a computer or are handwriting your work, underline all book titles and magazine or newspaper names that you might otherwise put in italics.)

Books

Author's last name, First name. *Title*. City of publication: Publisher, Year of publication.

Robinson, Eden. *Monkey Beach*. Toronto: Alfred A. Knopf Canada, 2000.

Newspaper Articles

Author's last name, First name. "Title of article." *Name of Newspaper*
  Full date: Page(s) of article.

Careless, James. "Getting Down to the Wireless." *The Toronto Star*
  August 17, 2000. K5.

Magazine Articles

Author's last name, First name. "Title of article." *Name of Magazine*
  Full date: Page(s) of article.

Mackie, Brian. "Frame by Frame: The Narrative Art of Comics." *The Lazy Writer*
  Fall 1997:12–17.

Encyclopedia Entries

Author's last name, First name. "Title of entry." *Name of Encyclopedia*.
  Year of publication.

Randall, Mary. "The Ozone Layer." *New Encyclopaedia Britannica*. 2001.

The Internet

Author's last name, First name. "Title of Work." Year or full date (if applicable) of publication. <Internet address> (Date of retrieval).

Ledes, Richard. "Housing Construction: The Challenges of Building Interactive Narrative."
1996. <http://www.intelligent-agent.com/aug_building.html> (20 Aug. 2001).

or

Name of organization. "Title of Work." Year or full date (if applicable) of publication. <Internet address> (Date of retrieval).

Canadian Broadcast Standards Council. "Canada Deals with Media Violence."
<http://www.cbsc.ca/english/canada.htm> (13 Oct. 2000).

Writing

MAKING AN OUTLINE

An **outline** helps you organize information before you write your first draft. It can help save you time, even though, at first, it may seem like an extra step. When you plan your writing with an outline, you will have a solid foundation for your composition.

Outline Headings

Use topics for your headings. Keep them short. If you are going to write a report on renting an apartment, your **topic headings** might look like this:

I. Introduction
II. Deciding what you want
III. Sharing or living alone
IV. Researching neighbourhoods
V. Using the want ads
VI. Using other sources
VII. Interviewing the landlord
VIII. Signing a lease
IX. Moving in
X. Conclusion

If you are writing an essay on a short story, your topic headings might look like this:

I. Thesis
II. Author's use of characters to develop theme
III. Author's use of setting to develop theme
IV. Author's use of narrator to develop theme
V. Conclusion

An outline includes more than just the topics you are going to discuss. It breaks down those topics and adds detail to them. There is a standard format for showing the breakdown of the parts. Let's go back to the report on finding an apartment.

I. Introduction
    A. Importance of taking time to find an apartment

II. Deciding what you want
    A. Location
        1. distance to work
        2. distance to public transit
        3. distance to shopping

III. Sharing or living alone
    A. Finances
    B. Privacy

IV. Researching neighbourhoods
    A. Safety
        1. presence of police
        2. safety at night

You can see the pattern of starting with the main idea and adding supporting details under each topic. Having thought out exactly what you are going to say, you simply have to put your ideas into sentences.

The same outline structure is used for an essay or any other type of writing that requires planning.

GRAPHIC ORGANIZERS

To help you organize your information before you write, you can also use **graphic organizers**. Following are examples of the types of organizers that you can use.

Time Lines

Time lines help you to organize events in chronological order. For example, you might assemble a time line like the one following from the information you have gathered about Jimmy's voyage in "Love Like the Ocean" (pages 161–165):

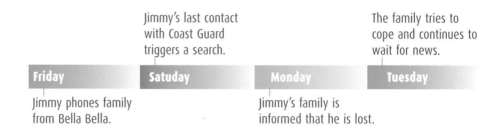

Jimmy's last contact with Coast Guard triggers a search.

The family tries to cope and continues to wait for news.

| Friday | Satuday | Monday | Tuesday |

Jimmy phones family from Bella Bella.

Jimmy's family is informed that he is lost.

Clustering

Clustering is a special form of representing-to-learn using a kind of graphic outlining. Put a key concept, term, or name in a circle at the centre of a page and then free-associate, jotting down all the words that occur to you in circles around the central idea in whatever pattern "seems right." Often, clustering reveals connections and relationships among pieces of information.

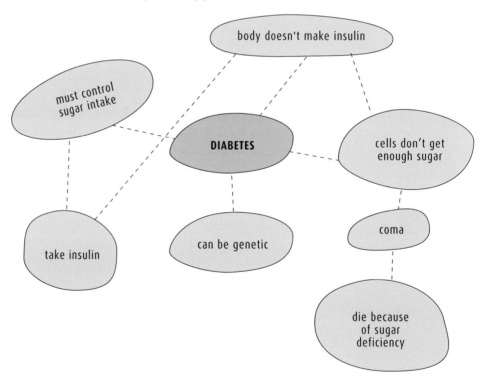

Drawing and Sketching

This is the graphic equivalent of freewriting. Create original drawings to illustrate ideas found in your reading, discussions, and inquiry.

Story Maps

Story maps are diagrams or maps of the events in a story or narrative, often done chronologically. They can apply both to literature and to historical narrative.

King Midas and the Golden Touch

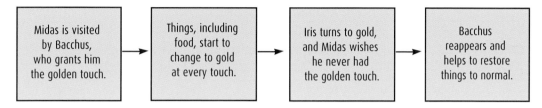

| Midas is visited by Bacchus, who grants him the golden touch. | → | Things, including food, start to change to gold at every touch. | → | Iris turns to gold, and Midas wishes he never had the golden touch. | → | Bacchus reappears and helps to restore things to normal. |

Venn Diagrams

When subjects—books, concepts, people, countries, and so on—have certain attributes that are *alike* and others that are *different,* you can use two or three interlocking circles to display the contrasts and similarities.

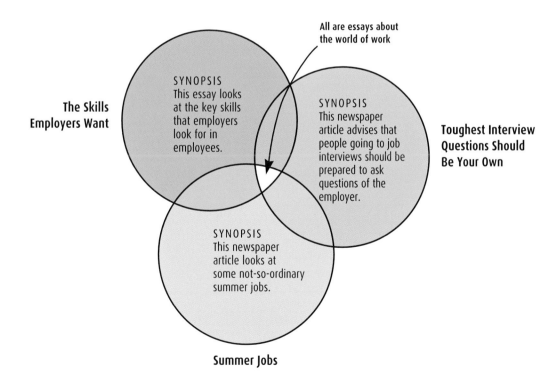

The Skills Employers Want

All are essays about the world of work

SYNOPSIS
This essay looks at the key skills that employers look for in employees.

SYNOPSIS
This newspaper article advises that people going to job interviews should be prepared to ask questions of the employer.

Toughest Interview Questions Should Be Your Own

SYNOPSIS
This newspaper article looks at some not-so-ordinary summer jobs.

Summer Jobs

SUMMARIES

In today's busy world, many documents are prepared in two versions: a full, detailed version and a summary, a short version of the original document. A good **summary** captures the main ideas and supporting details of the original accurately and clearly in as few words as possible.

Following are some tips for writing a summary:
- Use a highlighter to identify key concepts in the original.
- Stick to the key concepts in your summary.
- Try to keep the structure, tone, and style of the original intact.
- Leave out unnecessary words, examples, and information.
- Use one general word to replace several specific words.
- Use one example to represent a series of examples.

ORGANIZING YOUR WRITING

Essays

The word *essay* comes from the French verb *essayer,* meaning *to try* or *to try on*. In an essay, a writer "tries on ideas" about a single topic.

Introductory Paragraph: This opening paragraph may include some general information related to the topic or some background information needed to understand the topic.

The introduction includes the **thesis** or main idea statement, which is the idea you are going to "try on." A thesis is an opinion you arrive at by thorough research and thought. Like a hypothesis, it is an "educated guess" about a topic. You must prove your thesis using evidence that will convince your audience.

Body: This is the main section of the essay. It consists of paragraphs that develop the controlling idea or prove the thesis.

Methods of developing expository paragraphs include comparison/contrast and example/illustration, as well as cause/effect, analogy, definition, and classification.

The order can be **chronological** (beginning to end), **sequential** (for instructions), **spatial** (presenting details as you want the audience to see them), or **climactic** (using details, events, or facts in increasing order of importance).

Each paragraph in the body has a point and a proof and must relate back to your thesis or controlling idea.

Conclusion: This final paragraph restates your thesis and summarizes your evidence.

Bibliography: After the conclusion of the essay, the bibliography lists all the sources that were used, including print, electronic, video, audio, and human resources. (See pages 256–257 for examples of correct bibliographical formats.)

Reports

Some reports, such as laboratory and science reports, require specific headings. If headings are not given, use the same format as an essay: introduction, body, conclusion.

Introductory Paragraph: This opening paragraph defines your topic and explains the purpose of the report.

Body: This central section develops the topic in a series of paragraphs, and it quotes experts or uses quotations from a variety of sources. Quotations must be accurate, and footnotes must be used to show where the quotations came from. Visuals such as charts are often used to explain the information.

Conclusion: This summarizes findings and refers back to the introduction.

Bibliography: The bibliography lists all the sources that were used. (See pages 256–257.)

Case Studies

In business and social science courses, you may be asked to do a case study. A case study is an in-depth examination of a real-life situation that demonstrates a theory or supports a hypothesis.

A case study can be organized under many subheadings. It is important to consult your teacher about the subheadings applicable to your work.

Some common subheadings used for case studies are the following:
- **Problem/Issue**: This section states the problem or issue that your case study will examine.
- **Background**: This information is important to let the reader know how the problem or issue arose.
- **Facts**: This section includes the details about the issue. It may include facts from secondary sources or facts from observations.
- **Discussion**: In this section, facts are examined in light of the hypothesis or the theory you are examining.
- **Alternative Courses of Action**: If your case study calls for some action, this section allows you to examine a variety of actions.
- **Recommendations**: After studying the case, it is likely that you will make recommendations regarding your topic.

METHODS OF DEVELOPMENT

Although this section reviews five ways to develop individual paragraphs and essays, no matter which method you use, you must provide details. Details add credibility and substance to your writing and are essential to creating convincing expositions, narratives, and descriptions. Different types of paragraph development also increase the readability of your exposition.

Development by Definition

Developing an essay by definition is the process of explaining what is meant by a term, an idea, or an object. When developing a definition, start with a general statement; for example, "A hero performs an act that puts the welfare of others before that of himself or herself."

With each new example, start a new paragraph.

ACTIVITY

Choose a character from one of the stories you have read in this textbook, and, using definition, write a paragraph to prove that he or she is one of the following: dependent, a victim, a hero, courageous, ignorant.

Development by Chronology

Chronology is the order in which a series of events takes place. A personal essay may focus on a series of events leading up to an incident such as a car accident that has been preceded by several near misses. A news report may discuss the incidents leading up to an important event, such as decreases in budgets and reductions in staff resulting in an increased health risk for workers.

Caution: Using a chronological approach when writing about literature may lead to retelling the story instead of examining the various literary aspects of the story.

ACTIVITY

For one of the stories or novel excerpts in this textbook, write a newspaper report in which at least one paragraph is developed by using chronological order.

Development by Problem/Solution

Many writers use problem/solution as a method of organizing. This type of organization is particularly effective when writing a persuasive essay about a problem that may have a solution (e.g., a shortage of summer jobs for students, young children finding inappropriate sites on the Internet, violence on television).

As with cause and effect, the problem is posed (see below), its history or background is discussed, and a solution is proposed. Several solutions can be offered, but each should be accompanied by an explanation of its benefits and drawbacks.

When offering possible solutions, a writer must mention a solution's negative aspects because readers will often have already considered what the writer is proposing and will know the strengths and weaknesses of the arguments beforehand. The writer loses credibility if he or she does not acknowledge these weaknesses. It is up to the writer, then, to prove that the strengths far outnumber the drawbacks.

ACTIVITY

With a partner, research and discuss the pros and cons of genetically modified foods. Choose one of the major problems related to this issue (e.g., people not understanding the benefits of these new foods, businesses not appearing to care about the long-term effects these foods might have). Write a persuasive essay on the problem and the solutions you have found.

Development by Cause and Effect

Discussions of cause and effect are concerned with the reasons why something happens. Questions to ask about cause and effect include
- What has caused it?
- Where has it come from?
- Where is it going?
- What will happen to it?
- What is it used for?
- How does it fit into the larger scheme of things?
- What would happen if it didn't exist?
- Why does it exist?
- Could it be changed?

When organizing cause-and-effect paragraphs, you can either

- start with a cause and show or try to predict its effect (e.g., If handgun ownership is not regulated, more handgun-related deaths will occur.)

  or

- start with an effect and try to explain its cause (e.g., Fewer secondary schools offer classes in auto mechanics because of the expense of the program.)

Remember: The fact that one event follows another does not necessarily mean that the first event is the cause of the second. Examples:

I wore my red socks when I won my first tennis match.

Wearing those red socks did not necessarily cause my win.

I wrote two exams with the same pen and got over 80 percent on both exams.

Using that pen did not cause my success.

ACTIVITIES

Read the following paragraph.

As a result of modern society's shift from oral to print communication, just about every job today requires skills in reading and writing. Before written language, people transacted business orally within and between communities; however, as people travelled farther afield, the need for proof of business transactions became more important. Traders represented large companies and even royalty, both of which wanted assurances that their money was being spent in the way it was intended. Since that time, print has been used as a way of increasing the accuracy and reliability of ordering, invoicing, instructing, reporting, and reviewing.

1. List the cause and effect in this paragraph.
2. With a partner, create a list of five other causes and effects. Individually, choose one and write a short paragraph showing the relationship of the two events.

Development by Classification

Classification is used to show how something fits into a category or how it differs from a category. Some questions you might ask yourself are

- What other things are like it?
- What kinds of it are there?
- What is it part of?
- What goes along with it?
- How does it differ from others like it?
- What connects it to all the other things in the category?

If developing a paragraph or essay using classification,
- Be sure you have an adequate and accurate definition of the category.
- Ask yourself why it is important to look at the issue or idea as part of a category.
- Include both similarities to and differences from the category to create more interest.
- Make sure there is a point to considering your subject as part of a category.
- If the category is a literary genre, research that genre for accurate information.

ACTIVITIES

1. a) Work with a partner. For each of the following subjects, list 20 items that could be included in that category.
   - music
   - local restaurants
   - cars
   - school sports
   - movies

   b) Break each of the lists you've made into subcategories, creating a subtitle for each.
2. Examine your categories and subcategories. Create a topic sentence for an expository paragraph you could write on one of these categories or subcategories.

TRANSITIONS

In order for your writing to flow logically from one sentence to the next sentence —one point to the following point—you need to include **transitions**. Transitions connect your ideas, helping your readers to follow the logic of your argument. Transitions can be used between sentences in the same paragraph or as a logical bridge between paragraphs. They come in many forms.

Repetition

Repetition of a word or phrase from one sentence or paragraph to the next will signal a continuation of the same topic. Example:

While Grade 10 students are often very good at writing short stories, they sometimes find *writing essays* difficult. *Essay writing* challenges students' ability to think and write logically.

Remember, however, that overusing this technique can result in a repetitive or monotonous voice.

Substitution (Pronouns, Synonyms)

Substituting a pronoun or a synonym for the subject in your previous sentence connects the two ideas. Example:

Doing science is more exciting than just *reading* about science. *The former* shows students how scientific principles work; *the latter* tells students how the scientific principles work.

Be sure the antecedent of the substituted word(s) is clear. (For example: "Students like doing science, not just reading about science. *It* is exciting." The second sentence is unclear. What does the word "it" refer to: the doing or the reading?)

Transitional Words or Connectives

Transitional words or **connectives** show relationships between ideas. Here are examples of relationships and the kinds of transitional words that are used in each:
- to add ideas: *and, moreover, furthermore, further, similarly, too, likewise, again, in the same way, besides*
- to show cause and effect: *accordingly, therefore, as a result, consequently, hence, thus, for this reason, it follows that*
- to compare: *similarly, likewise*
- to contrast or introduce a limiting thought: *but, nevertheless, otherwise, on the other hand, conversely, on the contrary, however, yet, still*
- to introduce examples: *for example, for instance, such as*
- to indicate order: *next, in the second place, to begin with, first* (not *firstly*), *second, in conclusion*
- to show a relationship of time: *then, now, currently, at present, somewhat later, thereupon, thereafter, eventually, at the same time, meanwhile, presently (soon)*

- to show a spatial relationship: *to the right, in the distance, straight ahead, at the left, above, below, in between*

Example:

Many students love to study French; *furthermore*, they understand the value of learning to speak and write a second language.

REVISING YOUR WRITING

Whether revising your own or someone else's work, practise using a simple memory device, or mnemonic: RADS. RADS will help you decide whether or not your ideas are complete and in the best possible order. Use RADS to help you examine your entire composition, including each paragraph and sentence.

R   Reorder

❏   Are my ideas in the best possible order?
❏   Have I considered alternative orders (chronological, sequential, climactic)?
❏   Does one idea flow logically into another?
❏   Are there any ideas out of place?

A   Add

❏   Do I have enough ideas to make my work convincing?
❏   Do I need to add more details?
❏   Do I need to add some more examples?
❏   Have I used enough description, including adjectives, adverbs, and interesting verbs?
❏   Will my audience be convinced?
❏   Could I add some imagery, similes, or metaphors to create a stronger effect?
❏   Could I add some transition words to help link my ideas?

D   Delete

❏   Do I have any ideas that don't support my main idea?
❏   Do I have ideas that don't add to the point I am trying to make?
❏   Do I have some ideas that clutter up my work?
❏   Is my language too flowery or descriptive for the tone I want to set?
❏   Have I repeated ideas?

S Substitute

❏ Are there other ideas I have gathered that might be better than the ones I have?

❏ Do I have one weak idea? Should I continue my research to find a better one?

❏ Are there words that don't capture the feeling I want to create?

❏ Should I use a thesaurus to help find better words?

❏ Are there some linking words that are not working?

❏ Have I used the appropriate language for my audience?

Proofreading and Editing Your Writing

Good ideas are hard to read if a writer has not proofread and edited his or her work. Check the following before writing your final draft.

Sources

❏ Have I used quotation marks around any words or phrases I have borrowed from other sources?

❏ Have I named the source of those words?

❏ When I have used ideas from other sources, have I given credit to that author?

❏ Have I created a bibliography of all my sources?

Grammar and Usage

❏ Have I checked and corrected any sentence fragments, comma splices, and run-on sentences? (See pages 230–231.)

❏ Have I included a variety of sentence types (simple, complex, compound), sentence lengths, and sentence orders (natural, inverted, split)? (See pages 228–230.)

❏ Do all my verb tenses agree?

❏ Do all my pronouns agree with their antecedents in number and gender?

❏ Have I used a consistent point of view (not switching from *I* to *you* or *one*)?

❏ If I have used a thesaurus, have I checked the dictionary to be sure the connotation of my new word is correct?

❏ Have I written in the active voice and used the passive only when appropriate? (See page 223.)

❏ Have I written sensitively, avoiding racist, sexist, and homophobic language?

Spelling

❏ Have I checked my work for unintended errors, such as leaving out letters?
❏ Have I checked all my homophones, such as *their/there/they're; know/no?*
❏ Have I checked all my plurals?
❏ Have I used apostrophes correctly?
❏ Have I capitalized the correct words (especially in dialogue, scripts, and poetry)?
❏ Have I checked the spelling of specialized vocabulary?
❏ Have I used a dictionary or a spell-check program on my word processor?

Punctuation

❏ Have I used end stops and capitalization appropriately and correctly?
❏ Have I used commas, dashes, and colons appropriately and correctly?
❏ Have I used quotation marks for direct speech and quotations from sources?

Oral Communication Skills

GOOD LISTENING SKILLS

Good listening skills are essential to oral communication. Your success at communicating depends on how well you listen to others and receive their messages. Following are some do's and don'ts of listening.

DO	DON'T
• make eye contact with the speaker • review what the speaker has said • concentrate • try to recall facts and ideas • take notes • record instructions • ask questions • tune out outside noises • avoid distracting behaviours • use mnemonics (memory devices) • pay attention to non-verbal communication • pick up on message reinforcers such as charts, diagrams, photos, slides	• judge a person by appearance or delivery • fake attention • bring your prejudices to the presentation • avoid difficult ideas or concepts • tune out or let your mind wander • interrupt the speaker • use selective listening • make side comments to others or listen to or pay attention to the behaviour of others and their side comments

ORAL PRESENTATIONS

Just as it is important to listen while someone else speaks, whether in a formal or an informal group setting, so it is important that you speak well to convey your message effectively. As a student, you require good speaking skills for various oral activities, including

- debates
- demonstrations
- dramatic and/or choral readings
- group work
- independent study presentations
- performances – role plays, readings, storytelling
- symposia
- interviews
- meetings
- reports
- seminars
- speeches
- video presentations
- sales talks

A formal oral presentation is one of the most common activities that you will be involved in. Here are some suggestions to help you plan an effective oral presentation.

Planning Your Oral Presentation*

Know Your Purpose

What do you want to accomplish with your oral presentation?
- to inform
- to persuade
- to motivate
- to entertain

Know Your Audience

- their age groups
- their interests in your topic
- the reason they are listening to your presentation

Planning Your Content

Know Your Subject

- read — books, articles, electronic information
- talk — personal or phone interview, discussion
- view — movies, documentaries, interviews
- record — on tape, on cue cards, in your notebook, on your computer
- organize

* Based on S. Carlile Clark and Dana V. Hensley, *38 Basic Speech Experiences* (Topeka, Kansas: Clark Publishing, 1999).

- discard information that is not adding to your presentation
- add information where you find you have gaps
- replace information that might be weak with stronger points
- order your information in the most logical order, starting with a hook to get your audience interested and ending with a powerful conclusion
- think of ways to get your audience involved

Some General Tips for Presenting

- get the audience's attention
- make them want to hear what you have to say
- make it clear to the audience why the material is important to them
- if appropriate, involve your audience
- ask your audience to take some action (further study, a comparison with something they already know)
- appeal to their emotions and needs (love, wealth, self-preservation, nationalism, loyalty, religions, political beliefs, desire for recognition, desire for adventure)
- be sincere and enthusiastic
- use humour (words, anecdotes, body language, gestures, props) where appropriate
- incorporate visuals such as board work, posters, overheads, slides, electronic devices, presentation software

Avoiding Stress in Formal Presentations

Being nervous before speaking in public is not uncommon. The extra rush of adrenaline you get when you're nervous can work in your favour to keep your speaking energized and exciting.

Signs of Stage Fright

Those of you who have "stage fright" *may* experience one or more of these symptoms of stress:
- your breathing becomes faster
- your heart rate speeds up
- you perspire more
- you feel fidgety or as if you have butterflies in your stomach
- you feel nauseated or faint
- your mouth gets dry
- your knees feel weak

Getting Past Stage Fright

You can help to calm your nerves and get past your stage fright by doing the following things:

- *Speak in front of an audience as often as possible:* Start with small groups and move up to increasingly larger audiences.
- *Pick a topic that interests you:* If you are participating in a debate or making a presentation, choose ideas that will hold your attention. If you're not enthusiastic about your topic, you will not feel confident because you might feel the audience will not be interested either.
- *Prepare:* Most students who get stage fright are afraid they won't do a good job. Research thoroughly, create an outline, write out your oral presentation or speech, and try it out, first in front of the mirror or into a tape recorder, then on your family or friends. Say the speech as many times as possible. Of course, this means you can't be writing your speech the night before it is due! While you are rehearsing, visualize yourself in the room where you will be presenting, in front of your audience.
- *Memorize:* If you have to memorize your presentation, use mnemonics to help you remember the order of your points or key words in your presentation. **Mnemonics** are memory aids. One useful mnemonic is creating an acronym, a word in which each of the letters stands for another word. You probably already know some acronyms to help you remember. MRS VANDERTRAMP is an acronym for the irregular verbs in French. BEDMAS is an acronym for the order of operations in mathematics.
- *Think of the audience:* The speech isn't about you—it's about them! You are trying to persuade, entertain, or inform *other* people, not yourself. Focus on them. Some experts suggest imagining your audience in their underwear!
- *Move:* Facial expressions and some hand gestures keep you relaxed and use up some of that excess energy you feel. You can physically move around if it is appropriate to the type of oral presentation you are giving.
- *Wear appropriate clothing:* You don't want to be worried about the length of your skirt or the need for a tie. Think about your audience. Think about the formality of the occasion. Decide on your clothing ahead of time. Wear it while you are practising your speech at home.

THE ROLE OF THE AUDIENCE

When you speak in front of an audience, it is important to be aware that the way the audience perceives you will have an influence on the way your speech is received. You must be a credible speaker for the audience to stay with you. So how do you increase your credibility?

Competence

- Know what you are talking about.
- Know more about your topic than your audience does.
- Draw your audience's attention to your knowledge. This could be done by simply presenting enough facts that the audience can see immediately that you know what you are talking about. You could cite personal experience that demonstrates your understanding of your topic. Someone else could introduce you and draw attention to something in your background that shows you know about the topic.

Trustworthiness/Friendliness

- Tell the truth without embellishments.
- Present both sides to a story (just make sure your side is stronger).
- Use fair and persuasive techniques.
- Give your audience all the facts.
- Smile.
- Stay calm.
- Be friendly.

Relevance/Appropriateness

- Find out who your audience is.
- Match your topic, tone, vocabulary, and diction (level of language) to your audience and to the purpose of your presentation.
- Dress appropriately for the occasion.

ACTIVITY

Reread "Justin Trudeau: A Son's Eulogy" (pages 6–8). On the basis of this speech, who do you think is the intended audience? What is Justin Trudeau's purpose? What impact do you think the speech had on its audience? What can you observe about the level of language in Trudeau's speech? Is it appropriate for the speech's purpose and audience?

ORAL REPORTS

Oral reports are similar to written reports. They are organized by subtopic. When presenting an oral report, it is a good idea to have visuals to accompany your presentation.

Overheads

Here are a few reminders about using overheads.
- Plan ahead. Do not ask your teacher for an overhead projector at the last minute.
- Be sure you have the correct markers to create the overhead.
- The font size on your overheads should be large enough for the audience to see. (Do not expect regular-sized type from a word-processed document on an overhead to be read by anyone but you.)
- If you are handwriting an overhead, be sure to leave margins on all sides so that your handwriting will fit the image size.
- Colour provides interesting contrasts, if you can manage it.
- Be sure there are no errors on your overhead.

Posters

You can create eye-catching posters on Bristol board or chart paper to accompany your report.
- Put only a small amount of information on each poster.
- Make the poster's lettering large enough to be seen from the back of the room.
- Plan your layout so that you have large borders and so that your lettering is uniform in size and fits into the space on the page.
- Check all the text to ensure that there are no errors on your poster.

Blackboard

As old-fashioned as the blackboard may seem, you can use it as effectively as you can any other visual aid.
- Prepare your board work in advance, if possible.
- Write in large letters that can be seen from the back of the room.
- Use colours, if they are available.
- Print, rather than write.
- Check all the text to ensure that there are no errors on your board work.

Computer-Assisted Presentations

When planning a computer-assisted presentation, remember to
- Plan each of your slides to provide you with enough information to speak about the topic, but not all the information that you will convey to your audience.
- Add some graphics, if appropriate.
- Use a background that does not interfere with the information on your screen.
- Check all the text to ensure that there are no errors on your slides.

DEBATING

Debate Procedure

The Chair introduces the topic, introduces the speakers, explains the time limits, and announces the judges' decisions. It is up to the Chair to maintain the tone of the debate.

The First Speaker for the Affirmative   **4 minutes**

Give a brief introduction to the topic, define any necessary terms, note any points agreed on by all debaters, note any issues to be excluded, state clearly and briefly all the affirmative points, and prove the point you have chosen to deal with.

The First Speaker for the Negative   **3 minutes**

State agreements and disagreements with the interpretation of the topic by the first speaker, state the arguments for the negative side, indicate who will prove each argument, refute briefly the arguments of the first speaker, and present your own arguments.

The Second Speaker for the Affirmative   **3 minutes**

Refute the arguments of the first speaker for the negative and state your own arguments and proof.

The Second Speaker for the Negative   **4 minutes**

Refute any arguments for the affirmative as yet unanswered, state your own arguments and proof, and sum up the arguments for the negative side.

The First Speaker for the Affirmative   **1 minute**

Do not introduce any new arguments; refute arguments already made and sum up the affirmative arguments.

Debate Terminology

refute: to prove a statement or argument to be wrong or false
point of order: a question to the Chair regarding proper following of rules
point of personal privilege: a question to the Chair regarding a misrepresentation of your argument

BUSINESS PRESENTATIONS*

A **business presentation** is a speech in which you introduce your business to an audience and try to persuade them to buy a product or service from you.

To sell any product, you must be
• completely familiar with the product
• confident in the product and in yourself

Materials that you should have at the sales talk include:
• order forms
• pens and pencils
• receipts
• business cards

How to Organize a Business Presentation

Introduction

• Introduce yourself by name (have business cards available).
• Give some background information
  — about you (your education, qualifications, history with the company or with other companies like it)

---

* Based on S. Carlile Clark and Dana V. Hensley, *38 Basic Speech Experiences* (Topeka, Kansas: Clark Publishing, 1999), pages 74–76.

—about your company (how long it has been in business, its reputation for quality, how it stands behind its products)

Demonstration

- Explain the purpose of your product.
- Show its advantages, special features, improvements over other similar products or over previous models, dependability, beauty, ease of use, and economy.
- Be clear and concise—too much information overwhelms people.
- Mention any endorsements you have—what other people (especially if they have a relationship to your audience) have said about the product.
- Tailor what you say to suit your audience and their needs.

Information About How to Order

Provide your audience with information about
- where and when they can purchase what you are selling
- cost (indicate whether taxes and shipping are extra or included, depending on how you have calculated the price)
- how they can pay (cash, personal cheque, certified cheque, debit card, credit card)
- whether special prices apply if the product or service is ordered on the spot
- when they can expect delivery, or whether they can take the product with them from the sales meeting

Question Period

- Answer openly and honestly.
- If by chance you don't know the answer to a question, be sure to get the questioner's number and telephone him or her immediately with the answer.

Conclusion

- Thank the audience for their attention.
- Express an interest in speaking to them individually and telling them where you will be located for further questions.

Tips for Giving a Business Presentation

Here are some tips you may want to keep in mind for the sales talk:
- Look good; dress smartly. Remember this is the business world.
- Smile.

- Be confident, but avoid slipping into sounding boastful.
- Keep your language simple, descriptive, and vivid, but avoid jargon and technical terms.
- Use visuals whenever possible — these could be overheads, posterboards, handouts, computer-generated or, if small enough, the product itself.
- *Do not* criticize competitors. Praise their products, but show how yours is better.

ACTIVITY

Think about a product you really know about and believe in. Create a business presentation for that product. You can fabricate the background information if you cannot find information on the company that manufactures the product.

TELEPHONE COMMUNICATION

Whether you are using the telephone to request information or to have an interview, you need to be clear. You may have a "face that launched a thousand ships," but even the beauty of Helen of Troy would not be able to influence an unseen person on the other end of the telephone. No one can see your facial expressions or your gestures. Content is the key to clear and effective telephone communication.

Asking for Information

Before Calling

1. Write down the kinds of information you want to know.
2. Record the names and telephone numbers of the places where you think you can get the information.
3. Have paper and pencil ready to record information given to you.

On the Telephone

1. Identify yourself (name, where you are calling from).
2. Explain the reason for your call.
3. Ask for the person most likely to be able to help you.

4. Once you are speaking to the most appropriate person, make sure you take down his or her name.
5. Identify yourself again, and thank the person for taking time for your questions.
6. Ask your questions. Record the answers.
7. If necessary, ask the person to repeat any information you might have missed.
8. If the person cannot help you, ask if he or she knows who might be able to help.
9. Thank the person once again.

Interviewing over the Telephone

Sometimes you will call about a job and suddenly find that you are being interviewed over the telephone.

Before Calling

1. Be prepared with your résumé.
2. Think about what questions you might be asked in an interview and prepare answers for them.

On the Telephone

1. Explain why you are calling, and ask for the correct person if a name has been given to you.
2. If you do not know whom to speak to, explain why you are calling and ask for the name of the appropriate person. Jot it down.
3. Ask to speak to that person.
4. Introduce yourself and explain why you are calling.
5. Ask any questions you have. (Hint: It is always easier to ask about pay and benefits over the telephone.)
6. If the person starts to ask you questions, ask if this is an interview or if another interview will be scheduled. If the person says it is an interview, put your best interviewing skills into play.
7. If you are not being interviewed, and if you are still interested in the job, ask if there will be interviews and request an appointment.
8. Thank the person by name and assure him or her that you will be at the appointed place at the appointed time. (Hint: If you do not know the location of the interview, get directions.)

ACTIVITY

In a group of three, set up a situation in which information is needed or a job interview is being conducted on the telephone. Two members of the group can role-play the situation while the third person takes notes on how well the person seeking the information or the job is doing.

The Business of Life

INTRODUCTION TO COMMUNICATION

In college and in the workplace, you will be expected to communicate with teachers, colleagues, employers, older people, younger people, and people from different backgrounds. Your communication will be spoken, written, and non-verbal, including body language and facial expressions. You need to be effective at all types of communication in order to be successful.

Why is good communication important? It is good for
- building better relationships
- sharing what we know, think, and feel with others
- learning from others
- resolving problems, disagreements, and complaints in a way that will do us the most good
- avoiding misunderstandings
- responding to others without hurting them or getting hurt
- showing ourselves in the best light possible and bringing out the best in others

Good communication is

direct: Mean what you say; say what you mean. Don't "drop hints" or beat around the bush.

specific: Give all the information needed to get your message across.

tactful: Be polite. Think about the other person's feelings and rights before you speak. You want to avoid saying things accidentally that will hurt them or harm you. Remember, once words are out of your mouth or down on paper, they can't be taken back.*

---

* Herta A. Murphy, Charles E. Peck, and Sheila A. O'Neill, *Effective Business Communications* (Toronto: McGraw-Hill Ryerson Ltd., 1983), page 89.

clear: Use details to describe how you feel.

honest: Say what you really feel. Make sure what you say matches the facts.

LETTERS

As you get older and your experiences broaden, especially in the workplace, you will probably need to write a letter to a person you don't know or a business you have not dealt with before. You may be sending this letter by post or by e-mail. Whichever method you choose, the content and message of the letter will be the same, though the format of the e-mail may be less formal.

Business Letter Format

A letter with a **full block format**
- is justified left,
- has no indentations for paragraphs, and
- has one line space between paragraphs.

In an **open punctuation format**, there are no punctuation marks at the end of any line that is above the message (e.g., return addresses, dates) or below the message (e.g., the closing). There is an exception to the rule: if the last word in the line is an abbreviation (e.g., Blvd.), it should be punctuated with a period.

Wording

The most important part of writing a letter is your choice of words. Even if you are angry at a person or company, you must choose words that are calm and non-threatening. Yelling—in person, on the phone, or in a letter or e-mail—is rarely effective.

Often, when you write a business letter, you want something: information, a refund, a job, a sale. Sometimes, however, a business letter is what we call a "goodwill" letter—a letter of thanks or acknowledgement. Whatever your reason for writing, the basic principles of letter writing are the same.
- Be clear.
- Be concise.
- Provide details.
- Tell the truth.
- Be courteous.

Letters of Request

Following are some steps in writing a letter of request:

1. Start your letter by stating what you want from the person or company.
2. In your second paragraph, explain why you are requesting the information or item. You may include a compliment about the product or organization if you feel this is relevant to the letter.

Sample Letter of Request for Information (Full Block Format with Open Punctuation)

F. Linkslater
576 Jakes Ave., Apt. 1324
Markham, Ontario
L0G 9B6

January 31, 2002

Customer Service Department
"Sponsor a Moose"
1 Main Street
Unionville, Ontario
L6G 3F2

To the Customer Service Department

I would like to sponsor a moose for the year 2003. Please send me an information package with an application form to the address above. I also have an e-mail address, so a package could be sent electronically to linkslaterf@cyberspace.com.

I have heard through my colleagues that your organization has an excellent reputation and has been instrumental in preserving moose in Ontario. I look forward to having the opportunity to participate in this excellent program.

Sincerely

F. Linkslater

F. Linkslater

Judge the effectiveness of this letter on the basis of the criteria stated on pages 285–286. Do the same for the letter below.

Sample Letter of Request for a Refund (Full Block Format with Open Punctuation)

Janice Woo
111 53rd Avenue
Edmonton, Alberta
T2A 3H1

January 31, 2001

Customer Service Department
Kim's Clothing Company
500 11A Street
Edmonton, Alberta
T6A 1B7

Ned Phelps, Manager of Customer Service

I have been shopping in your department store for several years now and have always been pleased with the quality of the products you sell. Recently, however, I purchased a pair of shoes that I wish to return for a full refund.

On December 21, 2000, I bought a pair of Schneider sandals to wear on my vacation (copy of bill enclosed). I wore them for two days, and the heel strap broke. On January 6, 2001, when I returned to your store, I attempted to exchange them for a new pair. The manager, Chris Shoehorn, explained that, because the shoes were on sale, I did not qualify for an exchange.

The sandals were defective. They should not have broken after only two wearings. I would like to return them to the store for a full refund. Please call me at 555-4103 or e-mail me at janice.woo@networks.com to arrange for this return or to discuss the problem with me. Thank you for your time.

Sincerely

J. Woo

J. Woo

Letters of Goodwill

Following are some steps for writing a letter of goodwill:

1. Start your letter by acknowledging the person's, or company's, positive actions.
2. In your second paragraph, respond to the requests or comments the person or company has made. Then end on a positive note.

(Note: The Customer Service Department might have a standard letter that it sends out to all those who request information.)

Sample Letter of Goodwill

SPONSOR A MOOSE

Customer Service Department
"Sponsor a Moose"
1 Main Street
Unionville, Ontario
L6G 3F2

February 3, 2002

F. Linkslater
576 Jakes Ave., Apt. 1324
Markham, Ontario
L0G 9B6

Dear F. Linkslater

Thank you for your request to "Sponsor a Moose." We have been working diligently to protect Ontario's moose population for ten years now, and without people like you, we would not be successful.

Accompanying this letter is our information package and the application form you requested. If you know of others who would be interested in learning about our program, please forward their names and addresses to us or have them contact us. We would be happy to assist them in any way we can.

Thank you once again for your interest.

Sincerely

Egan Edwinter, Manager
Customer Service

RÉSUMÉS

Résumés should be
- limited to one page (if possible)
- complete
- accurate
- a good representation of who you are
- an accurate summary of what you can do

Sample Résumé

Roberta Smith
120 Victoria Avenue West
Winnipeg, MB
R3Z 6H6
(H) (204) 555-0295
(B) (204) 555-2879
roberta_smith@young.ca

Skills

Management	• Shift manager for fast-food restaurant in charge of five employees per shift
Cash	• Familiar with both ABC Model 5200 and XYZ Model 2280
Customer Service	• Served food in fast-food restaurant • Worked as a telemarketer selling storm windows
Group Leadership	• In charge of organizing the equipment and food for a group of 15-year-olds on a school-sponsored canoe trip
Teaching	• Responsible for creating Sunday School lessons and teaching ten 5-year-olds each Sunday

Work Experience

June 2000 – present
Shift Manager
Eat at Joe's Hamburger Emporium
Supervisor: Viveen Mallon
Phone: (204) 555-0345

January 1999 – present
Sunday School Teacher
Advent United Church
Supervisor: Maleen Worth
Phone: (204) 555-4782

. . . 1

Name
Address

Home phone
Business phone
e-mail address

In the skills section, highlight the types of skills you have acquired through the work you have done or the experiences you have had in school or in your community.

In this section, include your work history.

(continued)

The **skills résumé** is the most popular and currently thought to be the most effective way to present yourself on paper. Remember to tailor your résumé to suit the requirements of each potential job or employer. If possible keep your résumé in an electronic file, where you can revise it easily and at short notice.

The skills résumé has several distinct parts, as shown in the sample on these two pages.

(continued)

2/

March 1999 – May 2000
Telemarketer
Freezies Storm Windows
Supervisor: Elgin Felcone
Phone: (204) 555-3967

Education   1998
Graduated from Terry Fox Collegiate,
Brandon, Manitoba

Extracurricular   Soccer; choir; skateboarding
Interests

References on Request

If you wish to list your references, you can. (This section is optional.)

Both in our jobs and in our personal lives, we have to make decisions. Sometimes these decisions are minor and do not require much thought. Decisions about what to have for breakfast or what to wear to school may take time, but they are not life-changing.

Many decisions, however, will have a major impact on you. Their consequences may be life-altering. For example, your career may be influenced by the subjects you study at school. Think, too, about people you know who made a decision to drop out of school and consider how their lives have changed. Some will have been successful, others will not. Think about people who decided to drink and drive, and have injured themselves and others.

When you are trying to make an important decision, it is essential to plan — to think about the options and weigh all the alternatives. Many of us don't plan. Our decisions are made in a number of ways that may not be beneficial to us. Following are some ways in which people make decisions. Read through them with the class, and discuss their pros and cons. You may recognize several decision-making patterns that you have developed over the years. Recognizing your own patterns is the first step toward changing them.

Decision-Making Patterns *

Wish Pattern

Definition: Choosing an alternative that will lead to the desired outcome, no matter what the risks. You just "wish" things will go the way you want them to.

Example: Not studying for a test, wishing you will recognize what's on the test, and hoping you will do well.

Escape Pattern

Definition: Choosing an alternative that might not be the best alternative in order to avoid making the tough choice and facing the consequences or results.

Example: Accepting the answers for a test from a friend instead of studying, learning the material, and passing or failing the test on your own.

---

* Adapted from *Choices* (Santa Barbara: Advocacy Press, 1984).

Safe Pattern

Definition: Choosing the certain way to bring success even if the decision won't make you happy or satisfied.

Example: Taking a course you think is an easy credit instead of a more difficult course that you know the college you want to enrol in might require.

Impulsive Pattern

Definition: Choosing an alternative based on impulse.

Example: Accepting a ride, without thinking, from a driver who has been drinking.

Fatalistic Pattern

Definition: Leaving the decision up to fate: "Whatever happens will happen."

Example: Going out without permission and leaving the consequences up to fate.

Compliant Pattern

Definition: Letting someone else or a group make the decision for you.

Example: Going along with a group of your friends who have decided to skip math class, even though you enjoy math.

Delaying Pattern

Definition: Putting off the decision until it's almost too late, and then rushing through the decision.

Example: Not deciding what courses to take until the day the option sheets are due to be handed in to your counsellor.

Agonizing Pattern

Definition: Not making a decision because there are too many choices.

Example: Not submitting your application to a college or another post-secondary program because you can't decide what to take.

Intuitive Pattern

Definition: Making a choice based on a gut feeling.

Example: Choosing to work at a store that sells sporting goods, not because you have researched the store or its background, but because it "feels right."

PERFORMANCE REVIEWS

School is not the only place where your performances are judged. In almost every job you have, your supervisor will want to know how well you are doing. If you become the supervisor, you will want to know how the people who work for *you* are doing *their* jobs.

Some performance reviews will determine whether or not you get a raise. Other performance reviews will determine whether you will become a permanent worker at the company. Still others will determine whether or not you will keep your job. The following performance review guidelines are based on the skills that employers have identified as the most important to success in the workplace. They are also a good indicator of how well you work within your classes.

You can use these guidelines to evaluate your own performance on a project or a group activity, or to evaluate the performance of your peers. Your teacher may use these guidelines to evaluate your performance in class, on group work, or on a project.

Performance Review Guidelines

When you are completing your **performance review**, consider some of the following points. Not all of them will be appropriate for each project you undertake, and you may wish to add some things that you feel are important.

Communication Skills

- listening to understand and learn from others
- reading, understanding what you read, and using written materials (e.g., graphs, charts, visual material) to complete the job successfully
- writing clearly and effectively in the required format so that others can understand what you have written
- voicing opinions clearly without overpowering others
- applying your understanding of the sender/receiver communications model

Thinking Skills

- thinking critically, acting logically
- evaluating situations, using good judgement, and applying effective decision-making skills when faced with a problem
- using technology and information systems effectively
- applying any specialized knowledge that you have to the project

Learning Skills

- learning independently
- learning something new from the project
- improving on skills learned during previous projects

Attitudes and Behaviours

- completing the project with confidence
- feeling a sense of self-esteem from working through the process and completing the project
- having honesty and integrity
- having a positive attitude toward personal learning and growth
- persisting with the project in order to complete it

Responsibility

- setting goals and priorities and working toward them
- planning and managing time effectively
- being accountable for your actions

Adaptability

- recognizing and respecting the differences and talents of others
- identifying and suggesting new ideas and ways to get the job done—displaying creativity

Working with Others

- understanding the project and working as a group member toward completing it successfully
- understanding the dynamics of the group and working effectively within it
- planning and making decisions with the group and taking responsibility for outcomes (both positive and negative)
- respecting the thoughts and opinions of others
- having a give-and-take attitude within the group to achieve results
- working as a group member when appropriate and as an individual within the group when appropriate
- taking various roles in the group (leader, recorder, reporter, worker, decision maker) when appropriate

Sample Performance Review (Based on a Group Project)

Things I did well

I thought that I did a good job by putting my point across to the group members. My writing was clear and effective. I was understood while communicating. I learned to work as hard as I could to complete the assignment.

I thought that we worked very well as a group and put a lot of effort into the project. We had fun doing it, too.

We all put in effort on different aspects of the project. Monique did her share by typing everything out and working on the scenario. I wrote most of the script and acted as the lead character.

Things I didn't do well

(Not to brag) but there wasn't anything that I would have changed. Our final package for the project was put together well. I think that Jonah did not contribute as much as Monique and I did, but Monique and I shared equal responsibilities and left it up to Jonah to hand in his own work. Next time, we'd make sure we included him more all the way through the project. It might have been our own fault that we did more than he did.

The Media

ANALYZING VISUAL AND MEDIA WORKS

Elements of Visual Production: Television, Video, Film*

People who make television programs, videos, films, and other visual productions must deal with two main things: picture elements (what the production looks like) and sound elements (how the production will sound).

Picture Elements

- original live-action or dramatized footage
- stock footage: archival footage or footage from other films
- interviews
- re-enactments
- still photos
- documents, titles, headlines, cartoons, other graphics
- blue screen (for special effects)
- special effects

Sound Elements

- sound recorded at the same time as visuals (on-the-street interviews, at a live concert)
- sound recorded on its own and dubbed onto the film or tape
- voice-over: voices or commentary recorded separately from filmed visuals and then dubbed onto the film or tape

---

* Information based on Arlene Moscovitch, *Constructing Reality: Exploring Issues in Documentary* (Montreal: National Film Board of Canada, 1993).

- narration: scripted voice-over spoken by narrator, filmmaker, or participant
- sound effects
- music
- silence
- ambient noise (background noise)

Camera Terms

As you make storyboards (see pages 301–302) and prepare for filming, you will find the following camera terms helpful. These terms should help you to be very specific, so that others can understand exactly what you mean.

Camera Angle

- **high**: sometimes called the bird's-eye view. The camera is placed well above normal eye level. Viewers feel that they are looking down on the subject and many consequently feel superior to it, or the subject may give the impression of being overwhelmed and/or alone.
- **low**: sometimes called the worm's-eye view. The camera is placed below eye level. Viewers feel that they are looking up at the subject. This may make the viewers feel that the subject is more powerful than they are or that the subject is in control.

Camera Movement

- **tilt up**: the camera moves upward (from low angle to high)
- **tilt down**: the camera moves downward (from high angle to low)
- **pan**: the camera moves from right to left or left to right across an imagined horizon or panorama
- **dolly**: the camera moves in toward (dolly in) or out from (dolly out) the subject in a straight line. In this case, the camera is mounted on a tripod with wheels or on a makeshift dolly. The camera can be hand-held.
- **truck**: the camera moves right or left in a straight line and is usually mounted
- **zoom in or out**: the camera lens focuses in on or back from the subject (from wide angle to close-up and vice versa)

Camera Distance

- **extreme close-up**: a detailed shot of a very small area
- **medium close-up**: a shot that might include the head and shoulders of the subject
- **close-up**: a shot taken a short distance from the subject

- **medium shot:** a shot midway between a close-up and a long shot
- **medium long shot:** a shot that would have the subject in full view
- **long shot:** a shot in which the camera is placed far away from the subject
- **extreme long shot:** a shot that would have the subject in the distant background

READING CARTOONS AND COMICS

The meaning of the word "cartoon" has changed over time. Originally, it meant a full-sized, colour, preparatory drawing or painting on heavy paper. The drawing may then have been turned into an oil painting, an egg tempera painting, a mural, a fresco, a stained-glass window, or even a tapestry. Today, a cartoon is a drawing or series of drawings in which content, not the style of execution, is most important. The word "comic" implies that the drawing will be humorous or satirical, whereas a cartoon may be humorous, satirical, serious, or instructional.

Although cartoons often include text and may require the audience to read words, their visual aspect is most important. Understanding what makes the visual part of the cartoon effective can increase your understanding and enjoyment of what you are seeing. Whether a cartoon is one panel or several, most of the same rules apply.

Central Focus

The artist draws your attention to one part of the drawing. Here are some questions to help you look at how the artist has accomplished this.
- How large is the central focus compared with the objects around it?
- Is the shape of the central focus different from other shapes in the frame?
- Is the detail on the central focus more complex or simpler than that of the other objects in the frame?
- How does the colour used in the central focus differ from that used for other objects?
- Has the artist drawn attention to the central focus by creating strong lines leading toward it (someone pointing to it, lines from other objects leading the eye to it)?
- Is the central focus near the centre of the picture?
- Is the central focus in isolation — by itself?

Point of View

Cartoons are much like frames in a film. The artist draws the action from a specific point of view and distance. Review the sections "Camera Angle" and "Camera Distance" (see page 297) because they will help you to understand a cartoonist's point of view.

Movement

Movement may be suggested in many ways in a cartoon. The most obvious way is to use "speed lines," which suggest that someone is running, or to repeat a character in sequential frames following through on an action. If all the objects and characters are static in the cartoon, the artist can still suggest movement. A gesture such as an arm in the middle of a punch, a full figure in midstep, or an eye movement can let us know that a character is moving.

Unity

Unity within a cartoon causes you to focus on certain aspects of that cartoon — the ones the artist wants you to notice. Repetition within a frame or between frames draws the viewer's eye. The closeness of one shape or object to another also draws the eye. If an artist places one object so that a line or edge of one shape continues to another shape, the viewer's eye will be drawn along that line.

ACTIVITY

Examine any of the cartoons in this textbook. Describe how the artist has drawn attention to the visual aspects of his or her cartoon and how the drawing enhances the written message.

CREATING VISUALS AND MEDIA WORKS: POSTERS, STORYBOARDS, COLLAGES*

Just as writers gather information, organize it, and create drafts before producing their final version, visual artists plan each and every thing they produce, whether it is drawn by hand or created on a computer. If you are creating a visual product that requires drawing or putting together pictures and type, here are a few helpful hints.

Research

- If you need some background images, look through books and magazines to get ideas for these images.
- Photocopy the pages you like. (Never cut up a book that isn't your own!)
- Take photographs yourself.
- If you want to draw animals, go to the zoo or a pet store or rent a video with animals in it.

Create Thumbnail Sketches

- **Thumbnail sketches** are just for composition purposes. Do them quickly inside a frame that is the same proportion as the final work. They shouldn't contain any detail.
- Produce as many thumbnail sketches as possible so you will be sure to include your best and most creative ideas (which sometimes come later rather than sooner).
- Experiment with colour and value.
- Avoid tracing your research pictures. Try to change the angle or view of your subject. (Remember, most pictures and drawings, including cartoons, are the property of the artist.)

Choose a Focus

What do you want to put in the foreground, middle ground, and background of your visual presentation?

Create Rough Sketches

- Once you have your subject matter and your thumbnail sketches, you need to put them all together in a final rough layout, larger than the thumbnails but still in proportion to the final.

---

* Information based on Mark Thurman, *How to Plan Your Drawings* (Markham: Pembroke Publishers, 1992).

- Decide on your emphasis. Will it be the characters, the setting, an object, or the action?
- If you need more room, draw outside the border and then draw a new border, ensuring proportions are maintained.
- Ensure you create a definite centre of interest and subordinate the less important information to the special emphasis you've created.

Final Copy

- When you're pleased with your design, create a final, full-sized version of your masterpiece.

Creating a Storyboard

A **storyboard** is a series of drawings, often composed of thumbnail sketches, that show the camera shots in a video or film, along with the audio for each shot.

When you create a storyboard, you should provide all the necessary instructions for sound/audio and video. Make sure you have considered all six types of information listed below. However, keep in mind that certain types of information may not apply to every shot.

Draw the frames or shots as if you are looking through the lens of a camera. The artwork for the frames can range from stick figures to full-colour pictures. Each frame should represent a separate shot in your video or film.

Sample Storyboard

1. description of shot contents: person approaching mall entrance
2. camera distance: long shot
3. camera angle: eye level
4. camera movement: pan left as subject enters doorway
5. audio: traffic and footsteps
6. shot duration in seconds: five seconds

1. person carrying shopping bag
2. medium shot
3. eye level
4. pan right as subject walks to bus stop
5. footsteps
6. two seconds

(continued)

(continued)

1. shopping bag
2. close up
3. eye level
4. (no movement)
5. (no audio)
6. three seconds

Creating a Collage

A **collage** is a collection of visual materials—photographs, pictures, words, and advertisements from magazines and newspapers, along with other visuals—that create a mood or show a theme.

Here are some suggestions you might want to think about as you plan your collage to help make it interesting and thought-provoking.

Create a Background with Depth

Try using a colour background that suits the mood of the collage. You might collect material from magazines for visual backgrounds such as city skylines, farmlands and countrysides, or typical urban scenes. Placing your other visuals against such backgrounds will help you to create some depth.

Create a Variety of Emotions

Try to create a variety of emotions by
• using visual parallels—things that are similar
• using contrasts—things that are different
• putting together things that might seem to be unrelated

Use Repeated Images

Some of the best collages work well because they focus on repeated images. For example, a collage on the theme of guilt can create a strong impact by including 100 pairs of eyes along with a few simple visuals and text.

Use Words in Different Ways

Because many collages include some words, you should try a variety of approaches, such as contrast or irony or the use of clichés. You might look for quotations in collections of quotations, poetry books, and advertisements. If you have access to a computer, you might input the text and print it out using different fonts and point sizes.

Work with a Partner

Often it helps to work with someone else so that both of you can look for interesting contrasts and ideas as you plan and create your collage.

LAYOUT OF A PAGE

Different kinds of writing have different requirements for presentation on a page. The setup of writing on a page for production is called the layout of the page.

A number of elements are available to you as you prepare an appropriate layout for your work, especially if you are using a computer. Consider the best and most appropriate use of the following when preparing the layout of a page.

- **White Space:** How much space do you want to leave blank? How much space do you want to leave between lines and paragraphs, and for margins?
- **Point Size:** How big do you want the print to be? Do you want to use print of different sizes for titles, headings, and captions?
- **Fonts:** What font will be easiest to read? Do you want to use a variety of fonts for emphasis? Do you want to **bold**, *italicize,* or underline any of the words in your document?
- **Boxes and Sidebars:** Will these special features help your reader to find information more easily?
- **Icons and Illustrations:** Will visual features assist your reader to understand the information better?

> **TIP**
>
> To get ideas for the layout of your work, look at professionally prepared and published documents similar to the one you are producing. Very different layouts are used for advertisements, résumés, reports, and poetry. Select one that will work best for your audience and the information you are presenting.

THE PITCH: HOW ADVERTISERS DRAW ATTENTION TO THEIR PRODUCTS*

Advertisers know we will pay attention to the unusual, interesting, and unexpected. There are several ways in which they grab our attention.

Appealing to Our Senses

Advertisers use some or all of the following elements to appeal to our senses.

- motion
- colour
- lighting
- sound
- music
- visuals
- special effects
- action

Appealing to Our Emotions

When appealing to our emotions, advertisers use associations with an emotional state, such as happiness or sadness.

Appealing to Our Intellect

Advertisers appeal to our "thinking side" through

- news
- claims
- advice
- questions
- demonstrations
- scientific evidence
- real-life stories or testimonials

Building Our Confidence

Advertisers gain our confidence by
- using brand names we know and trust
- using people we think we know and trust (e.g., movie stars, people dressed like doctors, dentists, researchers)
- using cartoon figures, animals, and other friendly figures
- using words associated with trust

Stimulating Our Desire

The products advertised generally make at least one of the following claims:
- They keep a good thing going.
- They help users to obtain something good.

---

* Adapted from Hugh Rank, *The Pitch* (Park Forest, Illinois: Counter-Propaganda Press, 1982).

- They help users to avoid a bad thing.
- They get rid of a bad thing.

Advertisers claim that their products will provide us with something. The following twelve product claims are the most common:

- the best
- the most
- the most effective
- the most beautiful
- the rarest
- the newest
- the most classic
- the most reliable
- the easiest or simplest
- the most practical
- the fastest
- the safest

In addition, advertisers often suggest "added value" as a result of purchasing their products. The following four categories are the most common added values:

- basic needs (food, health, security, money, sex, comfort, activity)
- fitting in (religious acceptance, scientific research, being popular, being elite, being normal)
- love and belonging
- growth (success, respect, creativity, curiosity)

ACTIVITY

In a small group, find an example of one print advertisement, one radio commercial, one television commercial, and one Internet advertisement. For each of them, determine which audience the advertisement is targeting. Using the information above, create a chart demonstrating how each advertisement makes its audience pay attention to it. Be prepared to present your advertisements and commercials and your analyses of each one to the class.

> Glossary

act: A main division of a drama. *Medicine Woman* is a one-act play, while *Leaving Home* has several acts, of which Act One appears in this anthology.

adaptation: In literary terms, it refers to a work that has been modified or altered. For example, *Medicine Woman* is an adaptation of Richard Deming's story.

advertisement: A public notice in newspapers and magazines, on posters and billboards, in broadcasts (radio and television), and so on, designed to increase sales or draw attention to or promote organizations, goods or services, events, or ideas. See also **commercial**.

analogy: A comparison that focuses on something similar between two things that are otherwise not the same. An analogy is often used to explain a complex idea in terms of a simpler one. Some might argue that "King Midas and the Golden Touch" makes an analogy between the mythical king and modern human beings who are obsessed with gaining profit.

animated film: A film shot from a series of hand-drawn or computer-generated pictures that are shown in rapid succession resulting in the illusion of movement. Walt Disney's *Beauty and the Beast* and *The Lion King* are famous examples of such films. There are usually no live characters in an animated film.

anthology: A published collection of literary material including poems, short stories, novels, non-fiction selections, or other material. This textbook is an example of an anthology.

antithesis: A figure of speech in which words or ideas are set up in parallel structure or balance against each other to emphasize the contrast in their meaning. For example, "To err is human, to forgive divine": Alexander Pope.

argumentative essay: See **essay/magazine article/supported opinion piece/personal essay.**

article: See **essay/magazine article/supported opinion piece/personal essay** and **newspaper article/report/story.**

atmosphere (or **mood**): The prevailing feeling in a literary work created through word choice, descriptive details, and evocative imagery. The description of waking "to a yellow fire" in "Watching the Sun" creates an atmosphere of warmth.

audience: The group of people for whom a piece of writing, film, television program, or other work is intended.

author: A person who writes short stories, novels, non-fiction selections, or any other written material.

autobiography: The story of a person's life, written by that person.

bias: An underlying preference or prejudice for or against a particular idea, value, or group of people.

biography: The story of a person's life, written by someone other than that person.

brochure: A printed booklet, or pages that are folded into panels, used to advertise or give information about a business, product, place, and so on. It often contains colourful graphics or pictures.

caption: A heading or subtitle that accompanies a photograph, drawing, or cartoon.

caricature: An exaggeration or distortion of a character's most prominent features in order to ridicule him or her.

character: Refers to (1) an individual in a story, narrative poem, or play, and (2) the qualities of the individual. The latter are usually revealed through dialogue, description, and action. In "Marriage Is a Private Affair,"

for example, the father's prejudice is revealed through dialogue and his own actions.

cliché: An overused expression. For example, "*Tired but happy*, we came home."

commercial: A television or radio advertisement. See also **advertisement**.

conflict: A struggle between opposing characters, forces, or emotions, usually between the protagonist and someone or something else. The central conflict in "Marriage Is a Private Affair" is between the father and his son, who "married a woman who spoke a different tongue."

connotation: The implications or unstated associations conveyed by a word beyond its basic meaning. Connotations may be widely understood by many people, or may be personal and private, based on an individual's life experiences. See also **denotation**.

consensus: An agreement by members of a group that, although it takes into account individual points of view, focuses on what all members of the group can agree to in order to proceed with a task. For example, there has to be a consensus about the interpretation of a drama by all members of the cast and crew in order for a coherent production of the drama to occur.

context: The situation or background information that helps to explain a word, idea, character, or incident in a text. It could refer to the surrounding event(s) or information in a text, the background of the writer, or the social situation in which the text was written. As well, the context the reader brings to a text affects how a piece of writing is received and experienced.

covering letter: A letter used to introduce a package of materials. For instance, when someone submits a résumé as part of a job application, the covering letter identifies the sender, the position applied for, and the contents of the application (e.g., application form, résumé). It also highlights the applicant's most relevant skills or experience. Covering letters are short and written in a formal business style.

debate: A discussion or argument that pre-sents both sides of a topic. A debate can be formal, such as a televised debate between politicians. Formal debates take place in public, are guided by rules, and are overseen by a moderator. (See also The Reference Shelf, pages 278–279.)

definition: A statement or explanation used to clarify the meaning of words or concepts.

denotation: The basic or specific meaning of a word without associated ideas or emotions. See also **connotation**.

dialogue: A conversation between two or more characters. Dialogue is often used by writers and dramatists to reveal character and conflict. The dialogue between the characters in *Leaving Home* shows the conflicts among them.

diction: The deliberate choice of words to create a specific style, atmosphere, or tone. In "Watching the Sun," the poet uses words that evoke warmth and contentment.

direct speech: The exact words spoken by a character. Direct speech is almost always enclosed in quotation marks. (See also The Reference Shelf, page 236.)

drama: A story written in the form of dialogue intended to be acted out in front of an audience. It consists of plot complication and resolution, character revelation, conflict, setting, and theme. *Medicine Woman* and *Leaving Home* are examples of drama.

dramatic monologue: see **monologue**.

editorial: A newspaper or magazine article giving the opinion of the editor or publisher regarding a subject.

essay/magazine article/supported opinion piece/personal essay: Non-fiction prose that examines a single topic from a point of view. It requires an introductory paragraph stating the main or controlling ideas, several paragraphs developing the topic, and a concluding paragraph. The title often identifies the topic. Formal essays are usually serious and impersonal in tone. Personal or informal essays reveal the personality and feelings of the author and are conversational in tone. "Head Game" is an example of this type of non-fiction writing.

An **informational essay** provides information to the reader. It has supporting details and frequently involves some analysis of the information presented. An example is "The Skills Employers Want."

A **persuasive essay** uses supporting details and argumentation to persuade the reader to accept the writer's point of view.

An **argumentative essay** argues for or against a question or a position on a topic, issue, and so on.

etymology: The etymology of a word traces its historical origin and development. Most dictionaries provide the etymologies of words.

eulogy: A speech or piece of writing in praise of a person, action, and so on.

explicit meaning: An idea or a message that is stated directly by the writer. For example, David Suzuki explicitly states in his essay that the "media do not *reflect* reality but *create* it." See also **implicit meaning**.

exposition: A piece of writing that presents information, explains ideas, or presents an argument. It is a generic term for writing that is not drama, narration, or description. An example is "Why Write?"

extended metaphor: See **metaphor**.

fiction: Prose writing that is based on imagination rather than on fact.

flashback: A device that shifts the narrative from the present to the past, usually to reveal a change in character or to illustrate an important point. The excerpt from *Night* is presented entirely as a flashback by a narrator who looks back at the horror of Nazi concentration camps.

flyer: A printed notice used to advertise a product or service.

foreshadowing: Refers to clues that hint at what is going to happen later in the plot. Foreshadowing is used to arouse the reader's curiosity, build suspense, and help prepare the reader to accept events that occur later in the story. In "No-Pear-A-Bow," the voices of warning in the protagonist's head and the hush of the night all serve to foreshadow his encounter with the ghost.

glossary: A list of special, technical, or difficult words with definitions or comments.

graphic organizer: A chart, graph, Venn diagram, or other visual means used to record, organize, classify, analyze, and assess information.

hypothesis: A theory or a proposition assumed to be a likely and true explanation. Usually a hypothesis is created in order to test it out against all known information or through experimentation. In writing, a writer may develop or prove a hypothesis through written discussion and information.

image/imagery: A picture created by a writer using concrete details, adjectives, and figures of speech that gives readers a vivid impression of what or who is being described. The descriptions in "Catalogue" create different, but definite, images of cats. Similes, metaphors, personification, and symbols are all specific kinds of imagery.

implicit meaning: An idea or message that must be inferred by the reader. The theme of a short story or the qualities of the characters, for instance, are rarely stated directly, but can be inferred from details provided in the story. For example, we can infer from "Maths" the narrator's fear of the subject. See also **explicit meaning**.

informational essay: See **essay/magazine article/supported opinion piece/personal essay** and **exposition.**

interior monologue: See **monologue.**

interview: A recorded discussion, usually structured in a question–answer format. Examples of interviews are those between an employer and a job applicant (see The Reference Shelf, page 282), a reporter and a politician, or an immigration officer and a new immigrant.

invective: Writing or speech that denounces or is insulting to something or someone.

irony: A literary device that creates a contrast or discrepancy between what is said and what is meant, or between expectations and reality. For example, the reader is aware that the relationship between the narrator and Todd in "Everyone Talked Loudly in Chinatown" will likely not last. The narrator, on the other hand, is blind to this fact. (See The Reference Shelf, page 241, for common types of irony.)

journal: A notebook that contains personal reflections and responses to writing, events, incidents, and people.

layout: A plan or design of a page of a book, advertisement, newspaper, or other printed material that shows the placement of the words and illustrations or photos. Layouts can be done by hand or by using computer-design software.

live-action television program: A program that involves live acting (as opposed to animation) and may be televised as the event or action is taking place. News, sports, and sitcoms are examples.

memoir: A form of autobiographical writing dealing with personal recollections of people or events. "The Sentence" is a kind of memoir.

memorandum (memo): A brief, informal form of business communication used to convey factual information accurately and clearly. All memos identify the date, the person the memo is being sent to, the sender, and the topic. A typical memo template begins in the following way.

Date:

To:

From:

Re:

metaphor: A figure of speech that makes a comparison between two seemingly unlike things without using connective words such as *like* or *as*. In "Anne Frank," the narrator compares Anne Frank to a "crippled-winged" bird that "never flew." See **simile.**

Sometimes writers use an **extended metaphor** — a metaphor that develops its comparison over several lines or paragraphs or even throughout the entire composition. The poet in "Anne Frank" uses the extended metaphor of a trapped bird to describe the situation of the famous diarist.

monologue: A speech by one person telling a story, revealing character, or describing a humorous or dramatic situation.

A **dramatic monologue** is a form of poetry in which a character speaks to a definite but silent listener and thereby reveals his or her own character.

An **interior monologue** is a form of writing that reveals the inner thoughts of a character.

mood: See **atmosphere**.

narration: Telling a story or recounting an event or series of events.

narrative: Another word for story. Narratives have the following elements: plot, conflict, characters, setting, point of view, and theme. Narratives may be fictional or non-fictional, and include novels and (auto)biographies (or personal stories/narratives) as well as short stories and anecdotes.

narrator: The person or character who tells the story.

newspaper article/report/story: Non-fiction prose that informs readers about an event or issue. It has titles in the form of brief sentences (also known as headlines). The most important information appears at the beginning of a newspaper article so that the reader can stop reading once he or she has sufficient information on the topic.

opinion piece: See **essay/magazine article/supported opinion piece/ personal essay.**

panel discussion: A discussion of a particular issue by a selected group of people, usually experts, before an audience.

parody: A humorous imitation of a piece of writing, film, or drama that mocks the original by exaggerating or distorting some of its salient features.

pathetic fallacy: A literary device in which nature or inanimate things are represented as sympathetic to or prophetic about events or the emotions of the characters. Pathetic fallacy is evident toward the end of "Marriage Is a Private Affair" when the first rain of the year falls, marking the end of Okeke's resolution to shut out his son from his life.

personal essay: See **essay/magazine article/supported opinion piece/ personal essay.**

personal narrative: See **narrative**.

personification: A metaphor in which human attributes are given to inanimate objects. For example, in "Watching the Sun," the leaves of the mango tree are described as "playing."

persuasive essay: See **essay/magazine article/supported opinion piece/ personal essay.**

plot: A series of events and the thoughtful interrelations of these events, their causes and effects, and so on; the main story in a narrative or drama. The main plot in "No-Pear-A-Bow" tells about a man's encounter with a ghost. (See also The Reference Shelf, page 242.)

poem/poetry: A unique form of writing about experiences, thoughts, and feelings, frequently divided into lines and stanzas, which uses compressed language, figures of speech, and imagery to appeal to readers' emotions and imagination. There are a variety of poetic structures with different requirements of length, rhyme, rhythm, stanza formation, and so on. (See also The Reference Shelf, pages 246–248, for types of poetry.)

point of view: The perspective from which a story is told. (See also The Reference Shelf, pages 244–246, for types of point of view.)

proposal: A plan, offer, or suggestion put forward for consideration. The information in a proposal is organized to support the proposed conclusion.

prose: Ordinary language or literary expression not marked by rhythm or rhyme is called prose. As Molière put it in *The Bourgeois Gentleman*, "All that is not prose is verse. All that is not verse is prose." The protagonist of Molière's play is proud and pleased to find out that he has been speaking prose all his life and he didn't even realize it! This type of language is used in short stories, essays, and modern plays.

pun: A play on words. For example, in *Romeo and Juliet* (Act III, scene i), as Mercutio lies dying, he says, "Ask for me tomorrow, and you shall find me a *grave* man." The word "grave" could mean both "serious" and "dead in the grave."

purpose: The aim or goal of any piece of writing, including articles, advertisements, brochures, and so on.

realistic character: See **character**.

report: An oral or written account or opinion formally expressed, based on findings from investigation or inquiry. (See also The Reference Shelf, page 263.)

research report: A form of non-fiction writing intended to inform an audience about a particular topic. It contains factual information that is carefully researched from authoritative sources. (See also The Reference Shelf, pages 253–257.)

résumé: A summary of information about a job applicant's personal, educational, and work experience. There are many formats to choose from, but all require a neat, easy-to-read presentation of factual information. (See The Reference Shelf, pages 289–290 for a sample résumé.)

review: A form of writing that discusses the good and bad points of a book, film, work of art, and so on. It usually provides a synopsis or description of the work and focuses on a few key aspects, using evidence to support arguments.

rhyme scheme: The pattern of end rhymes. A rhyme scheme is indicated by assigning each new end rhyme a different letter of the alphabet. For example, the rhyme scheme of stanzas 1–3 of "Stopping by Woods on a Snowy Evening" is *aaba*: know, though, here, snow. (See also The Reference Shelf, pages 246–247.)

role playing: Assuming and acting the role of a character, fictitious or real, and using dialogue and/or gestures appropriate to the individual to present the character to an audience in an improvisation.

sarcasm: A cutting expression or remark.

satire: A literary work that ridicules human vices and follies, often with the purpose of teaching a lesson or encouraging change. "Reflections Dental" takes a satiric look at the appearance of people's teeth on television.

scene: The time, place, circumstance, and so on of a play or story, usually involving a particular incident. In a play, a scene is a division of an act, taking place in a single location. See also **act**. (See also The Reference Shelf, page 242.)

script: The written text for a play, video, film, or radio or television broadcast. It includes dialogue, sound effects, stage directions, and so on.

setting: The place and time of a story, play, or poem. The setting of "No-Pear-A-Bow" is at night, out in a lonely countryside. (See also The Reference Shelf, page 242.)

short story: A short fictional prose narrative having only one major character, plot, setting, and theme. The short story usually focuses on a single conflict, character, or emotional effect.

simile: A figure of speech that makes a comparison between two seemingly unlike things using a connective word such as *like* or *as*. An example occurs in "Catalogue," where cats are described in several ways,

including being "Like a good mat." See **metaphor**.

speech: A public address, usually given in formal language, often to persuade an audience. Justin Trudeau's speech was delivered at his father's funeral service.

stanza: A set number of lines grouped together to form units in poetry.

storyboard: A series of panels with sketches and dialogue, representing the shots in an advertisement, film, or television program, and used to plan a script for a film or video. (See also The Reference Shelf, pages 301–302.)

style: The particular way in which a writer expresses himself or herself in writing. It is the sum effect of the author's choice of voice, vocabulary, and sentence structure, and use of devices such as imagery, onomatopoeia, and rhythm.

summary: A brief account giving the main points of a story or article.

suspense: The condition of being uncertain about an outcome, used by writers to create tension, excitement, or anxiety. In "No-Pear-A-Bow," readers are kept in suspense as to whether or not the protagonist will actually meet the ghost.

syntax: The order or systematic arrangement of words in a sentence. Syntax will determine whether ideas expressed orally or in writing are clear and easy to understand.

theme: A statement of the central idea of a work, usually implied rather than directly stated. One theme of "There Will Come Soft Rains" is the destructiveness of war.

thesis: A main or controlling idea or statement about a topic that a writer proposes and supports in an essay. The thesis of "Pampered Teens Don't Have It Bad" is that "young people are marginalized because adults treat [them] with kid gloves." See **topic**.

tone: The attitude a writer expresses toward his or her subject. The tone of writing may be formal or informal, personal or impersonal, angry or cheerful, bitter or hopeful, and so on. The tone of "I and Africa" is a mixture of recognition, exhilaration, and joy.

topic: The subject that is being written or talked about. The subject of "Head Games" is shampoo. (Note: Topic and thesis are often confused: **topic** is the subject matter; **thesis** is the statement about the topic.)

topic sentence: A sentence that states the subject of a paragraph. The sentence "Writing helps you discover who you are" in "Why Write?" begins one of the paragraphs. The paragraph then explains why.

typography: The arrangement, appearance, or style of printed words.

voice: This word has three different meanings within this textbook.

Verb voice refers to whether a verb is active or passive. An active voice is usually recommended since it tends to be more direct, hard-hitting, or forceful. The passive voice makes writing more formal and a little bit distant, and is most appropriate in formal, objective reports. (See also The Reference Shelf, page 223.)

Voice is used in the context of oral presentations to discuss volume, clarity, and so on, when speaking.

Voice is also used to describe the distinctive style or tone of an individual writer or speaker. "Pampered Teens Don't Have It Bad" has the distinctive voice of a teenager trying to persuade readers to understand her point of view.

> Index

> Acknowledgements

Text

Family Circus/Comic Strip by Bil Keane. Reprinted with special permission of King Features Syndicate. **A Son's Eulogy** by Justin Trudeau. Courtesy of Justin Trudeau. **Stopping by Woods on a Snowy Evening** by Robert Frost. From *The Poetry of Robert Frost*, edited by Edward Connery Lathem. © 1951 Robert Frost, © 1923, 1969 by Henry Holt & Co., LLC. Reprinted by permission of Henry Holt and Company, LLC. **Busted** by Harlan Howard. From *Poetry of the Soul* by Harlan Howard. Reprinted with permission. **Pampered Teens Don't Have it so Bad** by Sarojini McKenna. Reprinted by permission of the Toronto Star and the author. **Small Change Can Add Up to a Big Loss** by Ellen Roseman. Reprinted with permission from The Toronto Star Syndicate. **Catalogue** by Rosalie Moore. Reprinted by permission, © 1940 (renewed 1968). Originally published in *The New Yorker*. All rights reserved. **The Best Kind of Fear** by J. William Knowles. From *Breaking the Surface* © 2000. Reprinted by permission of Sono Nis Press, Victoria, BC. **No-Pear-A-Bow** by Cathy Miyata. Permission granted by Arnold Gosewich. **Night** (excerpt) by Elie Wiesel. From *Night* by Elie Wiesel, © 1982 Farrar, Straus & Giroux. Reprinted with permission of the publisher. **What's in This Toothpaste?** by David Bodanis. From *The Secret House* by David Bodanis. Reprinted with permission of Simon & Schuster, Inc. **Hockey Stick is a Canadian Artefact** by Fabrice Taylor. Reprinted with permission of The Toronto Star Syndicate. **Reading With Purpose** from *Improve Your Reading, 4th edition* © 2000 by Ron Fry. Reprinted with permission of Career Press, Franklin Lakes, NJ. All rights reserved. **Why Write?** by Caryn Mirriam-Goldberg, excerpted from *Write Where You Are: How To Use Writing to Make Sense of Your Life* by Caryn Mirriam-Goldberg © 1999. Used with permission from Free Spirit Publishing Inc. All rights reserved. **The Sentence:** Excerpt from *Angel Square* by Brian Doyle. Text © 1984 by Brian Doyle. First published in Canada by Groundwood Books/Douglas & McIntyre Ltd. Reprinted by permission of the publisher. **The Skills Employers Want**. Reprinted by permission of The American Society for Training & Development. **Strategies—Decision Making Patterns**, © Girls Incorporated of Greater Santa Barbara. Reprinted by permission of Advocacy Press. Not to be duplicated in any other form. **Toughest Interview Questions Should be Your Own** by Michael Stern. Reprinted by permission of the author. **Summer Jobs** by Camille Bains. Reprinted from The Canadian Press. **Who Am I?** by Brian Henry. Reprinted with permission of the author. **I and Africa** by Lillian Allen. From *Nothing But a Hero*, © 1990 Well Vessel/Women's Press, Toronto. Reprinted with permission of the author. **Attitudes: How Will Yours Affect Your Future?** © Girls Incorporated of Greater Santa Barbara. Reprinted with permission of Advocacy Press. Not to be duplicated in any other form. **Values Survey,** © Girls Incorporated of Greater Santa Barbara. Reprinted with permission of Advocacy Press. Not to be duplicated in any other form. **Welcome to the Ark** by

Photographs

Illustrations